Let every student of nature take this as his rule, that whatever the mind seizes upon with particular satisfaction is to be held in suspicion.

FRANCIS BACON, *Novum Organum*, 1620

Three Seductive Ideas

Jerome Kagan

Harvard University Press
Cambridge, Massachusetts
London, England

First Harvard University Press paperback edition, 2000

Library of Congress Cataloging-in-Publication Data
Kagan, Jerome.
Three seductive ideas / Jerome Kagan.
p.   cm.
Includes bibliographical references and index.
ISBN 0-674-89033-7 (cloth)
ISBN 0-674-00197-4 (pbk.)
1. Psychology—Philosophy.   I. Title.
BF38.K23   1998
150′.1—dc21
98-8169

Contents

Three Seductive Ideas

Prologue

The true method of discovery is like the flight of an aeroplane. It starts from the ground of particular observation; it makes a flight in the thin air of imaginative generalization; and it again lands for renewed observation rendered acute by rational interpretation.

A. N. Whitehead, 1929

If you had lived in Europe as the fifteenth century came to a close, you would have believed that witches cause disease, that harsh punishment of a child creates an adaptive fear of authority, and that pursuit of sexual pleasure depletes a man's vital energy and guarantees exclusion from heaven. Today, five centuries later, the vital but still young sciences of human behavior are friendly to a number of equally fallacious assumptions. This book critically examines three of these potentially misleading ideas and suggests some of the reasons for their continued popularity.

The first flawed belief is that most psychological processes generalize broadly. Therefore, many believe it is not terribly important to specify the agent being studied, whether rat, monkey, or human, or the context in which the subject acts, whether laboratory, natural habitat, workplace, or home, because broad conclusions can be drawn regardless of the agent and context. Instances of this loose thinking can be found in every technical journal, but especially in books written for the general public. A quality called intelligence, for example, is applied to animals, human infants, college students, and software programs. The evidence used to infer this quality includes rats running mazes, the survival of species, infants staring at novel pictures, possession of a large vocabulary, fast decision times, the ability to recall a long string of numbers, and correct application of logical rules. The notion that one mental process could mediate such a diverse set of phenomena should strain the imagination of the most open mind.

This permissive attitude is widespread. When a man pushes ahead of us in a queue, we are prepared to attribute a general trait of aggressivity to him, believing that he is similarly aggressive at home, in the office, and on family picnics. Not surprisingly, perhaps, we are much more conservative when we ourselves commit the very same act. If I push ahead in an airport line, I will explain my rudeness as an uncharacteristic reaction that happened to be provoked by special conditions—the flagrant incompetence of the airline's booking agent, or snarled traffic in the airport tunnel, or a last-minute medical emergency at home. Social psychologists call this type of asymmetric logic, in which we assign broad stable traits to others but explain our own behavior as due to local conditions, the attribution error.

Our attraction to broad categories is most obvious when we name concrete things in the world. A mother points to a tall, crimson-leafed maple and says, "Look at the tree," not "Look at the big, colorful maple." The preference for underspecifying an event and, therefore, overgeneralizing is probably rooted in the biological nature of the human mind and is one of the oldest and best-established phenomena in the psychological laboratory. If a rat or human is shown a red light, followed a second later by a reward—food for the rat and perhaps money for the human—each agent will display a conditioned excitability to a variety of red hues, not just the particular wavelength of red used in the original conditioning. The human brain, like the brain of a rat, is biased initially to attend to generality rather than particularity. Experience must teach us to prune our initial understanding.

This fine-tuning is a seminal purpose of the empirical sciences. Over the last five hundred years much of our progress in the study of nature has occurred because investigators analyzed abstract concepts and replaced them with families of related but distinct categories. The cosmos, we now know, contains not just the visible stars in galaxies but also the mysterious, massive "dark matter" that surrounds them. Reproduction occurs sexually in some species, asexually in others, and both ways in a few. Viruses are distinguished from retroviruses, and sharks are not close relatives of whales.

Scientists have just begun to appreciate the advantages of analysis for cognitive phenomena. For example, the unitary competence that psychologists had regarded simply as memory is now recognized to consist of a set of distinct processes mediated by different brain circuits. Despite these few victories, too many social and behavioral scientists retain a deep affection for big concepts like learning, fear, depression, communication, love, and consciousness, trusting that each term faithfully describes a coherent commonality in nature. The first chapter of this book probes this problem by analyzing four popular words that are used so abstractly as to render them almost useless: fear, consciousness, intelligence, and temperament.

A second seductive premise favored by those who study human behavior is infant determinism, which holds that some experiences during the first two years of life are preserved indefinitely. One of the great moments in child development occurs in the middle of the second year, when a toddler who fails to find a toy she had seen an adult hide under a cloth looks purposefully for the object in nearby places. If the toy were under the cloth a few seconds earlier, and she did not see it removed, she knows that it must be somewhere, for objects do not disappear. This universal event, which Jean Piaget called "object permanence," implies that the human mind is prepared to believe that things do not just vanish unless some agent or force intervenes.

Given the universality of this belief, we should not be surprised to find it frequently applied to the psychological products of the first years of life: things—in this case the products of the child's earliest experiences—do not just vanish. To most people, the premise that the first mental structures created by experience are preserved indefinitely, like a scratch on a table, seems reasonable. But in fact many early ideas and habits either vanish or undergo such serious transformation that they cannot be retrieved in later life, any more than the first strokes of a seascape can be discerned from the larger scene, once a painting is complete.

The private reorganizations of images and ideas that occur over development are hidden from observers. An infant's representation of his mother's face changes imperceptibly with each passing year, so that no adolescent is able to reconstruct the earliest schema of his parent. Similarly, the nine-month-old's cry of terror when picked up by an uncle she has never seen before vanishes by the second year with no sign of heirs. These early mental events can be likened to names written in the summer sand that disappear with the tide. As Chapter 2 will show, the impermanence of first structures is as likely an outcome as preservation, whether in evolution, psychological growth, or language.

One trio of authors writing over sixty years ago told parents that an adult's aesthetic sense was established in the first year of life. Other writers have advised parents not to take their infants to the movies, lest they be harmed by the experience. Readers who wonder whether these beliefs are old-fashioned and have vanished should read the February 3, 1997, issue of *Time* magazine. The cover story, "How a Child's Brain Develops," probably worried many working parents, for it implied that if mothers do not remain home to play with their infants, their child's future psychological integrity would be compromised. "In an age when mothers and fathers are increasingly pressed for time . . . the results coming out of the labs are likely to increase concerns about leaving very young children in the care of others. For the data underscore the importance of hands-on-parenting, of finding time to cuddle a baby, talk with a toddler, and provide infants with stimulating experiences."[1]

The same advice was a frequent theme in Sunday sermons in America delivered over two hundred years ago, and it continues to generate unnecessary anxiety among perfectly competent parents. Of course, infants who are neglected, abused, and rarely played with will be slowed or seriously retarded in their psychological growth; whether the retardation will be permanent should the child's environment change is less clear. But most neglecting or abusive parents do not read *Time* magazine, while the vast majority who do are providing their infants with adequate love and stimulation. It is not fair to tell them, in science-fiction rhetoric, that every time their baby looks up at their smiling face, "tiny bursts of electricity shoot through their brain, knitting neurons into circuits as well defined as though etched into silicon chips." Even though the essay acknowledged later that children are malleable during the opening years of life, the prose exaggerated what we know.

There are good reasons why many believe in the preservation of early structures. First, infant determinism has the illusion of being mechanistic. It is easier to state a cause–effect sequence if each new quality is preceded by one that makes a substantial contribution to it than if a new behavior suddenly emerges because of a traumatic event or maturational changes in the brain. Second, a belief in infant determinism renders the parent's first actions useful. If the bases for adult traits were not established until later childhood, the first years would seem to have no special purpose. But a third, and perhaps the most potent, reason why Americans believe in the preservation of early structures is that this doctrine is in accord with egalitarianism. Each historical period is dominated by a philosophical view—an intellectual electric fence—that most scholars try to avoid breaching. From the early medieval period to the eighteenth century, philosophers and naturalists were reluctant to reach conclusions that would contradict the Bible. Although few contemporary scientists worry about the implications of their work for Christian doctrine, a majority are concerned with the implications of their findings for the ethic of egalitarianism, and in the field of child development that anxiety makes the doctrine of infant determinism attractive. If society could arrange growth-enhancing experiences for all infants and if the resulting psychological products were preserved despite the slings and arrows of later life, we might approach the ideal of a society of equals. But if, on the other hand, the frustrations of poverty or prejudice could produce psychological discontinuities in adolescence despite a benevolent infancy, the egalitarian premise would be threatened. Thus community sentiment surrounding the idea of equality maintains this assumption.

Loyalty to the doctrine of infant determinism is also sustained by the ambiguity of the phenomena we wish to explain. As long as the adult qualities supposedly determined by infant experience remain general—like being well-adjusted or free from mental illness—we have no way to refute the notion that early experience is contributory. As long as adherents of infant determinism are unable to specify a particular outcome for a given class of infant experiences—say, a phobia of animals, introversion, suicide, substance abuse, or poor school performance—they make testing the hypothesis difficult.

Biologists, by contrast, usually begin with robust, observable outcomes and then try to explain them. The ratios of wrinkled to smooth peas in Mendel's herbarium motivated the idea of genes as a cause of heredity. Spoiled wine was the hard fact that led Pasteur to posit the existence of microbes. In these and other examples the facts came before the explanatory concepts. Too many students of development reverse this sequence by positing causes—like playing with an infant—before they specify what it is they wish to explain.

No serious investigator of human development challenges the claim that the social experiences of the first two years sculpt to some degree the profile we see on a child's second birthday. Infants who are neglected are obviously less alert, less verbal, and less enthusiastic than those who receive predictable care, affection, and playful encounters. However, the profile observed at age ten is the result of a decade of experiences, not just those that occurred in the first two years. If two-year-old children living in less stimulating environments suddenly found themselves in growth-enhancing homes, their minds would grow quickly. It is unfair to blame uneducated mothers living in poverty for not playing with and talking to their infants as frequently as they should. If these mothers knew that their indifference harmed their infant, they would alter their actions. The problem is that they do not appreciate that they can be effective agents in their child's growth; many of them have become fatalists. We will help them more by muting their fatalism than by impugning their character. The second chapter questions the faith in infant determinism and describes three important influences on development that do not emerge until later childhood.

The final chapter of this book addresses the assumption, popular among psychologists and economists, that most human action is motivated by a desire for sensory pleasure. Philosophers, by contrast, award greater power to a different motive—the universal human wish to regard the self as possessing good qualities. More philosophical works have been written on morality than on any other human quality because it is a unique and distinctive characteristic of our species. Every species inherits potentialities that make the acquisition of particular competencies easy. Talking comes readily to humans, while reading usually requires special tutoring. Assigning the symbolic labels good or bad to experience also comes easily to humans, and this disposition permeates our actions, beliefs, and emotions.

A person asked why he ordered chocolate cake may describe the pleasant sensation the dessert creates, but when asked why he cut his vacation short in order to visit his mother in the hospital, his reply, "I had to," makes no reference to sensory pleasure. Those who feel minimal guilt recognize that something is wrong with them. A female murderer out of prison on parole told an interviewer, "I never had a strong sense of sin . . . somewhere along the line I missed out on guilt."[2]

The only competing goal that scientists pit against a felt moral imperative is the claim that all volitional actions are directed at maximizing pleasure or minimizing pain. As behaviorism and psychoanalysis gained adherents, the nineteenth-century belief that the child knew right from wrong and could use his will to maximize the former was replaced with the suggestion that all moral values were conditioned habits acquired through praise and punishment. Hence, humans had less freedom of choice than they believed. By the middle of this century, this deterministic philosophy dominated most scientific explanations of moral behavior. The ancients would not have understood this gloomy, robotic description of human conscience.

Although all persons want to regard themselves as belonging to a category of "good people" as each defines that concept, this motive is vulnerable to dark forces. Philosophers, novelists, and playwrights who have attempted to capture the vulnerability have had difficulty finding the right balance between the lion and the lamb in each person. Social scientists have awarded a little too much power to the obvious desire to maximize self-interest and attain sensory pleasure and not quite enough to the universal need to be kind, loyal, and loving. This chapter does not compete with philosophical works by defending one set of ethics over another, for I ask only why humans hold any ethical position at all.

Each chapter illustrates a basic psychological principle. The seminal idea in Chapter 1 is that all behavior is influenced by the person's psychological construction of the immediate situation, which in turn is influenced by the objects and people in the perceptual field and by memories of both the immediate and the distant past. For example, if a college student is asked on a questionnaire, "Are you happy?" an affirmative reply is more likely if he had not been asked moments earlier, "How many dates did you have last month?" A child who is shy with an unfamiliar adult often laughs spontaneously with unfamiliar children. The first chapter argues that an indifference to the local influences on behavior leads some social scientists to write about psychological processes as if they were like the fingers and toes that each person carries from one situation to the next.

The principle that permeates Chapter 2 is that events which are discrepant from what has been experienced, or what is expected, are the most important causes of thought, feeling, and action. Surprises motivate interpretations, and interpretations are the critical determinants of what will be felt, remembered, and done. The child who is scolded continually for yelling becomes accustomed to the punishment; the child who is not scolded most of the time will react with considerably more feeling when a parent unexpectedly chastises him for raising his voice. Humans continually compare self with others, and the products of the comparison create beliefs about the self. If everyone in a town is dirt poor, poverty has far less serious psychological consequences than if only a minority lives with disadvantage.

This principle bears on the doctrine of infant determinism because children do not compare their personal qualities with those of others in any systematic fashion until they are five or six years old. That fact is one important reason why the events of the first two years are of less significance than psychologists or the media have claimed. And over the course of later experience, discrepant events continue to shape the psychological profile of the developing child and adolescent.

The principle which informs Chapter 3 is that humans would rather avoid the varieties of regret that follow a loss than gain the variations on joy that follow attainment of a desired goal. Put simply, most humans tend to be risk averse. Investors usually hold stocks losing value for too long a time and prefer investments in which loss is minimized over those that maximize large gains. When people must choose between avoiding a future state of sadness, fear, anxiety, shame, or guilt, or attaining the state that follows possession of power, wealth, or sexual pleasure, most have a preference, not always honored, for the former because the dysphoria usually lasts longer than the joy. Suppression of behaviors that might bring on guilt and shame serves a motive—Thomas Aquinas called it an aptitude—for virtue that is the basis of human morality.

The three chapters collectively argue that *Homo sapiens* possesses a small number of unique qualities that are present in no other animal. Uniqueness is common in biology. Snakes shed their skin, dogs do not; bears hibernate, cats do not; monkeys form dominance hierarchies, mice do not. Humans experience guilt, shame, and pride, anticipate events far in the future, invent metaphors, speak a language with a grammar, and reason about hypothetical circumstances. No other species, including apes, possesses this set of talents.

However, because a great deal of important, informative research is performed with animals, scientists feel considerable social pressure to generalize conclusions based on evidence from animals to the human condition. This strategy is successful for many phenomena. Vision and hearing, for example, are very similar in monkeys and humans. But equally confident generalizations are not possible for all human qualities. Only humans engage in symbolic rituals when they bury kin, draw on cave walls, hold beliefs about the self and the origin of the world, and worry over their loyalty to family members. Thus, it is useful to examine critically the generalizability of some current psychological concepts that rely primarily on research with animals, in order to decide which extrapolations may have gone too far. I suspect that many extrapolations, like Don Quixote's conviction that he was attacking giants rather than windmills, will turn out to be seriously inaccurate.

Although the ancients wondered about the features that define human nature, systematic empiricism in psychology is only a little over one hundred years old, and understanding is necessarily immature. If we let

Galileo's discoveries mark the birth of systematic experimentation in the physical sciences, then the social and behavioral sciences are over three hundred years behind and by analogy should resemble the physics of the seventeenth century. Robert Boyle's *The Skeptical Chymist*, written in 1661, seriously criticized the conceptions of his day. Boyle came to realize, for example, that the ashes left after a log had burned were not present in the log before it was put in the fireplace.

Three Seductive Ideas was written with Boyle's skepticism. My conclusions—that many psychological processes do not generalize broadly; that most adaptive adult characteristics are not determined by experiences of the first two years; and that the majority of our daily decisions are issued in the service of gaining or maintaining a feeling of virtue—challenge assumptions that can be traced to the philosophical foundations of the contemporary social and behavioral sciences. My selection of these three topics for examination should come as no surprise. I am a developmental psychologist, and abstract concepts like temperament, fear, attachment, and intelligence are popular in research on child development. Furthermore, controversy over the deterministic role of early experience is at the heart of many debates in this field. Finally, the universal emergence of a moral sense at the end of the second year is so striking to those who study children that its significance is difficult to ignore. A scientist who studied only college students might agree with a statement once made by Van Quine, one of the world's most respected philosophers, that human conscience is essentially a socially constructed product built from slaps and sugarplums. But no one who has seen a three-year-old's face become tense as she fails a difficult task, or heard a small child say "Yukky" to a dirty cloth lying on a laboratory floor, would find this argument persuasive.

A willingness to question these three premises must overcome strong defenses. Four conditions aid the commitment to a particular belief. The most obvious is a set of incontrovertible facts drawn from observation and experiment. Newton's contemporaries knew that the greater the force with which a stone is thrown, the farther it will travel. Thus, when Newton wrote the equation that formalized this incontrovertible fact, he encountered little resistance. Equally compelling is the power of logical explanation. Parents accepted the fact that injecting young children with a bacterium or virus could be prophylactic once the logic of the antigen–antibody interaction was presented to them in a coherent argument. The ease with which a person can imagine an explanation also aids its receptivity. How the foods we eat might influence our mood is easy to imagine, but how our genes might accomplish the same goal is more difficult to visualize. Finally, we are always friendly to explanations that are in accord with our ethical standards—what we prefer to be true. The sixteenth-century Portuguese who shipped slaves from West Africa to Brazil salved their consciences by reminding themselves that God had made Christian Europeans more civilized and virtuous than those they were exploiting.

A critique of ideas popular in the social and behavioral sciences cannot take advantage of the first two conditions and is seriously hampered by the last two. There is no large body of impeccable, interrelated facts surrounding human emotions, the role of early experience, and morality that can be arranged into logically powerful arguments. Further, psychological processes, like the equations of quantum mechanics, are inherently nonvisualizable. Faced with the failure of facts, elegant logic, and visualizability, scientists and nonscientists alike fall back on pleasing explanations that affirm their ethical standards. The popularity of infant determinism, for example, is not based on logic or a rich set of facts but on its fit with contemporary ethical views.

A critique of these three themes is by necessity philosophical in nature. Sadly, philosophical arguments have lost favor during the past half century as technically complex and counterintuitive discoveries in the physical sciences, compounded by an explosion of information and historical and cultural upheavals, have generated doubt over the possibility of objective knowledge. As a result, many have become pragmatists. Whatever works best—which often means whatever feels best—is the usual rebuttal to philosophical critiques.

But the social and behavioral sciences have not enjoyed the dramatic theoretical and methodological advances that mark the last two decades in biology, chemistry, and astrophysics and, as a result, are not working well. One reason for their halting progress is a reluctance to question the trio of ragged ideas that is the subject of this book.

CHAPTER ONE

A Passion for Abstraction

When a person, plate, or poplar tree falls to the ground, our verbal description of the event is usually accurate, and almost all listeners know what we mean. Statements like "Mary had an argument with her mother-in-law" are less certain, because the nature and intensity of the argument are not completely clear; nonetheless, most adults will share a common conception of what happened. But understanding recedes quickly if a sentence refers to invisible qualities that are attributed to large numbers of people, animals, or objects. These are the sentences of science.

What distinguishes scientific language from most conversation is the use of words to describe hypothetical events not perceived directly but intended to explain those that are. Trouble arises, however, when psychologists, sociologists, economists, and others in the social and behavioral sciences use abstract words for hidden psychological processes. Often, these words fail to specify critical information such as the type of agent, the situation in which the agent is acting, and the source of evidence for the ascription. All three are critical to understanding. Whether the phenomenon is learning, communication, depression, externalization, extroversion, cooperation, avoidance, fear, regulation, or memory, scholars who study animal and human behavior prefer to use words suggesting that a psychological process operates in essentially the same way in different agents acting in varied situations. And they stubbornly resist replacing the single abstract word with a set of related but specific terms that fit nature more faithfully.

Examples of this passion for abstraction abound, not just in popular writing but in the technical literature as well. For example, a recent book on cooperation implies that insects, fish, birds, monkeys, and humans all engage in a behavior ("cooperation") that shares a common evolutionary mechanism. Similarly, in a paper recently published in one of psychology's premier journals, the authors concluded from a laboratory study of college students playing a gambling game that "people select the gamble that minimizes negative affect."[1] This unconstrained statement ignores the age, social class, and ethnic background of the subjects, the specific nature of the gambling situation, the artificiality of a laboratory setting, and the specific emotion the students experienced. By using the adjective "negative," the authors appear to be telling us that it is not very important whether the subject's emotion was guilt, shame, fear, anger, anxiety, or boredom.

The contrasting view, held by Whitehead and Wittgenstein, insists that every description of a phenomenon should refer to both the event and the circumstances of the observation. There is no guarantee, Whitehead warned, that a particular concept always represents "the immediate deliverances of experience." The psychological state of a fleeing mouse, a grimacing monkey, and a worried college student are sufficiently different that we should be suspicious of the suggestion that each is in a similar psychological state. Wittgenstein's metaphor for the inexact use of language was a pair of tight shoes that deformed the object it was intended to fit.[2]

This chapter examines four popular but controversial psychological concepts that illustrate this habit of ambitious overgeneralization. They are fear, consciousness, intelligence, and temperament—each word an abstraction hiding a set of diverse phenomena that would be better described with families of related but decidedly different terms. I chose these ideas from the potentially large number that could have been chosen because two of the four—fear and consciousness—have become recent targets of elegant research by neuroscientists, who have begun to give new meanings to these old words. The other two—intelligence and temperament—were selected because they are currently centers of intense debate both inside and beyond the academic community. After a short period of relative silence on the importance of IQ, the publication in 1994 of *The Bell Curve* by Richard Herrnstein and Charles Murray provoked widespread societal discussion of this idea. Similarly, after seventy years of exile, the notion of temperament has returned to challenge older theories of personality development and psychopathology that ignored the influence of the person's biology.

All four terms refer to phenomena that are of critical contemporary interest. But because each word is being used without specification of either the class of agent or the context of actualization, it can claim only partial insight into the phenomena we wish to understand.

Fear and Anxiety

Imagine a psychologist who asks 1,000 people to answer two dozen questions about their fears, worries, and anxieties. The sources of concern include money, status, friends, violence, public speaking, strangers, illness, death, nightmares, storms, animals, and their child's future. Each person checks yes or no to each query. Over two-thirds of the informants report less than three apprehensions, but 15 percent admit to ten or more. These 150 people differ in age, gender, social class, ethnicity, and actual stress in their lives, and they worry about different things. One is an unmarried, poor, 35-year-old single mother of three children who lives in a violent urban neighborhood of a large city; a second is a 45-year-old man with stomach cancer; and a third, a 25-year-old woman from a wealthy family, has just graduated from law school. The circumstances of their lives diverge drastically, yet the different reasons for each profile of worries are lost when the psychologist categorizes all three as "anxious."

Almost half of American adults report a bout of depression, anxiety, alcoholism, or substance abuse during their lifetime, and the incidence of these psychological problems is greatest among economically stressed parents who have young children. It does not take great wisdom to appreciate that this group of adults has some reason to worry about the future of their families and that some might become depressed, temporarily, or be tempted to abuse alcohol as a way to cope with the actual stress in their daily lives.[3]

Social phobia, too, is most prevalent among those with marginal income and education. A psychiatrist diagnoses a person as a social phobic if the patient says she feels so uncomfortable with strangers that she avoids social gatherings such as restaurants where strangers might evaluate her behavior. Poor, less-educated women from rural areas are most likely to describe themselves this way and therefore to receive the diagnosis "social phobia."[4] However, it should not be surprising that a twenty-year-old high school dropout who is embarrassed about her education, unskilled job, and social position would want to avoid meeting those with more wealth and education. On the other hand, a female physician who is afraid of meeting strangers is likely to present a different history and psychological state; yet both women receive the same diagnosis. The meaning of the word "anxious" is not like the adjective "blue-eyed," for its meaning can vary when it is applied to people from different ethnic or national backgrounds who have lived under dissimilar circumstances.

Most investigators who study "anxiety" or "fear" use answers on a standard questionnaire or responses to an interviewer to decide which of their subjects are anxious or fearful. A smaller number of scientists asks close friends or relatives of each subject to evaluate how anxious that person is. A still smaller group measures the heart rate, blood pressure, galvanic skin response, or salivary cortisol level of their subjects. Unfortunately, these three sources of information rarely agree. Many adults who show a large rise in heart rate and increased sweating on their palms while watching slides of dangerous scenes deny that they feel fearful or anxious while viewing the pictures. And many of those whose friends describe them as anxious do not show a rise in heart rate or increased sweating in their palms when looking at the pictures. Each way of assessing anxiety yields a different answer to the question, "Who is anxious?"[5]

Historical events have eroded an earlier distinction between fear and anxiety. The contrast between the two is sharpest when we compare the emotional state created by brake failure, as one is hurtling at 60 mph to-ward a truck stopped at a red light, with the emotional state created by anticipation of an important job interview one week hence. The two feeling states differ not only in intensity and quality but also in the content of thoughts about the future.

The dissolution of the semantic barrier between fear and anxiety has a complex history. Fear assumed greater prominence in Christian Europe during medieval times because of a preoccupation with God's wrath. Saint Augustine nominated fear as a fundamental emotion but distinguished between the fear of being punished for a sin, either by God in this life or by the Devil in the next, and worry over being forsaken by a beloved or by God (which seemed to fall midway between guilt and anxiety over social disapproval). Augustine regarded fear of divine punishment as a blessing because it helped humans behave morally, and John Bunyan, writing almost a thousand years later, reasserted the belief that fear of God permitted one to love the Deity.

The modern view, by contrast, holds that fear restricts the capacity for love. We have Freud to thank for this perspective, for he distinguished between the fear created by a present danger and the anxiety created by anticipation of a possible one and indicted the latter as the culprit in all of the neuroses. Neurotic symptoms, according to Freud and his followers, were learned behaviors whose purpose was to reduce anxiety produced by conflict over sexuality. By arguing that anxiety could be resolved if one emptied the unconscious of its repressed wishes, Freud implied that anxiety was not a necessary emotion and that everyone, potentially, could be freed of this feeling. It was pleasing to entertain the possibility that, with effort, we could all be rid of this enemy of serenity. Who would not welcome such a lovely state?

Another important strand in the tangled history of the relation between fear and anxiety was Darwin's naturalization of the human emotions, as described in *The Expression of the Emotions in Man and Animals* (1872). During succeeding years, scholars regarded the animal's state as the more natural one; and animals, they observed, behave as though they might be fearful. Because the imminent threat of harm elicits distinct reactions in both animals and humans (primates and humans even show similar facial and postural expressions in the presence of danger), the emotion of fear was treated as an inherent aspect of human nature, and was freed from its long-standing moral connotations. It was far less obvious that animals can become anxious, for they do not seem capable of worrying about the distant future. Thus, fear was naturalized, but anxiety was not.

Our evaluation of whether fear is functional or dysfunctional has changed even within this century. During the thirty-year ascendancy of behaviorism in American psychology—roughly 1930 to 1960—fear was regarded as an uncomfortable but natural state, originating in pain, that nevertheless motivated the learning of new, often adaptive, habits. But during the last two decades, as neuroscientists studied the brain events mediating fear and as public and private funding agencies became more concerned with mental illness, fear has once again become the villainous cause of psychological disorders and, as such, has been marked with the stigma of abnormality.

If life's assignment is to control hedonistic desires, as in Saint Augustine's century, fear is an ally and not an alien force. But if the day's assignment is to gain friends, seduce a lover, and take risks for status and material gain, fear is the enemy. As history altered the daily scripts people were to follow, fear displaced desire as the emotion to subdue. If humans must restrain greed, lust, competitiveness, and aggression, then self-control, in the form of will, is a prerequisite. But each person's will is less potent when fear is the demon to be tamed, for it is more difficult to rid oneself of fear than to control an action aimed at gaining a desired state of affairs. Thus history relegated will to the same ash heap of ideas where Newton's ether lies gathering dust. The belief that humans can and should be free of anxiety is one of the distinguishing illusions in Western thought in this century.

Contemporary neuroscientists would like to believe that eventually the neural bases for fear will be discovered, to be followed by pharmacological interventions that could eliminate anxiety from human experience. The neuroscientists also imply that neurotic symptoms—for example, obsessive thoughts or avoidance of people—are direct reactions to the fear state itself and need not have any therapeutic value. The contrast between this and the older view reflects the new belief that biolog-

ical processes, whether genes or brain states, have direct effects on behavior that are not modulated by history or cultural setting. The claim
that a man's avoidance of parties is a direct product of his brain state dif-
fers from the earlier claim that he learned to avoid parties because he
felt less anxious when he stayed home.

Psychiatrists and psychologists continually survey the prevalence of
human anxiety about public speaking, high places, large animals, or
leaving home, on the premise that anxiety is unnatural and unhealthy.
But, surprisingly, they do not gather comparable information on the
prevalence of anger at friends, employers, relatives, drivers, policemen,
or public officials, because presumably they tacitly believe that anger is
natural and possibly even healthy. Among the ancient Greeks, by contrast, anger was of greater concern than anxiety because it interfered
with societal harmony.[6]

The modern assumption that anxiety is abnormal and maladaptive
has to be incorrect. A feeling of apprehension before speaking to a large
group of strangers is as natural, and quintessentially human, as is anger
at being cut off by a motorist at an intersection. Thus, we must ask why
contemporary psychologists and psychiatrists regard anxiety, but not
anger, as a potential sign of mental illness. One part of the answer is that
anxiety, particularly social anxiety, seems to be a greater burden than
anger in modern society; it is less adaptive in a world where taking risks
and meeting people are often required for vocational success. An ill-
tempered employee may not go as far in his career as an even-tempered
one, but both will probably do better than a person who finds it difficult
to talk to strangers.

Other events in this century helped to fold the ideas of fear and anxiety into each other. The world lived for almost fifty years with the
chronic worry that America and the Soviet Union might launch nuclear warheads that would destroy civilization. Was worry about this
terrible possibility an instance of fear or of anxiety? The answer was
not clear. The media have also warned the public about the threat of
overpopulation, AIDS, polluted water, tainted food, smog, cigarette
smoke, and global warming. Do these dangers create a state of fear or
anxiety? Finally, antianxiety drugs, like Valium and Prozac, turned out
to be effective whether one was afraid of driving over long bridges or

worried about being watched in a restaurant. If fear and anxiety were distinctly different states, the drugs should not be effective with both of them. Perhaps they were the same state. Authors of popular personality questionnaires, who believe they have finally discovered the foundations of human personality, collapsed the varied forms of fear and anxiety into a single factor called *emotionality*.

Laboratory research on animals has reinforced the idea that fear and anxiety are close relatives. Elegant experiments with mice and rats have now identified the neural circuits that are activated when an animal acquires a conditioned fear reaction to a tone that, in the past, signaled a painful electric shock. Consequently, fear reactions such as bodily freezing (that is, not moving) or a rise in heart rate when the tone is heard are now interpreted as a sign of an acquired state of fear that was created earlier by the close temporal association between the tone and the shock. Because few scientists were willing to say that rats experience anxiety—meaning they anticipated future pain—it became easier either to dismiss the importance of that state in humans or to assume, without detailed argument, that fear in a mouse was closely related to anxiety in a human.[7]

It is reasonable, however, to wonder whether rats that suddenly freeze in place when they hear a tone which in the past had signaled painful electric shock are in a brain state that is essentially the same as the one experienced by a passenger being told that the plane will have to make a forced landing on water in the next few minutes. Rats will also freeze to a tone that, in the past, had signaled a loud noise rather than shock.[8] Surely, anticipation of a loud noise generates a state different from the state created by the threat of painful electric shock; yet the animal's reaction—freezing—is the same. One good reason for distinguishing between the state following a painful shock in rats and in humans is that the latter have a much larger frontal lobe. When humans hear a tone that had been associated with electric shock, the frontal lobes are activated and the person quickly acquires control of the biological signs of fear after only two exposures to the tone. That phenomenon could not occur in rats.

Pavlov conditioned dogs to salivate to a sound by placing food powder in their mouths after the sound. But Pavlov did not suggest that the sound created a state of hunger that was indexed by salivation in the conditioned animals. Analogously, women who watched erotic films often experienced engorgement of the vaginal wall as a conditioned physiological reaction, but the degree of engorgement was not positively correlated with the women's reports of the intensity of sexual arousal they felt. Many women reported feeling no sexual arousal when the engorgement occurred.[9]

The extensive corpus of evidence on the role of the amygdala in emotion suggests that this neural structure, located in the medial side of the temporal lobe, is activated by a diverse set of events that psychologists call aversive—for example, electric shock or a loud noise—and produces a family of reactions that can include freezing, retreat, biting, a rise in heart rate, and the release of chemicals, including cortisol and opioids. But it is less clear that these brain events always signify, or create, a fear state if fear means an unpleasant feeling different from the one created by the shock or loud noise itself. When adults were exposed very briefly (only 3/100 of a second) to pictures of faces with either a fearful or a happy expression, followed immediately by a longer exposure to a face with a neutral expression, they reported seeing only the latter and they did not report feeling anxious during the period when the invisible fearful faces were presented. Nevertheless, measures of their brain states revealed a significant increase in activity in the amygdala when the fearful faces appeared.[10]

It may be a conceptual error, therefore, to assume that the circuit which mediates the acquisition of a conditioned response like freezing, salivating, or engorgement of the vaginal wall is identical to the circuit that mediates the conscious emotional states of fear, hunger, or sexual arousal. I trust no one believes that being passionately in love is nothing more than a circuit involving the hypothalamus, autonomic nervous system, and engorged circulatory vessels in the genitals. It is not obvious that a conditioned freezing response in an animal is sufficient evidence to assume that the animal is in an emotional state of fear. The scientists who condition animals to freeze to a tone are treating fear as an essence, much like nineteenth-century physicists treated space, time, and matter. I suggest that we replace the question "What are the brain bases of fear?" with "How do different species react, in brain and body, to events that signal danger?"

During the period between the two world wars, psychologists thought that the study of hungry rats learning to traverse a maze to get food was a good model for the study of human intelligence. That promise was never kept because the phenomena that comprise human cognitive talents are too different from those that help a rat figure out the correct turns in a maze. I suspect there may be a similar frustration of the hope that a rat's freezing upon hearing a tone associated with electric shock is a useful model for human worry over loss of a loved one, poor performance on an exam, competitive pressure from one's co-workers, or finding a lump in one's breast. Richard Feynman suggested once that no one understands quantum mechanics; I suspect no one understands fear, either, at least not yet.

Every time investigators believe they have finally found a biological or behavioral marker for fear or anxiety, subsequent research undermines their optimism. Twenty-five years ago, many psychologists believed that the galvanic skin reflex—that is, activity of the sweat glands—measured human anxiety. It turned out that almost any change in the external environment or any intrusive thought produced this reflex. Increases in heart rate, blood pressure, or cortisol level in the presence of a threat also enjoyed a short period of enthusiasm but, as with the sweating response, subsequent evidence vitiated their sensitivity as indicators of anxiety.

Potentiated startle has become, in a relatively short time, a candidate for this important responsibility.[11] The rationale for selecting this reaction originated in work with animals. A rat exposed to an unexpected brief loud burst of noise shows a bodily startle of a given magnitude. The rat undergoes a series of conditioning trials in which the onset of a light becomes the signal for delivery of a painful electric shock. It is presumed that after many such trials the light eventually is able to provoke a state of fear in the conditioned animal, as evidenced by the fact that the rat freezes and shows a heart rate rise when the light is flashed. When rats conditioned in this way were exposed to a light followed three seconds later by a burst of loud sound, the magnitude of their startle reflex was larger than it had been before undergoing conditioning—for example, instead of the original four units, it was now six units.

This robust result has been interpreted as indicating that the light created a state of fear which, in turn, enhanced the startle. If this hypothesis were true, then if a person startles more than usual in the presence of an aversive stimulus, the enhanced startle might mean that the person was indeed in a fear state.

The reasonableness of this exciting idea motivated investigators to implement two changes in the procedure used with animals.[12] A reflex eye blink following a sudden loud noise is an essential component of every bodily startle, and it is easy to measure by placing electrodes under the eye to detect the magnitude of muscle contraction. However, because human subjects do not like to be shocked (even for the sake of advancing science), pictures of very unpleasant scenes replaced the light and shock combination, on the assumption that an adult staring at a bleeding soldier should be in a state analogous to a rat that has seen a light that had been associated with shock. It turned out that adults did have larger eye blink reflexes when the loud noise occurred while the person was looking at an aversive picture, compared with a neutral or pleasant one. This fact was heartening, and it looked as though scientists finally had discovered a way to measure fear in humans. But over the years, as with the galvanic skin reflex, heart rate, and cortisol, the dream has begun to fade.

First, experiments revealed that hungry college students showed larger eye blinks when viewing pictures of food than did nonhungry subjects. It is a bit tortuous to argue that a hungry twenty-year-old looking at a picture of ice cream is in a state of fear, and more reasonable to believe that the pictures of food elicited thoughts of eating in hungry subjects. Other experiments indicated that the magnitude of the eye blink was larger if the loud noise occurred ten seconds after an unpleasant picture had appeared on the screen rather than two seconds.[13] If a picture of a bloodied soldier elicits fear, it should do so quickly and not require ten seconds to develop. These facts suggested that perhaps the blink reflex was larger when the person was engaged in thought; we know from anecdotal experience that people are most likely to startle to an unexpected noise when they are sitting at a desk deeply engrossed in a mental task. This assumption would explain why the magnitude of the blink was greater when hungry adults saw pictures of food or when the noise burst occurred ten seconds after the appearance of an unpleasant picture.

This possibility finds support in a study in which adults were told that a series of circles or ellipses would appear on a screen. They were instructed to ignore the circles but to count the number of times an ellipse remained on the screen for a relatively long period of time. Thus, the adults were more likely to be engaged in thought when an ellipse was present than when the circles were on the screen. It turned out that the startle reflex was larger to ellipses than to circles. A person trying to remember the number of times an ellipse was on a screen for more than a few seconds is in a thoughtful state, not a fearful one. Apparently that cognitive state facilitates a potentiated startle reflex in humans.[14]

One important reason why no single behavior, including potentiated startle, can be relied on to index a person's (or an animal's) state of fear is that each response is controlled by a variety of brain mechanisms and can serve more than one purpose. When infant squirrel monkeys were separated from their mother, no correlation was found between the magnitude of change in their behavior and the magnitude of change in levels of the stress hormone cortisol circulating in their blood. Most of the time the relation between the presumed intensity of a fear state and the magnitude of a particular response is nonlinear. For example, rats showed potentiated startle to a light that had been paired with an electric shock of moderate intensity but showed a smaller potentiated startle when the light had been paired with a shock of very high intensity. If the magnitude of a startle is supposed to index the intensity of fear, then surely the startle should be greater to a light that had been associated with a very painful shock.

However, the mammalian brain was not constructed to make scientific research easy. It turns out that when the shock is of moderate intensity, activation of the ventral periaqueductal gray—a collection of neurons that sends axons to the brain stem—leads to a hypervigilant state that prepares an animal for the possibility of danger. The potentiated startle is one component of this state, in part because the central nucleus of the amygdala sends projections, via the ventral gray, to a nucleus in the brain stem that innervates the motor component of the bodily startle. However, when the shock used in conditioning is intense, the dorsal periaqueductal gray—a different set of neurons—is activated, and as a result the vigilant state and its correlated behaviors are replaced with reactions that are more appropriate when danger is imminent. It appears that the potentiated startle is one of the responses that is attenuated, in part because the dorsal gray may inhibit the amygdala. Humans would report greater fear, but would show a smaller potentiated startle, to the anticipation of intense rather than moderate levels of pain.

Perhaps these findings explain why some seven-year-old children who possessed a temperament characterized by high levels of fearfulness in the second year were unlikely to blink to a sudden loud noise delivered at a time when they thought they might experience an aversive event—in this case, a blast of air to the throat. These same children also found it easy to ignore the meaning of pictures symbolic of fear—for example, a picture of a snake—when they were asked to name the color of the picture's outline. By contrast, the children who showed the largest potentiated startle when they thought they might experience the aversive blast of air were least able to ignore the meaning of the picture when they had to name the color of its outline quickly. And these children had been minimally fearful to unfamiliarity and challenge during their early childhood.[15]

Thus, we are faced with what appears to be a paradox. Children whose ordinary behavior implied a high level of fearfulness reacted to two laboratory procedures that were supposed to index fear as if they were not very fearful, while children who were not behaviorally fearful in the world reacted to the procedures as if they were fearful. It is impossible to avoid the conclusion that the word fear must have multiple meanings.

A sudden unexpected noise, a grizzly bear peering at you from two hundred yards away, the bear lunging at your throat, a light that has been associated with shock, and worry about losing one's job while walking in a quiet meadow probably involve different brain circuits and therefore represent different psychological states that should not be placed on a continuum that might be called intensity of fear. By analogy, the psychological and bodily states of a person who has not eaten for twelve hours are qualitatively different from the state of one who has not eaten for four days. The latter is not just hungrier.

Another reason why no single index can be trusted to reveal either the quality or intensity of fear—or any emotion, for that matter—is that humans and animals differ genetically, from species to species and from individual to individual, in the magnitude of the reaction used to index fear. For example, a strain of mice called DBA showed greater potentiated startle than a related strain called C57, even though both strains were conditioned in exactly the same way.[16] Similarly, different species of monkeys differed in their reaction to the stress of being removed from familiar animals; crabeater monkeys became much more disturbed than rhesus, for example.

The prize of finding the procedure that will measure intensity of fear or anxiety continues to elude us because we have not acknowledged that it is a family of states and that no single reaction could reflect all members of the family accurately. Indeed, psychiatrists and psychologists now believe that each of the so-called anxiety disorders is genetically heterogeneous. If there are distinctly different types of human anxiety, then conditioned fear in an animal cannot be a model for anxiety states in humans.

The central problem is that fear is being used in two different ways. Most people use the word fear to name a subjective conscious experience. Most scientists, by contrast, use this word as a hypothetical construct to explain an empirically demonstrated relation between an incentive event (such as a light associated with an electric shock) and some reaction (such as bodily freezing or a rise in heart rate). These two circumstances require different words.

A person's interpretation of their feeling as fear is an event in nature that we wish to understand; it is not simply epiphenomenal to the firing of a circuit that involves the amygdala. The scientists' construct of fear, on the other hand, names a hypothetical set of processes that tries to account for a relation between real events, until the term is replaced by a better one. Confusion arises because we tend to confer onto this explanatory use of fear a set of features that belong only to a person's conscious state.

I would propose at least three different sources of the states that we now call fear, and each is different from the sources of a state we might call anxiety. One source of fear, popular among ethologists, consists of the biologically prepared tendency of every vertebrate species to withdraw, attack, become immobile, or issue a distress call in the presence of any one of a small class of events that signal potential harm, even though no prior conditioning or learning has occurred. For example, a head containing eyes with a pupil-to-eye ratio that is slightly over 0.5 produces immobility in chickens.[17] Prolonged exposure to a bright light enhances the startle reflex to loud sound in rats. A looming object makes infants cry. The varied stimuli that have this power to produce a response in the absence of learning are called *innate releasers* or sometimes evolutionarily significant stimuli, and they are thought to be more numerous in animals than in humans. These events have features that interact with the structure of a particular species' nervous system to produce freezing, startle, distress calls, or flight without any prior experience.

A second source of fear consists of discrepant events—events that are similar to familiar ones but are not assimilated immediately. Just as the ability to detect the energy in light or in touch has been preserved from mice to humans over the course of evolution, so too is the ability to detect an event that is different from one experienced in the immediate past—say, during the last few seconds—or one that is a transformation of a representation acquired in the deep past. A face with only one eye is likely to make us afraid because it is a discrepant transformation of what human faces look like; we call such a creature a monster. Some animals and children who are placed in new surroundings often freeze or retreat in the less familiar location. When four different dog breeds—Labrador retriever, sheep dog, boxer, and German shepherd—were observed in varied settings, the behavior separating the species most clearly was avoidance of unfamiliar objects on a busy street. German shepherds were the most avoidant; Labradors the least.[18]

Tibetan villagers believe that the fear created by a discrepant event is dangerous for it can cause the soul to leave the body, resulting in lethargy and loss of energy. A similar belief was shared by many nineteenth-century European physicians. A Glasgow physician sent a short communication to a medical journal describing a woman who was looking out the window when a man passing on the street "thrust a singed sheep's head close to the window pane. She screamed and her screams brought her mother, who found, as she got her quieted, that her mind was completely deranged and has remained in that state till this time."[19]

Fear of the unfamiliar is not present at birth because newborns have no acquired knowledge and therefore no expectations of what is normal. Fear of discrepant events appears in puppies at about six to seven weeks of age, in birds at two to four days, and in humans at seven to ten months. That is why fear of strangers and fear of separation from the caretaker emerge toward the end of the first year. Sometimes, as in the human fear of snakes, minimal experience is needed to create a state of fear, possibly because snakes' shape and form of movement are unusual and therefore discrepant. Isaac Marks, a British psychiatrist who has written an informative book on fears, recalls an incident with his 2½-year-old son:

He had never seen snakes nor did he know the word for them. I carried him over rocky terrain from a car to a beach at low tide. On the dry sand were exposed thousands of dried skeins of brown, black seaweed about a foot long looking like myriad dead eels or tiny snakes . . . As soon as the boy saw the dried seaweed on the sand, he screamed in terror and clutched me tightly trying to stop me from sitting on the sand. When I touched the seaweed, he shrieked and refused to do the same . . . The next day he touched the seaweed a bit more readily but was still obviously afraid. A week later he was able to throw the fronds away but was still unhappy to leave them in his hand. He gradually lost his terror with continuing exposure to the frightening situation.[20]

The ability to detect discrepancy has obvious evolutionary advantages because mismatches between past and present are often clues to a dangerous situation or to an opportunity to gain desirable resources.

Every mammal is capable of detecting such mismatches, and valuable new information about the world is acquired most often when a mismatch is detected.

Some neurons, in both the cortex and the brain stem, are devoted solely to detecting these mismatches. One important function of a collection of neurons in the brain stem called the superior colliculus is to initiate eye movements that track a moving target. Consider a tennis player tracking the trajectory of a tennis ball hit to his right side. Neurons in the superior colliculus permit the player to maintain his fixation on the moving ball, by detecting a mismatch between the place where the eyes are focused and the changing position of the moving ball. These neurons do not cause the eyes to move; they simply determine when there is a discrepancy and send that information to other neurons that make the correction in eye movement.[21] This finding implies that detecting difference is built into the oldest and most fundamental structures of the brain.

A third, and the most popular, source of fear derives from classical conditioning. In 1920 John Watson and his assistant, Rosalie Rayner, became famous for reporting that they had conditioned an infant to cry when he was shown a rat by presenting a very loud sound as the rat was presented. The two scientists even speculated on the free associations this child might confess to his psychoanalyst twenty-five years later.[22]

The acquisition of conditioned fear responses is mediated by a well-delineated neural circuit that includes the thalamus, basolateral and central areas of the amygdala, and the amygdala's projections to target structures that produce the behavioral and autonomic signs of fear. Some neuroscientists believe that this circuit is the biological foundation of all states of fear, including those caused by innate releasers, discrepant events, and classical conditioning. This claim resembles Pavlov's hypothesis that the conditioned salivary reflex was a good model for most acquired human behaviors. However, these three different states of fear are probably mediated by different biological structures and circuits.

For example, the enhanced startle a rat shows to a light that has become a conditioned stimulus for pain requires the central nucleus of the amygdala. But the enhanced startle reflex that occurs when a rat has first been exposed to twenty minutes of bright light does not require the central nucleus but a different structure, called the bed nucleus.[23] When mice were exposed to five different incentives that typically produce freezing—for example, an unfamiliar object, an unfamiliar environment, and a bright light in a dark compartment—mice that froze to one of these events were not more likely to freeze to a different one. The five situations, which were supposed to elicit the same state of fear, did not produce similar behaviors in the animals. That fact suggests that each situation elicited a different state.[24]

An experiment with the same purpose involved six inbred strains of rats that were exposed to varied discrepant situations (for example, being placed in a novel, open field or in a maze with open and closed arms), including exposure to unfamiliar animals. As with the mice, the rat strains did not behave similarly in these situations. One strain of animals that explored the open field (suggesting minimal fear) avoided the unfamiliar rats (suggesting high fear).[25]

One experiment provides persuasive support for rejecting the notion of a single fear state. Rats placed in a maze that had some brightly lit alleys avoided those alleys and went to a darker one, presumably because the light provoked a state of fear. Rats also avoided an object that delivered an electric shock when they contacted it. The avoidance is also presumed to be the result of fear. However, the avoidance of the brightly lit alleys requires a brain structure called the septum but does not require the amygdala. The avoidance of the object that delivered shock requires the amygdala but not the septum. Even though the rats avoided both the brightly lit alleys and the object that delivered an electric shock, the brain circuits mediating these behaviors were not the same. When rats whose amygdala had been removed were placed in a location where they had previously experienced electric shock, they showed less behavioral signs of fear but higher levels of plasma corticosterone—a hormone that often accompanies a fear state—than rats whose amygdala was intact.[26]

Similarly, young rhesus monkeys who had their amygdala removed showed less avoidance of some unfamiliar situations but more, rather than less, avoidance to the approach of other monkeys than rhesus whose amygdala had not been removed.[27] This result suggests that the brain states that mediate fear in unfamiliar places are not the same as those that produce fear to other animals, at least in monkeys. This possibility is real because rats do not require their hippocampus in order to learn to freeze to a tone that had been followed by shock but do require this structure in order to learn to freeze in the place where they were shocked. The acquisition of a conditioned freezing reaction to a tone or to a place are the consequences of different brain states.

When scientists observed that rats avoid brightly lit places, they related this observation to the fact that when people avoid a place, they often explain their behavior by claiming they are fearful. As a result, the scientists studying rats assumed that rats in a brightly lit alley were also in a state of fear. But the fact that two phenomena share a single feature—in this case, avoiding a particular place—is an insufficient basis for assuming that a similar process mediates both phenomena. This criticism applies whether we are attributing depression to two-year-olds or consciousness to animals. Darwin insisted that no species can be defined by a single characteristic.

The concept of a single fear state, therefore, should be replaced with a family of terms for related but distinct states, each with its own class of incentives, neurophysiological profiles, and behavioral reactions, and each should be clearly distinguished from human anxiety. Sentences containing the word fear that do not specify its environmental origins and the animal's (or person's) specific reactions are not helpful. This position shares features with Sartre's *Sketch for a Theory of Emotions* which rejected the usefulness of emotional words that did not specify a target.[28] Scientists who work with animals and psychiatrists treating patients use very different evidence to infer a state of fear. The former rely on brain circuits and behaviors, while the latter use the person's reports of their feelings and their judgment of the patient's adaptation to his or her setting. The two forms of evidence are so different it is unlikely they refer to the same event in nature. To borrow an idea from Hilary Putnam, if psychology (like philosophy) is to be informative, it has to descend from a global to a more local level.[29]

Societies invented words in order to communicate efficiently about everyday events. If I tell a friend, "I'm angry," he will understand that something occurred recently to lower my threshold for a hostile act.

That terse statement is sufficient for the pragmatics of our interaction, but it does not permit the listener to differentiate my anger at a thief who stole my car from anger at myself for losing my keys. Similarly the surprise that follows seeing a muskrat in my kitchen is not the same surprise that follows learning that a colleague is much younger than I had believed. The first surprise originates in violation of a perceptual expectation. The second originates in a disconfirmation of conceptual structures. In everyday conversation, words stuff dissimilar phenomena into the same drawer for the sake of efficiency. Scientists, by contrast, make advances when they open those drawers and separate the distinctive objects inside.

"Fear" is in desperate need of such an analysis. People who read that "fear is due to a neural circuit that requires the integrity of the thalamus and amygdala" will extract a meaning from the statement; unfortunately the meanings they extract may be different. Neuroscientists will think of the rat freezing in the presence of a tone that had been associated with shock; clinical psychologists and psychiatrists will think of a patient describing her fear of going to restaurants. The ambiguity is reduced considerably if the first sentence is replaced with, "A rat's acquisition of a conditioned freezing reaction to a tone associated with shock requires the thalamus, amygdala, and central gray." Now the truth value is ascertainable. The problem with a great deal of the scientific literature is that scholars more often use sentences of the first than of the second type. They rarely specify the class of agent (rats), the context (a conditioning procedure in a laboratory), and the source of the evidence (freezing to a tone).

It is likely that a variety of events, some aversive and some discrepant, can activate the thalamus, amygdala, and its projections, even though the outcome of those activations need not always be a state of fear. A person would feel fearful if a large animal were about to attack but would feel annoyed by the noise of a jackhammer, disgusted by an unpleasant odor, and excited if he were about to make his first parachute jump. The thalamus, amygdala, and their projections could be active in all four states.

Many years ago most psychologists believed that select nuclei in the hypothalamus were the site of hunger because animals ate when these neurons were stimulated, even though they were not food deprived and the eating probably did not create pleasure. However, recent investigators have demonstrated that these neurons were actually the basis of a more diffuse state that led to different behaviors depending upon the immediate context. If food were available, the animal ate; if water was presented, the animal drank; and if small wood chips were placed on the floor of the cage, the animal retrieved them.[30] I suspect that a similar story might be told for the amygdala.

Imagine an experiment in which the amygdala of male rats was stimulated when the context was either a sexually receptive female, an intruder, or a perceptual challenge requiring the rats to discriminate between a large rectangle and a small sphere in order to get a food pellet. If the stimulated animals showed more vigorous mating behavior, more effective biting of the intruder, and faster discrimination, which are possibilities if the stimulation was not intense, we would have to acknowledge that the amygdala, like the hypothalamus, participates in multiple states and mediates different behaviors depending on the context. As with activation of the hypothalamus, stimulation of the amygdala need not always create a state of fear. The pheromones secreted by ewes in estrus, which excite olfactory structures, also excite the amygdala of male sheep, and projections from the amygdala to the hypothalamus lead to hormonal changes that create sexual arousal, not fear.[31]

Recognition of the significance of the local context may bring the disciplines of neurobiology and psychology closer together. The recent rapprochement of evolutionary and developmental biology, after a century of separation, provides a fruitful analogy. The former field is concerned with the many forces that created the thousands of species that represent the diversity of life, while the latter is concerned with the processes involved in pre- and postnatal growth of the individual. The student of evolution knows that gene mutations are critical for the emergence of a new species, but until recently the student of development had regarded genes as stable molecules that were equally potent in all bodily tissues simultaneously. This older conception of genes was inconsistent with the dramatic brain and behavioral changes that mark individual development. However, when molecular biologists discovered that genes were not always active in all cells at the same time but were selectively turned on and off in a dynamic temporal pattern, it became clear that genes contributed to both evolution and development.

A tension exists today between those neuroscientists who believe that the structure of the body and brain constrains the number and nature of human emotional states and those social scientists and humanists who believe that culture can expand or contract substantially the number and variety of possible psychic states. No one questions that the structure of the human visual system limits the range of wavelengths that humans can perceive. However, a painter can construct a large variety of different shades for each of the visible hues. The same can be said for emotions like fear. Students of culture are impressed with the differences in phenomenology and coping reactions among those who fear illness, death, witches, rejection, God, dangerous animals, and task failure. A useful maxim in the natural sciences is: When you encounter a contradiction, make a distinction.

A compromise position argues that activation of a particular brain circuit, producing an accompanying physiological state, is the biological foundation of a family of related but nonetheless different human emotions. The brain does constrain the number and quality of possible human emotions, but no brain state is linked in a deterministic way to any specific human emotion. The events of the individual's past and the context of the present can produce different psychological experiences, thoughts, and actions in individuals who are, for a period of several seconds, in the same brain state. This possibility is analogous to isomeric crystals that have exactly the same chemical composition but different properties. In a sense, the difficulty of discovering the connection between behaviors and emotions, on the one hand, and brain processes, on the other, is analogous to a similar frustration faced by physicists trying to find the connection between Newton's laws of mechanics for large objects and the electrodynamic events that occur at the subatomic level. Much behavior is punctate, goal-directed, and influenced by feelings. None of these properties applies to neurons or circuits.

Recent discoveries in molecular evolution are relevant to the discontinuity between brain and psychic phenomena. It appears that many small changes in DNA sequences have no functional consequences for the animal's physiology or anatomy.[32] Analogously, one might speculate that many spontaneous changes in synaptic configurations have no functional consequences for the feelings, thoughts, and actions of the individual. Should that speculation prove true, we would expect a theoretical gap between brain and mind, as there is between the DNA sequences that comprise the genome and the features of the phenotype.

No physiologist would confuse the blood level of lipids or glucose, each of which contributes to a state of hunger, with the subjective experience of being hungry. Similarly no one should assume that the neural circuits that are correlated with, and may be necessary for, a conscious feeling of fear are identical with, or account completely for, the individual's subjective experience of being afraid. Being afraid is not just the addition of awareness to the discharge of the limbic system.

The biology of the brain provides the basis for an envelope of psychological outcomes, just as a large outdoor pen constrains the animals inside but does not determine any one arrangement of the animals. The psychological outcome that is actualized from a particular brain state is a function of what philosophers call boundary conditions. The thoughts of a person lying quietly in a PET scanner are not predictable from the pattern of metabolic activity because boundary conditions, stated in psychological language, determine which thoughts will be realized. The psychological event has a structure that is derivative of, but different from, the structure of the brain events. Moreover, a particular brain state—for example, activation of the amygdala, sympathetic nervous system, and central gray—can be the foundation for more than one psychological state, just as a particular gene can contribute to more than one bodily feature or physiological process.

The scientists who would like to believe that a state of fear is created every time a particular brain circuit fires fail to award sufficient influence to the immediate context and to the person's history. The diaries of John Cheever, who died in the second half of this century, and the diary and letters of Alice James, William and Henry James's sister, who died about one hundred years earlier, suggest that both writers inherited a very similar, if not identical, diathesis for a chronically dysphoric, melancholic mood.[33] But Cheever, whose premises about human nature were formed when Freudian theories were ascendant, assumed that his bouts of depression were due to childhood experiences, and he relied on drugs and psychotherapy to overcome the conflicts that he imagined his family had created. Cheever interpreted his depression as a function of his past experience. "The truth here is that because of my mother's business and my claim to having been neglected, I have always been oversensitive to a woman who is less than wifely . . . I mean to cure myself, not the world, and yet I feel, wrongly perhaps, that some of my anxieties can be traced back to this."

By contrast, Alice James, born in the summer of 1848, believed with the vast majority of her contemporaries that she had inherited her nervous, dour mood and that her childhood encounters were irrelevant. Public and medical opinion assumed that women, and especially those who were well educated, were susceptible to neurasthenia and depression because they inherited an insufficient supply of psychic energy. When Alice James had a serious breakdown at age nineteen, she wrote: "I saw so distinctly that it was a fight simply between my body and my will . . . When all one's moral and natural stock and trade is a temperament [that is] forbidding the abandonment of an inch or the relaxation of the muscle 'tis a never-ending fight . . . What is living in this deadness called life is the struggle of the creative in the grip of its inheritance." Because Ms. James could not change her heredity, she decided, after a decade of suffering, that she wished to die. The cultural contexts in which these two creative writers lived exerted profound influences on their understanding of their moods and the coping strategies they selected and, therefore, on their private emotional lives. Even if Cheever and James had inherited exactly the same genetic diathesis, they could not have experienced identical emotional states because they lived in different historical eras.

The meaning of all descriptions assumes, implicitly, a contrast. The insight of relativity theory was that one cannot know the velocity of an object unless one selects a frame of reference. When Cheever thought about the causes of his depression, he selected as a contrast a family environment where children's emotional needs were met. For Alice James, on the other hand, the contrast was the inheritance of a serene temperament. Each chose a different frame of reference for their mood, and so approached their work, relationships, and future in different ways.

The contrast principle applies to all explanations of events, even one as simple as a maple leaf fluttering in the air. Attributing the cause of the moving leaf to the decrease in light and temperature in late September assumes, as a contrast, the tree's state in July. However, if the leaf were torn from a tree on a windy day in late May, the correct contrast is a mild day, and the explanation involves air currents, not changes in light and temperature. Specification of the context supplies the necessary contrast and reduces ambiguity.

Every causal ascription of a psychological process has at least one other reasonable contrasting ascription. Imagine a college senior who has frequent bouts of apathy, sleepless nights, failing grades, no satisfying hobbies or athletic skills, and no girlfriend. Should this young man consult a college counselor, he would probably be classified as depressed because of the assumption that his emotional state is the major cause of his difficulties. But at other times and in other places, an observer might select his poor grades, lack of a hobby, or absence of a romantic partner as the cause of his emotional difficulties. Each classification, of course, implies a different curative regimen. If the therapist for the college senior focuses on his subjective feeling of anxiety, she will prescribe drugs or a therapy directed at altering his mood. But if she focuses on the poor grades, she will recommend a tutor, and if she focuses on his lonely love life, she might encourage the young man to find a romantic partner.

Our contemporary categories for human personality are based on contrasts that are local to North American and European psychologists in this historical moment. Personality does not, and perhaps cannot, have a universal meaning because historical era and culture exert nontrivial influences on the behaviors and moods that best differentiate the members of a particular community. During the first half of this century, personality types like hysterical and obsessive represented profiles that Freud believed were derivatives of classes of childhood conflict. When Freud's theory lost favor, psychologists changed the definition to refer to classes of social behaviors and moods of concern to Americans and Europeans. Today, the so-called primary personality types refer to the continuous qualities of extroversion (vs. introversion); conscientiousness (vs. disregard for civility); agreeableness (vs. irritability); neuroticism (vs. emotional stability); and an openness to experience (vs. a lack of intellectual curiosity). This small set not only ignores context but omits a large number of personality types that are less frequent. For example, a small group of adults is characterized by an extreme degree of narcissism, self-aggrandizement, and minimal empathy for or emotional involvement with others. These adults cannot be easily assigned to any of the five major personality categories.

The personality terms that would have differentiated among the Chinese living during the Ming Dynasty would probably have included variation in a desire for sensory delight—a category missing from the current set of personality types. The Spartans of ancient Greece would have made courage a major personality trait, and the ancient Hebrews might have emphasized variation in the belief in idolatry. In a sense, types of personality resemble types of weather. The categories that capture the major weather events in New England—blizzard, rain, cloudy, cold, sunny—do not differentiate among most days in the Sahara Desert. Perhaps one day psychologists will discover some human characteristics that represent the same blend of biological and experiential influences in every culture—a universal of human nature analogous to the velocity of light. But that time, if it ever comes, lies far, far in the future.

Consciousness

The recent flurry of writings on consciousness is a good reason to choose it as a second example of the problems that trail the use of unconstrained words. Although most of our actions, thoughts, and moods are the product of processes that never reach consciousness, one of its functions is to impose an interpretation on the barrage of information that finally pierces awareness. The absence of a single word for consciousness in the vocabulary of the classic Greeks might mean that they too recognized that no single term could capture the multiple phenomena that the English word lumps together. The fact that brain-damaged patients can discriminate different visual figures while claiming they cannot see anything—they have no conscious awareness of what they are doing well—gives special meaning to being aware.[34]

A second example comes from the study of a brain-damaged adult who could recognize swatches of color but could not match a color word to its proper swatch; that is, he did not consciously recognize the meaning of the word. Nonetheless, when a color word was printed in a different color ink—for example, the word red was printed in blue ink—and the patient was asked to name the color of the ink and ignore the meaning of the word, he showed the same delay as normal individuals, suggesting that at a nonconscious level the meaning of the color word was recognized.[35]

The current philosophical debate centers on whether consciousness is nothing more than a special profile of brain physiology or whether consciousness, more likely its plural forms, is an emergent event with autonomous principles and psychological descriptors. Daniel Dennett's solution to this knotty problem of the relation between the psychological and the neurophysiological is the proposal that awareness is not located in any one place in the brain but is rather the outcome of a number of competing brain circuits. While this idea forces us to entertain the fruitful possibility of multiple states of awareness, at the same time it comes very close to suggesting that consciousness is no more than a particular profile of neural activity. Awareness, at any given moment, is simply a victorious circuit. Not only does this conclusion fail to explain the very thing we wish to understand—one's awareness of feeling and thought—it also fails to specify the psychological features that differentiate the varied forms of consciousness from other psychological products of brain states, such as surprise, understanding, or apathy, that are not synonymous with consciousness.[36]

Dennett sees language as the seminal competence that gave humans their biological advantage but also as the talent that is most critical to consciousness. Gerald Edelman, who also emphasizes the role of language, differentiates between primary consciousness, characterized by a categorization of the present that is joined to a comparison with the past, and a higher-order consciousness that involves language. The latter requires primary consciousness but adds an act of reflection on the self. Edelman, like Dennett, believes that we cannot understand consciousness, or its plural forms, without major insight into the evolution and neurophysiological functions of the brain, especially the reciprocal connections among varied collections of neurons.[37]

The fact that human consciousness became possible because of evolutionary changes in the brain does not mean that all true or theoretically useful statements about consciousness must include descriptions of brain states. Boyle's gas laws accurately describe the relations among the pressure, volume, and temperature of a container of air without any reference to the laws of quantum mechanics. Both Frege and Russell had to admit failure after years of trying to derive mathematics from an underlying set of logic statements. Mathematics remains an autonomous body of knowledge, useful and beautiful but without an obvious foundation in elementary logic.

Consciousness is best described as a set of emergent phenomena that require particular brain processes but are not equivalent to them. A child's perception of a gull swooping down on the sea is not synonymous with a description of the neural circuits that make that perception possible. The forces responsible for atoms and molecules act to preserve them and to resist change in the status quo. But living things, which are emergent from these atoms and molecules, thrive precisely because of their ability to detect both internal and external changes and to react by altering their state.[38] Neurons respond to changes in the concentration of neurotransmitters and alter their activity; circuits react to changes in sensory input and alter their projected targets; organisms respond to energy changes in the environment and alter their behavior. Sensitivity to change is the key to an organism's survival, yet this quintessential quality is not inherent in its constituent atoms and molecules. It is likely that consciousness is as fully emergent from activity in neural circuits as the circuits themselves are from the atoms and molecules of which they are constructed.

In an elegant series of experiments demonstrating the partial independence of brain events and awareness, adults were shown an emotionally aversive film with a special apparatus that permitted the investigator to show the film either to the subject's right or left hemisphere. It was already known that when emotionally aversive material is presented to the right hemisphere—by showing information in the left visual field—cortisol and blood pressure, which are physiological markers of increased stress, rise to higher levels than if the information is presented in the right visual field. The subjects in this study, as was expected, showed larger increases in cortisol when the aversive film was presented to the right rather than the left hemisphere. But when the adults rated their degree of emotional arousal, they did not report greater arousal when the aversive film was presented to the right rather than the left hemisphere. That is, their conscious emotional state was not at all correlated with their brain's physiological reactions.[39]

Despite similar findings which indicate the partial independence of conscious awareness and brain state, some neurophysiologists write as though sentences describing the brain's physiological state are more accurate than those describing the psychological one and should replace them. One trio of investigators used the phrase "rewarding events" to refer to the consummation of all desired goals, as though food, sex, safety, and warmth followed the same neurobiological rules simply because neuronal tracts that use dopamine as a primary transmitter appear to be involved in the processing of desirable events. However, more recent evidence suggests that dopamine has more to do with focusing attention on a novel or salient event than with the state of pleasure the event produces.[40]

In another experiment, adults were asked to decide whether a word appearing on a screen did or did not refer to a living thing. The profile of brain activity displayed while the subjects were making their decision depended on whether the person had been asked to speak his answer aloud, click a button, or think about the answer silently. The particular form in which the respondent communicated his conscious attempts to solve each problem affected his brain state. The patterns of muscle tension, heart rate, brain waves, skin conductance, temperature, and breathing also vary with the specific task, whether a person was speaking, paying strict attention, or looking at a picture designed to elicit fear, anger, or joy. And there was no relation between the degree of dilation of facial blood vessels when a person blushes and the person's report of how embarrassed he felt at that moment.[41] None of these results should have occurred if a person's conscious thoughts or feelings were slaved in a deterministic way to what was happening in his brain.

Dramatic advances in neuroscience have persuaded many that psychological phenomena might eventually be understood, perhaps fully, in biological terms. The current enthusiasm for reducing consciousness to neural processes recalls a similar mood at the end of the last century, when stunning advances in physiology threatened Europeans with the metaphor of humans as machines. The power of this idea rested on scientific advances that had reinforced materialistic interpretations of human morality and the urban anomie that followed industrialization. Some scientists were suggesting that human spirituality would eventually be reduced to the actions of atoms and molecules. Anne Harrington has argued that this attitude motivated the rise of a holistic philosophy in German biology, physiology, and neurology.[42] The biologist Hans Dreisch raised the hopes of the holists by showing that if one cut the two-cell stage of a fertilized sea urchin egg to produce two discrete cells, each half grew into a whole organism. A machine could never do such a marvelous thing.

Today, the extraordinary discoveries of neuroscientists and molecular biologists are once again fanning a tiny flame of holistic rebellion reminiscent of the Gestalt movement in early twentieth-century Germany. David Magnusson and Robert Cairns, leaders in this new movement, have proposed two premises based on the Gestalt principles of Max Wertheimer and Wolfgang Kohler.[43] The first premise is that the unit of analysis—the event to be explained—must be a person in a context, rather than an isolated characteristic of that person, like a memory, feeling, belief, or motive, because each characteristic affects all others. Profiles of reaction to a situation, not single, isolated processes, are the entities that are either preserved or change with time.

Second, although the new advocates of holism acknowledge the important influence of genes and physiology, they insist that the behavior of an organism is not fixed by its genes. A particular strain of rats, for example, possesses genes that predispose them to develop hypertension. However, the hypertension is only actualized if the infant rat is nursed by its biological mother. If it is nursed by a surrogate who does not have the genes for hypertension, the symptom does not develop. A related illustration involves strains of mice bred to freeze, rather than attack, when confronted by an unfamiliar mouse. But the freezing occurs only if the animals are raised in isolation. If these same mice are exposed briefly to other mice during their development, they fail to freeze and may even attack an unfamiliar animal who intrudes into their territory.[44] The genes that bias these animals to freeze requires a specific rearing environment. Change the environment and the outcome is changed. One could not ask for a more persuasive example of the idea that many promises are locked in an organism's genes, and those that are kept depend on which particular events occur during the life course.

There is the story of a king who asked his heralds to bring to the palace all of the books in his kingdom. The volumes occupied over half of the palace, and after the king had perused them over a period of several years, he called his wisest counselors and asked them to reduce all of the wisdom in all of the books to one volume. They protested that this was impossible but when ordered to do so, they began the work. About a decade later they brought the king a volume of 600 pages that, they claimed, distilled the wisdom in all of the books. The king read the volume, invited the councillors once again to the throne room, and told them he wanted the contents of the book reduced to one page. Once again they protested but complied with the king's wish. Five years later, they brought him a single page. After reading it he called them again and ordered them to reduce the page to one word. They protested as before but accepted the assignment. One month later they gave the king a single piece of paper that contained the word "Maybe."

The evidence implies a partial autonomy of psychological and biological events. No matter how powerful brain scanning machines become in the future, scientists will be unable to determine the specific content of a subject's thoughts, neither the mathematical equation he was imagining nor the tune he was recalling, even though investigators might be able to infer that the person lying quietly in the scanner was generating mathematics rather than melodies. But the content of the person's thought will retain some unpredictability because each level of analysis strikes a barrier beyond which the scientist cannot predict the next emergent event. That is why there is a bit of indeterminacy in predicting the speed with which a monkey will move its eyes to a spot of light from the rate of change in electrical activity in the neurons that permit the eyes to move, and why a cat will stop orienting its head to a discrepant tone after only a few presentations, even though neurons in the hippocampus continue to react every time the unexpected tone occurs.[45] In both of these examples there is a dissociation between what is happening in the brain and the animal's behavior.

Some scientists are uncomfortable with this level of uncertainty because they seek facts that are unlikely to be proven wrong. They resemble hunters who, having trapped a secret of nature, want it to stay fixed on the trophy wall forever. Other scientists are chess players who derive joy from following the many complex rules for doing science—the correct assignment of subjects, the proper balancing of conditions, the most appropriate statistical analyses. Those who are butterfly chasers— a third group—are willing to work years for an aesthetic moment that follows a discovery, no matter how infrequent or transient. These investigators accept the temporary nature of all scientific generalizations and are bothered least by the message "maybe." Einstein described Bohr as such a person, for he "utters his opinions like one perpetually groping and never like one who believes he is in possession of definite truth."[46]

States of consciousness cannot be reduced to the language of physiology and must be described in psychological language. The concepts and principles that eventually explain awareness will be different from those that describe the brain circuits that sustain the varied forms consciousness assumes. This position has been pejoratively described as "dualist": dualists, it is claimed, are possessed by the devil because they secretly believe in two different kinds of events, mental and physical. But biologists are not called dualists when they use the language of proteins rather than DNA base pairs to describe the constituents of a fertilized egg. Nor are physicists dualists when they describe a vessel of water in terms of specific gravity, surface tension, and freezing point but describe the individual water molecules in terms of molecular weight. If a person notices a water stain on a tablecloth, would it be reasonable to say to that person that since neither hydrogen nor oxygen can stain cloth, their perception must be mistaken? I am puzzled by those who are frustrated by the necessity of using one language for brain processes and a different vocabulary for psychological events. All the phenomena of nature cannot be described in one language.

Scientists who treat consciousness as if it were only a biological event, like the propagation of electrical impulses from retina to visual cortex, want the book of behavior to be written in only one language. The possibility that one vocabulary could describe all brain and psychological processes has extraordinary aesthetic appeal. But it is worth quoting Vernon Mountcastle, acknowledged by neuroscientists as one of their most illustrious colleagues: "Every mental process is a brain process, but not every mentalistic sentence is identical to some neurophysiological sentence."[47] No language can capture every aspect of the events in nature. Language cannot capture completely my perception of the Seine on a summer morning; that is why I admire Monet and take color photographs. There is a permanent gap between the perceptual phenomenon and the sentences intended to describe it, even when we restrict the experience to a single sensory modality. If we add information from hearing and smell to the scene of the Seine, the impotence of language becomes more apparent.

Statements containing words like feel, hope, move, hit, and eat cannot be rendered completely into statements containing words like NMDA receptors, glutamate, synapse, circuit, kindle, and dopaminergic tract without considerable loss in meaning, even though we will find many correspondences between the two. As the scientific disciplines developed over the last century and a half, each took different aspects of nature as their foci of interest. Chemists who wished to understand forests studied plant photosynthesis; evolutionary biologists probed the emergence of new species; behavioral biologists studied the predatory behavior of animals in this special niche. All are features of forests, and it is not possible to describe them with the same language. The heart of the controversy, therefore, is between language purists who are made uneasy by the messiness of multiple vocabularies and pluralists who accept, without an excessive feeling of uneasiness, the fact that no one set of terms will be able to cover all we might observe or try to explain.

The events now covered by the term consciousness will eventually sort themselves into different concepts, with different names. One feature that is always ascribed to consciousness is an awareness of present sensations, from without and within the body. We are aware of and usually categorize the sweet taste of chocolate, the soft touch of velvet, and the heady aroma of perfume, as well as sensations that originate in the body (a feeling of relaxation after exercise or the discomfort of stomach cramps). This category of consciousness, which one might call *sensory awareness*, rests on a special brain state that Edelman regards as primary consciousness; Ned Block calls it P-consciousness.[48] When adults were exposed to two distinctly different tones—one 80 percent of the time and the other 20 percent of the time—they showed reactivity in the sympathetic nervous system only when they were consciously attending to the tones, not when they were ignoring them. However, the acoustic energy of the tones was processed by the brain whether the subjects were or were not attending to them.[49]

Further, if a low-voltage electric shock to the skin is increased gradually, the voltage necessary to make a person say "I feel something" is remarkably consistent from individual to individual across different laboratories. By contrast, when the person is asked to say when the electrical stimulation hurts, there is minimal agreement from individual to individual or laboratory to laboratory, because deciding whether an event is painful involves a complex judgment. It appears that a part of the brain called the anterior cingulate cortex participates in this judgment, while the sensory component of pain is mediated by sensory areas of the brain.[50] An athlete who breaks a bone in a competitive soccer game may continue to play and be unaware of any sensation of pain until the game is over. Similarly, three-month-old infants perform difficult visual discriminations despite the fact that they are totally unaware of what they are doing. That is why it is not necessary to attribute consciousness to animals who act adaptively with obvious perceptual and motor skills.

A distinction between sensory and cognitive awareness—reflection on one's experiences or thoughts—is analogous to the difference between raw experience and a narrative description. The awareness that we behaved in a particular way in a particular place at a particular time in the past is a state that Endel Tulving believes is unique to humans.[51]

Cognitive awareness can involve images but more often relies on words. Sensory awareness, however, need not involve the participation of any symbols. A word, phrase, or sentence distorts experience by awarding salience to those sensory features of the event for which a semantic meaning exists and is necessarily indifferent to features for which appropriate terms are unavailable. A cognitive awareness of "feeling annoyed" can be produced by a jackhammer, a faucet dripping in a hotel room, the smell of cigar smoke in a small waiting room, or a bright pair of headlights, even though these events produce very different forms of sensory awareness. Similarly, the sensory awareness of three sharp knocks on the door of one's bedroom evolves into distinctly different states of cognitive awareness depending on whether the knocks occur at 9 a.m. in a Maine bed-and-breakfast or at 3 a.m. in a Moscow hotel.

The difference between sensory and cognitive awareness can be captured in the laboratory. Adults who viewed a series of pictures symbolic of danger, death, and illness showed increased tension in the muscles above the eyes as the series progressed, implying a cognitive awareness of the fact that unpleasant scenes were being shown repeatedly. But at the same time, these adults showed a decreasing number of skin conductance responses because the sensory awareness of surprise was muted as the series of unexpected pictures progressed.[52]

Unlike sensory awareness, no external stimulus is necessary to provoke cognitive awareness. Individuals can be aware of the flow as well as the logic and coherence of a train of ideas. Future plans are members of this category of consciousness. The ability of humans to generate ideas of events that might occur years in the future might explain why we are the only species to have populated so much of the world. Presumably, the early migrations of hominids were motivated by their ability to imagine a better place to live. The brain profile associated with the awarding of meaning to an event is probably not the same as the profile that forms the basis of an awareness of the sensory components of an experience. Hence, a distinction between sensory and cognitive awareness is likely to be useful, even if the two occur almost simultaneously.

A third form of consciousness involves awareness of the ability to choose a particular behavior as well as the control of one's actions and emotions. The nervous adolescent on a school stage who instructs himself to gain control of outward signs of fear is one illustration. Individuals recognize the possibility of several possible responses, reflect on the advantages and disadvantages of each, and choose one of the alternatives. We might call this aspect of consciousness *awareness of control;* nineteenth-century writers called it "will." Awareness of control, unlike cognitive awareness, is often provoked by a feeling of urgency that is missing from cognitive awareness, as well as a competition among different urges. A feeling of anger presses for one response, while the wish to control a hostile act presses for another.

Finally, individuals are aware of some symbolic categories that apply to self. Many psychologists call this process self-consciousness; I prefer the phrase *awareness of self's features.* Although people are not aware of all of their qualities, most are conscious of their gender, age, health, ethnicity, religion, talents, and feeling tone. Reflection on any one of these categories need not be accompanied by an emotion, urge to action, or selection of a plan.

These four forms of consciousness probably did not evolve simultaneously. Chimpanzees might have a sensory awareness of the taste of particular foods and of varying patterns of light and shadow on the forest floor, but it is unlikely that they possess the other three forms of awareness. I doubt that apes are aware of the distant future, reflect on the past, and wonder whether they will be able to control a fear-motivated flight from a future threat. Weiskrantz notes that "the ability to make a commentary is what is meant by being aware and what gives rise to it."[53] I suspect that apes cannot generate commentaries.

It is also relevant that the four forms of consciousness do not emerge at the same time in human development. Sensory awareness is absent at birth but clearly present before the second birthday. However, cognitive awareness and awareness of control do not emerge until four or five years, at the earliest. Two-year-olds are incapable of remembering where they were and what they were doing at lunch a week earlier. Further, most young children are not able to exert moderately consistent control over their fear or anger until they are six or seven years old and do not become conscious of most of the important symbolic categories to which they belong until they are nine or ten years old.

As each form of consciousness emerges and is elaborated over the course of development, it adds a new quality to human functioning, just as language adds a distinct component to thought. A person without symbolic language experiences the sweet taste of chocolate and the warmth of a fire but these sensations remain separate. A person with language categorizes both experiences as good. The application of that category term changes the representation of the taste and warmth as both become clustered around a shared symbolic quality. Neither experience was good before the emergence of language; both are good after.

The symbolic labeling of experience contributes in a major way to the probability that past events will be remembered. When adults were asked about their earliest memories, few could recall any experience before the second birthday.[54] The vast majority remembered events that occurred after age three. This fact implies that the quality of awareness that exists following the second birthday, after language is in place, is qualitatively different from the states of consciousness during the prior two years.

Do these four forms of consciousness share a sufficient number of features to warrant treating consciousness as a unitary phenomenon, or is it useful to treat them as qualitatively different? The answer will depend on our purpose. The perception of color, shape, and motion involves activities in different parts of the brain. The neurons activated upon seeing the skyward motion of a red balloon are not the same as those activated when one looks at a stationary spot of light. This fact invites a distinction between two kinds of visual experience, even though activation of the thalamus and area V1 of the visual cortex is common to all visual experience.

Imagine an isolated country whose citizens know nothing about the biological causes of diseases. There is no understanding of viruses, bacteria, cardiovascular lesions, or cancer. The adults in this community recognize that a small proportion of the population occasionally reports feeling unhappy, tired, in pain, or less vital than ordinary, and they call this state illness. They know that those who are ill require rest, sympathy, and relief from daily responsibilities, but they believe that all illnesses are mediated by one mechanism, namely, eating spoiled food. In this frame, illness is treated as a unity, even though it assumes different forms. However, we know that humans are vulnerable to a large number of distinctly different illnesses with varied origins, physiological conditions, prognoses, and compromise of function. These differences are so salient that we have agreed on the wisdom of parsing the term illness into qualitatively different states. A similar analytic strategy will aid understanding of consciousness.

As with the concept of fear, support for assuming separate forms of consciousness comes from recent discoveries in neuroscience. The vigilant state of attention that follows an unexpected event—the screech of a bus or a sound on the roof—is mediated, in part, by norepinephrine-containing axons that originate in the locus ceruleus and project to the cortex. By contrast, the longer-lasting state of alertness that accompanies the memorization of verbs from a new language is mediated more completely by acetylcholine projections to the cortex. And the state of a person playing the piano is mediated more completely by dopamine projections to motor centers. People may say consciously that they feel "alert" under all three conditions, but I suspect that they could differentiate between the conscious state that accompanies a sound on the roof in the middle of the night and the feeling that accompanies memorizing Russian verbs. And physiological measurements would probably reveal two distinct profiles. If the different forms of consciousness rest on different neurochemical patterns, it is reasonable to argue that there is not one consciousness but many.

Intelligence

Every society invents words to describe variation in the talents that happen to be valued at that time. Therefore, no date can be assigned to the origin of the idea of a continuum of intelligence. However, the twin notions that intelligence is inherited and can be measured objectively, as one measures height or weight, are usually attributed to Darwin's cousin, Francis Galton, and his 1869 book, *Hereditary Genius*, even though Galton used the phrase "general ability" rather than intelligence.[55]

As is often the case with psychological ideas, historical conditions made the notion of differences in intelligence necessary. Almost all children and adults in rural, agricultural societies composed of small villages can perform the tasks necessary for survival—planting, harvesting, cooking, cleaning, and caring for children. Therefore, the variation that exists in the speed or alacrity with which the tasks are learned or performed is relatively unimportant, and there is no pressing reason to pay special attention to them.

But nineteenth-century industrialization created a special set of conditions. Some tasks now required more skill than planting, cooking, or washing, and European cities had large numbers of people who were unprepared to enter a technological work force. Citizens recognized, as we do, that formal education was necessary for most children. But learning to read, write, and do arithmetic comes to children far less naturally than carrying wood or caring for infants, and attempts to teach those scholastic skills revealed extraordinary variation in children's abilities. The startling clarity of that fact had to be named, and Western society called it intelligence.

The tests of general ability that Galton had invented—good vision and hearing and the ability to react quickly to a stimulus—did not predict life success. Almost a century ago, an American psychologist showed that variation in performance on these tests did not predict variation in grades among students attending Columbia University, and none of Galton's talents is measured on the modern intelligence test. That failure should have put an end to the concept of intelligence, but it could not die because society needed a way to explain why some children learned to read and do long division easily, while others had difficulty. That stubborn fact would not go away.[56]

The French psychologist Alfred Binet realized that tests of memory, learning, and reasoning, which resembled more closely the talents needed for school success, might be better predictors of who would find academic work difficult. He was right. The problems Binet developed in 1905, with Theodore Simon, are the origin of the modern test of intelligence.

Binet and Simon did not construct a complex theoretical argument about heredity or the meaning of intelligence. They were content with the pragmatic fact that a set of graded problems accomplished the goal for which it was intended: predicting how educable the child was in a school setting. The one- or two-word summary on the upper right side of the first page of a newspaper does better than chance in predicting tomorrow's weather, and most of us do not care why the terse phrase is generally accurate.

However, scientists after Binet and Simon did care about the meaning and origins of the phenomena being measured by intelligence tests. Two of the most important figures in this investigation were Charles Spearman and L. L. Thurstone, who did their work over seventy years ago.[57] Spearman believed that a unitary quality of reasoning was the heart of intelligence. Thurstone, less certain of a general ability, argued that individuals varied on seven different cognitive skills: perceptual analysis, numerical ability, verbal ability, spatial ability, memory, induction, and deductive reasoning. This controversy motivated psychologists to try to determine whether rats had a general learning ability or a number of different ones. Robert Tryon's rats seemed to show general intelligence (called *g*), while Frederick Mote's rats did not.[58]

Despite the reasonableness of Thurstone's argument, his ideas never replaced the simpler notion of *g*, even though Howard Gardner's popular 1983 book, *Frames of Mind*, a derivative of Thurstone's writings, has attracted many followers.[59] The defenders of *g*, like those who believe in one fear state or one type of consciousness, fail to appreciate that organs and physiological systems develop independently. No single general factor can represent the growth rates of the diverse classes of cells, tissues, and organs in animals or humans.

The descriptor "intelligent" is frequently found in sentences that are indifferent to the age and background of the person (or sometimes the animal species) or the evidential basis for the assignment. The statement "Intelligence is inherited" is used in the psychological literature to refer to rats, one-year-olds, or eighty-year-olds, even though they had been administered different tests. The following three statements can be found in many textbooks: (1) Intelligence predicts academic success. (2) Intelligence passes through developmental stages. (3) Intelligence increases with phylogeny. The term intelligence has dramatically divergent meanings in these three sentences because it refers to different agents in varied contexts producing different behavioral evidence. Sentence 1 would be more accurate if it were rewritten to say "Scores on IQ tests and school grades in children 6 to 17 years of age predict academic success," and a clearer version of sentence 3 would read, "When we test and compare the memory skills of mammals, we see that memory for past events increases from mice to apes to humans."[60] The unspecified term intelligence is mischievous because it permits readers to impose a variety of interpretations on sentences in which it is a component.

Why is the word intelligence so difficult to eliminate from our vocabulary? The answer is that facts demand explanations, and it is a reliable fact that second grade children who learn to read, to add, and to write stories early and easily obtain better grades in high school and college than second graders who have difficulty mastering these skills and, as a result, hold jobs with more status and a higher income. That fact is true in the United States and in every other nation studied. We have several explanatory choices. One is that families differ in the encouragement of academic mastery; children who have been encouraged early will be more highly motivated throughout their school careers. That explanation would fit much of the data were it not for the fact that the more closely two people are related, the more similar their IQ scores. Monozygotic ("identical") twins have more similar IQ scores than dizygotic ("fraternal") twins or two siblings of different ages. This robust observation means that something more than family encouragement is at work, and that something involves the biology of the child.

In a study of twin pairs who were eighty years or older, investigators concluded there were genetic effects on "general cognitive ability," even though only seven tests were administered to the identical and fraternal twins who participated: understanding the meanings of words, factual knowledge, ability to recall a list of numbers, ability to recognize a series of pictures seen earlier, ability to detect a figure that is different from five similar ones, ability to make a set of colored cubes match a pattern on a card, and, finally, the speed with which the person matched a number to a geometric pattern. The subjects' ease of learning new facts, inferring new concepts, deducing conclusions, or evaluating the quality of decisions were not tested. More surprising is the fact that the authors did not comment on the subjects' hearing and vision. Genes affect sensory integrity, and impairments in hearing or vision, which are common in old age, could have influenced test performance if some of these older subjects could not hear the instructions clearly or see the designs accurately.[61]

It is also odd that the heritability values were relatively low for the ability to make a pattern from colored blocks and to detect a distinctive figure, while the heritability values were high for understanding the meanings of words and fund of general information about the world. This pattern is common in most studies of adults, but not in two-year-olds. Verbal ability and information about the world are usually more heritable than other adult cognitive skills; indeed, the size of an adult's vocabulary usually has the highest correlation with the total IQ score and therefore with g. However, in two-year-old twins the number of words understood is not very heritable; rather, attentiveness to pictures and motor skill show higher heritabilities.[62] One implication of these facts is that intelligence does not have the same meaning in young children and adults. If that implication turns out to be true, the biological contribution to intelligence would not be the same across the life span.

I am not alone in the judgment that the exact nature of the biological contribution to intelligence test scores is at the moment a mystery. John Carroll, a respected psychologist who is neutral in this debate, wrote in 1982, "I have always thought that it would be difficult to assess the genetic influences on scores from tests that are so patently functions of specific learning experiences as typical IQ tests . . . Given the difficulty of controlling environments it will probably be very hard to provide convincing evidence for genetic influences even through twin or kinship studies."[63]

The statement that variation in intelligence is largely inherited is based on the application of the "heritability equation," which assumes that the effects of the relevant genes, environmental experiences, interactions of genes with experience, and the interactions among the person's genes are additive: the more genes relevant to cognitive skills and the more supporting the environmental experiences, the more intelligent the person will be.

Unfortunately, this assumption is rarely met in the life sciences. Genetically distinct mice strains differ in degree of exploratory behavior, but these differences are due to interactions of genes at different loci and not to additive genetic and environmental factors.[64] Neither do the EEGs of identical and fraternal twins fit the assumption of additivity. The brain wave profiles, too, are best explained by interactions among the individual's genes—called epistasis—rather than by adding genetic and environmental factors.[65] If this index of brain activity is inconsistent with the assumption of additivity, it is unlikely that the genetic contribution to the variation in cognitive abilities is additive either.

Most readers of media reports on the inheritance of intelligence may not appreciate that the statistic used to estimate the degree of heritability—called h^2—primarily measures the degree to which high or low IQ scores are influenced, in part, by genetic factors. That is, heritability is higher when there is a great deal of variability in the characteristic of interest. If there is minimal variability—for example, being born with five fingers—heritability will necessarily be low. Thus the heritability of IQ is high when the sample studied has some individuals with very low scores and some with very high scores. Heritability will be low if everyone in the sample has an IQ between 95 and 105. This fact leads to an important conclusion: If, as is likely, the biological bases for low IQs (under 80) are different from the biological bases for high IQs (over 120), that would mean that different sets of genes are responsible for different levels of intelligence. We know this is true for children born with Down syndrome.

A more serious issue is that investigators rarely assess the interaction between genetic and environmental factors because it is difficult to do so; hence, they are forced to assume it is small. Yet most outcomes in nature are influenced by interactions between the animal's biology and the context in which it lives. When song sparrows and swamp sparrows are raised in the laboratory, the former are more avoidant of novel objects than the latter, but if both species are raised in the wild, the differences in avoidant behavior disappear.[66] The context of rearing has a dramatic effect on all genetically influenced behaviors. Children who are born with the genes that are presumed to produce high scores on intelligence tests but who are raised in isolated rural villages without schools will have much lower intelligence scores than children with the same genes raised by professional families in an American suburb that supports excellent schools. The principle that outcomes vary dramatically as a function of combinations of causal events applies to all psychological qualities, including intellectual abilities.

An appeal to logic also compromises confident conclusions about the outcomes of the many genes that contribute to high or low IQ scores. The number of genes that control the shape of the wings of the fruit fly *Drosophila* are far fewer than those that control human cognitive abilities. However, flies who possess a pair of genes that leads to short, vestigial wings if the insects are reared at a normal laboratory temperature of 20° centigrade will develop almost normal wings if reared in a warmer environment of about 30° centigrade.[67] If a difference of 10° in room temperature can influence an important anatomical feature controlled by only a pair of genes, surely children's social environments must have a profound influence on the many intellectual abilities that are affected by a much larger number of genes. That is why biologists agree that the consequences of any gene(s) must take into account both the total genetic constitution of the person and the history of their rearing environments. Because neither of these is well understood for any aspect of human intellectual development, strong statements about the genetic or environmental determinants of cognitive competences have to be premature. It strains credibility to assume that the mode of inheritance of a person's answers to questions on intelligence tests, which are cultural constructions, fit a simple additive model.

An important source of support for the argument against *g* is a recent imaginative study of children with an inherited disease called PKU. These children—about 1 in every 10,000 births—have a genetic defect which leaves them unable to metabolize an amino acid present in most foods, called phenylalanine, to another amino acid called tyrosine. As a result, the level of tyrosine in the brain remains lower than it should be and often fluctuates. Almost all American children who have PKU are diagnosed at birth and placed on a special diet that contains low levels of phenylalanine. Because most of the children on the diet have adequate IQ scores, pediatricians tell the parents that all is well. But Adele Diamond and her colleagues have found that this advice is not completely accurate when the blood levels of phenylalanine approach five to six times the normal level.[68]

Tyrosine is needed to produce the neurotransmitter dopamine, and dopamine is especially important for the adequate functioning of the prefrontal cortex but less important for the functioning of psychological processes mediated by the temporal or parietal lobes. Thus children with PKU who are on a proper diet and have adequate IQ scores should perform more poorly than normal children on tests that require the full integrity of the prefrontal cortex but might perform adequately on tests that do not require the involvement of the prefrontal cortex. The former tasks require children to relate two or more events in "working memory" and to inhibit an incorrect response that is automatic. For example, the examiner asks a five-year-old to tap three pegs in the order red, green, yellow, although the pegs are arranged in front of the child in the order green, yellow, red. Thus the child has to remember the instruction and to inhibit a natural tendency to touch the pegs in the order in which they appear. Another task that involves both memory and inhibition requires the child to say the word night to a picture of the sun and to say the word day to a picture of the moon. The child has to remember the original instruction and to inhibit a natural tendency to say night to moon and day to sun. On the other hand, saying day to one design and night to a different design does not require the inhibition of an automatic but incorrect response. The children with PKU who were on the prescribed diet but had higher-than-recommended blood levels of phenylalanine did poorly on the peg test and the night/sun test, which required the prefrontal cortex, but performed as well as normal children on tests that did not depend on the integrity of the prefrontal cortex.

A similar conclusion follows from a study of poor inner city black infants whose mothers used cocaine. Scores on an infant intelligence test, called the Bayley Scales, could not differentiate the infants born to heavy users from those born to light users, but the infants born to the former group were comparatively impaired in their ability to recognize a series of photographs seen earlier.[69]

In a third example, children born to poorly educated parents living under economic stress are usually far behind middle-class children in their ability to read words and simple sentences when they begin school, and they typically obtain lower IQ scores. The poor reading skill is usually attributed to their low intelligence. One presumptive sign of the impaired intellectual ability is the fact that these children are not able to read several rows of letters quickly when instructed to do so. Some educators have interpreted this failure as reflecting a more general deficit in processing information in an automatic, efficient fashion. However, a study of children in Boston and India revealed, surprisingly, that most reading-retarded first grade children read rows of colors and pictures of familiar objects as quickly as children who were excellent readers. The more sluggish naming speed occurred only when they were reading letters. These children did not have a general intellectual deficit; rather their lack of familiarity with print prevented them from reading the letters quickly.[70]

These results indict the concept of general intelligence. The PKU children did well on some difficult mental tasks but poorly on others; cocaine-exposed children showed poor recognition memory but were not impaired on other cognitive skills; and poor children who cannot read are only slow in naming rows of letters, not rows of colors. The decision to average the performances on a varied set of tests that require different talents in order to come up with one value called intelligence is not logical. Averaging cognitive performances that rely on different parts of the brain distorts the true nature of cognitive abilities and is an inaccurate way to describe a person's profile of mental talents.

There is no question that children inherit different profiles of brain physiology which affect mental functioning. Genetic factors do influence psychological functions. But intelligence is not the best term to describe the complex products of inherited biological processes. There is a correlation of about 0.4 between the duration of attention to a novel stimulus in six-month-olds and IQ score at six years of age.[71] Some psychologists have interpreted that fact to mean that an abstract quality of intelligence is preserved over the five years. The more correct conclusion is that about 10–20 percent of infants who fail to attend to a novel stimulus have lower IQ scores than a majority of infants who show adequate attention to novelty and have normal IQ scores when they are older children. This simple change in the description alters the meaning of the original conclusion in a nontrivial way.

Cognitive functions include, at a minimum, perceptual recognition and discrimination and varied types of memory, inference, reasoning, and reflection. That one set of genes—those presumed to explain why genetically related children are similar in IQ score—influences all of these cognitive processes in a similar way is improbable. It is a theoretical mistake to use the concept of intelligence to represent each person's profile of cognitive talents.

The most popular intelligence test, the Wechsler Intelligence Scale for Children, assesses a small number of mental skills, including the size of the child's vocabulary, short-term memory for numbers, ability to make inferences from pictures, and a talent for solving puzzles. If intelligence were a unitary competence, the correlations among the scores on these four tests should be very high, but they are not. The test that measures short-term memory on the standard intelligence tests has a low correlation with the total IQ score. If one administers tests of very different intellectual abilities to 1,000 children, each test tapping a different cognitive skill, the correlations among the scores are modest, usually less than 0.4. That fact is inconsistent with the notion that intelligence is a unitary characteristic.

There is good reason to believe that linguistic skills make a more important contribution to an individual's IQ score than memory or perceptual talents. Most children with low IQ scores have poor vocabularies but are usually not deficient in their ability to perceive shapes, colors, or sounds or to make very subtle perceptual discriminations. A small proportion of boys who do not begin to speak until they are three or four years old are very talented at music and mathematics when they become older. By contrast a small number of children who have Williams syndrome, a genetic defect that occurs in about one in 20,000 births, can be proficient in their speech.[72] They will tell long coherent stories to adults, despite extremely poor spatial skills and low IQ scores. These sharp differences between verbal and nonverbal skills challenge the concept of general intelligence. It is likely that the unknown genetic factors which contribute to high IQ scores are due in part to biological differences in language talents. But even language skill is not a unity in two-year-olds, for quantity of spoken language is more heritable than the number of words the child understands at the end of the second year.[73] However the statements "Mary inherited a biology that made her speak early (or late)" or "Mary is verbally productive" have different connotations than "Mary is intelligent." The latter statement implies a broad biological influence on all cognitive functions.

Gerd Gigerenzer provides a persuasive example of how the quality of a person's reasoning depends on as simple a condition as the way the problem is worded.[74] Humans are poor at making correct inferences about the likelihood of an event when the problem is put in terms of percentages but are much better when the same problem is stated in terms of frequencies. For example, consider the following problem described in percentages: "During most years in New England, 10 percent of the days from June 1 to August 31, and one percent of all other days of the year in New England have temperatures over 90 degrees." If asked: "What is the probability that if the temperature on a particular day is over 90 degrees, it is a day in June, July, or August?" most persons say, incorrectly, about 10 percent.

However, subjects are considerably more accurate if the problem uses frequencies. When asked, "If 10 of the 90 days from June 1 to August 31 have temperatures over 90 degrees and 3 of the remaining 275 days have temperatures that high, what is the likelihood that a temperature over 90 degrees is occurring in June, July, or August?" most subjects mentally divide 10 by 10+3 and reply correctly that the probability is about 0.7 that a day that warm occurs during the three summer months.

Philosophers and cognitive scientists have debated in books and essays whether humans are rational or irrational. But humans reason correctly in some contexts but not in others. We can ask meaningful questions about human rationality only after we have specified the context. For example, brain activity is exquisitely sensitive to the specific laboratory procedure employed. When adults, who had seen earlier a particular list of words, were presented with a block of familiar words followed by a block of words never seen before, they showed a pattern of brain activity that was different for the familiar and new words. This fact implied that a special brain state is created when a person is confronted with a familiar or novel word. But a simple change in procedure led to a different conclusion. When the familiar and the new words were mixed together and the person was asked to say whether each word was familiar, the brain state was very similar for both old and new words.[75] As in

Gigerenzer's studies, the specific form in which a question was asked influenced the brain's response.

Scientists who continue to believe in the utility of the idea of intelligence are not persuaded by this evidence and counter that there must be a core ability being measured on all intelligence tests, along with a small number of more specific talents. If a child possesses the core ability in excess, she should perform well on all of the tests. This position is based on the results of a technique called factor analysis which is presumed to discover these core factors. When scores on a variety of tests are analyzed with this statistical technique, a first factor usually emerges and investigators name it general intelligence. But the first factor could have been labeled verbal ability because scores on vocabulary tests are the best predictor of the total IQ, and the heritability of "intelligence" rises dramatically between ages three and four, when verbal skills become major parts of the test. The first factor might also reflect a motivation to do well on tests combined with low anxiety over failure; both traits produce higher scores on all cognitive tests. Thus, it is not obvious that general intelligence is the most accurate way to name the first factor.

Consider an analogy with diseases. A factor analysis of the twelve most frequent symptoms associated with the diseases that affect most humans—both consciously reported symptoms as well as evidence from laboratory procedures—would yield a first factor that would be highly correlated with patient complaints of fatigue and discomfort. However, the fatigue and discomfort were caused by an extraordinarily diverse group of biological conditions, including viruses, bacteria, tumors, lesions, disturbance in the body's chemistry, and ruptures of blood vessels. This diversity is the reason why no biologist suggests that humans inherit a vulnerability to fatigue and discomfort but argue instead that persons inherit distinct genetic susceptibilities to very specific diseases.

This analogy is apt because, like IQ, vulnerability to most diseases, such as stroke, heart attack, and diabetes, is inversely correlated with social class.[76] People with less than a high school education and low incomes are more vulnerable to most diseases than well-educated, wealthy persons. However, scientists do not conclude from this that poor people's genes make them more vulnerable to all diseases than wealthy people. Rather, they acknowledge the critical role of personal habits, diet, availability of medical care, and psychological mechanisms linked to a person's social class.

The quality called leadership provides a related example of the confusion that follows an indifference to specifying context. The many books describing the qualities of leaders acknowledge that every leader requires a large number who are willing to follow. Thus, the mind of the community is a significant determinant of who becomes a leader. Sigmund Freud had qualities usually regarded as necessary for leadership—particular verbal talents, considerable energy, and courage. But if the young Freud had grown up in Calcutta at the end of the last century, where beliefs about the relation of sexuality to anxiety were very different from those in Vienna, he would not have invented the idea of a repressed libidinal motive causing a phobia of horses. And even if he had, this suggestion would have been ignored by the Indian community. Mendel's discoveries on the genetics of peas lay undiscovered for several decades because biologists were not prepared to accept them.

The term leader, therefore, is more like the adjective beautiful than the adjective freckled. The latter quality belongs to the individual no matter where she lives; the former describes a relation between a person and the local community. Sartre's existential philosophy, which emphasized the present and encouraged rejection of the past, contained a message that French society wished to hear after World War II because many citizens were feeling some guilt over their country's collaboration with the Nazis. The same philosophical stance in the People's Republic of China in 1955 would have been satirized; Mao continually reminded Chinese peasants that they must never forget the bitter past.

Some may reply that if Sartre had lived in Beijing his verbal talent and ambition would have led to a different philosophy, perhaps one in accord with the premises of the Chinese revolutionary community, but he still would have been acclaimed a creative person. There are, however, too many examples of men and women with Sartre's talents and energy who were not celebrated by their society because of a poor fit between their views and those of their society. Raymond Cattell is a brilliant, hard-working retired American psychologist who devoted his career to a factor analytic approach to personality. But because these ideas were not popular in the 1950s, when he did his major work, Cattell's ideas were ignored by most psychologists. His approach has become more popular during the last decade, and if he had worked half a century later perhaps Cattell would have been more highly celebrated by most of his contemporaries.[77]

Recent research on human memory and attention provides persuasive examples of the progress that can occur when faith in a unitary cognitive quality is abandoned. In the 1970s human memory was regarded as a single process. Individuals were described as having a good, average, or poor memory, regardless of what they had to remember. Some clinical psychologists continue to ask children and adults to repeat a series of numbers read to them by an examiner. If an eight-year-old child cannot remember a series of four numbers, the psychologist concludes that the child has an impaired memory, on the assumption that if he cannot recall four numbers he will also be poor at remembering words, scenes, story plots, facts, and his friends' names. We now know that this assumption is incorrect. It is not just a little wrong, it is wildly incorrect.

Scientists have discovered that memory is not a unitary talent but a variety of distinctive psychological processes. One process refers to the conscious recall of facts—the capitol of Texas, the meaning of shilling, the winner of last year's Super Bowl—called *declarative memory*. Further, within the category of declarative memory, there is an important distinction between conscious recall of isolated facts or events—called *semantic memory*—and conscious recall of the place where or time when the fact was learned or the event occurred, called *episodic memory*. The neural circuits that mediate semantic and episodic memory are different. Adults with damage to the hippocampus have seriously impaired episodic memory but can recall language, function adequately in school, and retrieve facts.[78]

A second form of memory is the ability to remember old motor habits, like riding a bicycle, called *procedural memory*. Remembering the name of one's first grade teacher— an example of declarative memory— is mediated by circuits in the medial temporal lobe that are not involved when one remembers how to ride a bicycle.

A third type is called *implicit memory*. Some people with damage to the medial temporal lobe, called amnesic, have very poor declarative memories. An aphasic who has just seen a list of two familiar words is unable to recall any of them. But if the patient is shown a list of fragmented words, like __g_n for wagon or d_at_ for death, which he had seen moments earlier, along with some words he had not seen, and is asked to guess the word that best fits the fragment, the patient's guesses are more accurate for words that were seen moments earlier, even though the amnesic is unaware that his guesses are correct. When school-aged children were shown photos of children they had played with in nursery school four years earlier, they did not recognize their prior playmates—their declarative memory was poor. However, when their skin conductance response was measured, the children showed more bursts of sweating in the palms to the photographs of the children they played with years earlier than to the photos of children they had never met—an example of long-term implicit memory.

Finally, a distinction between short-term and long-term memory is important. In short-term memory the individual has to remember the information for a brief interval, usually less than thirty seconds. A typical example is remembering a new telephone number long enough to dial it. Long-term memory refers to the recall of information acquired in the distant past. Amnesics have seriously impaired short-term memory but can remember many facts acquired years earlier.

Given these findings over the past quarter of a century, no contemporary psychologist would say of a person, "She has a good memory," without specifying whether the procedure assessed declarative, procedural memory or implicit memory; isolated facts or contexts; short-term or long-term memory; and the forms of information remembered, whether words, numbers, scenes, melodies, or nightmares. It should be noted that the standard intelligence test measures only declarative-semantic memory for facts and does not assess episodic, implicit, or procedural memory.

The concept of attention had also been regarded as a unitary process until scientists discovered the importance of distinguishing among the initial orienting to an event, the subsequent perceptual analysis of the event, the initial interpretation, and finally the motor readiness to act.

Different neural circuits mediate these different processes. Activity in circuits in the prefrontal cortex that are dependent on the neurotransmitter norepinephrine probably accompanies orienting to an unexpected event, while acetylcholine monitors more completely perceptual analysis, and dopamine contributes more to motor readiness. Further, deciding where an event is located in space is different from deciding what it is. The circuits that are activated when a person tries to determine the direction from which a voice is coming are different from those activated when a person tries to determine the category of an ambiguous shape lying on the road at dusk.

If memory and attention, both of which are critical components of cognitive abilities, must be decomposed into separate competences, intelligence cannot be a useful construct. Unless there are large numbers of individuals who are very competent, moderately competent, or impaired on every component of language, memory, attention, and reasoning, then averaging a person's scores on a restricted sample of these cognitive talents distorts, in a serious way, the nature of an individual's intellectual abilities. It follows that if intelligence does not name a phenomenon in nature, statements about its genetic bases are of uncertain value.

The diametrically opposed conclusions among varied scholarly groups reflect the wild nature of the debate on the reasons for differences in intelligence. Neuroscientists demonstrate the dramatic consequences of experience on the malleable young brain and, therefore, on the child's cognitive abilities. Further, a team of French scientists found a large number of working-class families who had given up one infant for adoption by an upper-middle-class family during the first year of life. The IQ scores and school performances of the adopted children were seriously different from those of their siblings who had remained at home.[79] The differences in IQ were as large as those found between working-class and upper-middle-class children in France or America. These facts make it difficult to defend the statement that most infants are born with brains which guarantee that some will become geniuses, some smart, some average, and some dumb, independent of the environments they encounter.

Developmental psychologists affirm the conclusion of the French scientists by demonstrating repeatedly the profound influence of depriving or enriching home environments on children's performances on intelligence tests. Yet, surprisingly, a group of respected behavioral geneticists came to what appears to be a contrary conclusion. After reporting no correlation between the IQ scores of adopted children and those of their adoptive parents, they wrote, without waffling, that although parents influence their children's abilities, "environmental factors related to parents' cognitive abilities have no consistent long term effects that make the cognitive development of one couple's children different from the cognitive development of children in other families."[80]

Reflect carefully on this conclusion. It claims that if a pair of identical twins were separated at birth and one twin was reared by parents with IQs under 85 who never went to high school and the other twin was cared for by two parents with IQs over 120, the children's IQ scores at age ten would not be influenced by the different intellectual capacities of the two sets of parents but might be affected by other parental characteristics. This view assumes that a parent's intelligence can be treated as a quality separable from their motives, values, and rearing practices.

Such polarized views on the role of the environment suggest that something is seriously wrong with the concept of intelligence. Imagine an opaque cylinder with shelves containing holes of different diameters and shapes. Objects of different shapes and sizes are dropped into the cylinder and fall to an open tray at the bottom, where an observer sees only small spheres. The observer wonders, but cannot know, whether the feature that permitted these objects to pass through the cylinder was shape or size, when in fact it was the combination of being both small and spherical that was critical. Similarly, parental social class and children's IQ score are always correlated with each other and with vocational success in our society, and the two factors act reciprocally. Indeed, the social class of a boy's father is a better predictor of the child's future vocational attainment than his IQ at age four years.[81] But the advocates of *g* write as if only the IQ score were critical, as if only size permitted the successful passage of the object through the opaque cylinder.

The relative importance of social class and cognitive abilities on adult success will vary with the community of adaptation, even though a child's IQ accounts for only 10 percent of the variation in vocational success in the United States. A child's social class is more critical in America and Europe than in small isolated villages in Brazil where, because there is less variation in class, differences in cognitive talents can be more important. Ernst Mach was correct: "No point of view has absolute permanent validity. Each has importance only for some given end."[82]

When a scientific domain is young—and psychology is one of the youngest—its practitioners are vulnerable to thinking in ways that the human mind finds attractive but which, unfortunately, fail to fit nature very well. Three of the hardiest preferences are for ideas that imply stable essences, possess symmetry, and are simple. The notion of g, or general intelligence, is graced by all three.

The human mind is biased to think that the world consists of unique arrangements of stable elements that are the essences of the objects. The classic Greek philosophers Thales, Plato, and Democritus did not appreciate that although their ideas referred to essences, nature did not honor that view, and they posited essences as the foundation of all matter in the world. Even though the sharp edges of rocks wear away, burning logs turn to ash, leaves turn brown, and animals grow and die, we insist, nonetheless, that the surface change disguises an invisible layer of unchanging forms underneath. The biologist Ernst Mayr has railed against this idea of essentialism, in part because it is inconsistent with evolution. Before Darwin, it was believed that each species possessed a primary set of features that defined its essence. Darwin's great insight was to realize that there is no most perfect dog, just generations of animals that changed, albeit slowly, over time. The concept of general intelligence is treated as an essence; profiles of cognitive talents cannot be so described.

The idea of general intelligence also meets the criterion of symmetry. Although the ancients preferred symmetrical patterns and infants look longer at symmetrical than asymmetrical designs, symmetry is actually rare in everyday experience. The distribution of clouds in the sky, trees in a forest, cows in a pasture, daisies in a meadow, and lily pads on a pond is asymmetrical. Yet when introductory textbooks display the symmetric distribution of IQ scores, with an average of 100 and roughly equal numbers below and above that invented value, the symmetry of the bell curve persuades us of its truth. The notion of a human quality that is symmetrically distributed across all the peoples of the world must generate the intuition that scientists have finally detected one of God's intentions.

Finally, the notion of general intelligence is simplicity itself. The number of human cognitive talents, probably as numerous as the number of diseases to which we are vulnerable, include perception in varied modalities, distinct memory processes, imagination, inference, deduction, evaluation, and acquisition of new knowledge. All of this extraordinary diversity is ignored when one declares a commitment to *g*.

Biologists are far less foolish. They do not suggest that humans differ genetically in a quality called "general health" and that people inherit either a high, moderate, or low vulnerability to all known diseases. Genetic effects on life functions are extremely specific most of the time. Nonetheless, some psychologists refuse to give up the idea that each individual inherits a quality that will determine whether they possess high, moderate, or low intelligence.

A persuasive argument that *g* represents an invented rather than a natural phenomenon is the fact that scores on tests that are supposed to measure this robust quality have risen in America and Europe over the last six decades. If today's American ten-year-olds took the IQ test that was used in 1932, one-fourth—ten times the number in 1932—would attain scores indicating superior intelligence. And if children who were age ten in 1932 took the IQ test used today, one-fourth would be classified as intellectually deficient.

The description "highly intelligent," Neisser argues, reflects a comparison between a particular person and all others of the same age from the same culture tested during the same historical era.[83] This ascription is nothing like the statement, "Mary's eyes are brown" or "Mary's body temperature is 98 degrees Fahrenheit." The intelligence measured on an IQ test has coherent meaning only when applied to individuals of the same age cohort who understand the language of the test questions. One can say nothing about the intelligence of an unschooled ten-year-old living in an isolated village in Tibet who has deaf-mute parents.

However, one can say what color that child's eyes are, what her body temperature is, and how much she weighs.

The arbitrariness of IQ scores is appreciated when one realizes that if a mysterious force reduced the IQ of everyone in the world by ten points, the heritability coefficients and the correlation between IQ and academic grades would remain exactly as they were before the change. A similar outcome would be impossible for natural phenomena. If human resistance to disease were changed by reducing everyone's T-cell count by 10 percent, serious health consequences would follow.

I do not question the fact that inherited biological factors affecting brain physiology contribute to the more similar scores of identical as compared with fraternal twins, and siblings as compared with unrelated individuals, on the tests used to study intelligence. The nub of the quarrel is over the inference we should draw from those hard facts. This is not a trivial issue. Ptolemy and Kepler were aware of very similar facts about the stars and planets, but the former inferred that the sun revolved around the earth, while the latter claimed that the earth moved. The difference in inference is not an arcane academic quarrel.

Some fifteenth-century citizens came down with the plague; some twentieth-century citizens contract AIDS. But the former believed that the cause of their illness was a witch; modern citizens believe that the cause of AIDS is a virus. Individuals differ in their performances on cognitive tests and in brain physiology. It would be extremely important if the cause of these differences was a particular set of genes that made some persons more competent on all tests. If this is unlikely, the concept of g does not refer to a natural phenomenon and, like Newton's ether, is retarding theoretical progress.

That is why at least one group of scientists asked by the American Psychological Association to prepare an objective evaluation of the concept of general intelligence concluded, "Standardized tests do not sample all forms of intelligence . . . the study of intelligence . . . needs self-restraint, reflection, and a great deal more research."[84]

It is not unimportant that the concept of intelligence has strong ethical connotations. Individuals who are of low intelligence are less likely to adapt to our society. That fact implies to some observers that those who possess low intelligence also possess a flawed biology. Once a concept acquires a moral connotation, it becomes difficult to criticize the logic of its application for it fills the important function of accounting for adjustment failures. Too critical an analysis of its meaning will compromise its utilitarian and ethical advantages and mar the feeling of certainty that renders it immune to criticism.

The attribution "intelligent" is often used in ways similar to the biologist's use of "fitness" for an animal species. But evolutionary biologists understand that the relative fitness of an individual animal depends on the specific ecological niche in which it lives. The availability of resources and competition with others living in the same place for those resources affect the fitness of all animals living in that area. Those who favor the concept of intelligence are friendly to the idea of relative fitness, but they reject the constraints that are part of that notion. Most important, these scientists do not seem to be aware of the value judgment inherent in the celebration of the verbal skills that is at the core of all intelligence tests.

Despite the many legitimate critiques of the controversial book *The Bell Curve*, most critics did not suggest that the term intelligence was not scientifically useful.[85] Most found fault with the authors' conclusions but did not question the legitimacy of the concept itself. However, David Wechsler, the inventor of the most widely used intelligence test, argued that a person's intelligence must always be understood in the context of a particular culture; therefore, people classified as "intelligent" in one society might not be so in another. This wise caveat was ignored because of a widespread conviction that each person—infant to octogenarian—has a relatively fixed amount of a complex mental quality that is—like Galen's mysterious black bile—a material, indestructible part of their personhood. Because no other psychological quality possesses that feature, this premise is likely to be incorrect.

Temperament

The belief that children inherit physiologies that bias them to develop particular psychological profiles rests on three observations. (1) Siblings raised by the same parents in the same home and neighborhood are usually different in their motives, moods, and talents. (2) Identical twins separated at birth and raised in different homes resemble each other more closely than they should in their motives, moods, and talents. (3) Correlations between particular emotional and behavioral qualities, on the one hand, and physiological features like heart rate, blood pressure, eye color, and body build, on the other, imply the influence of genes on a person's psychological features. Scholarly writing on children's temperaments is replete with terms like shy, avoidant, sociable, active, reactive, self-regulating, and irritable. Each word fails to specify the age or prior history of the child or the context in which the child is observed.

Many young children are initially quiet and subdued with unfamiliar adults. However, most of these same children will not be shy when they are with unfamiliar children. Only about 10 percent of two-year-olds are quiet and timid in both of these social situations, and only about 15 percent are sociable in most unfamiliar situations. These two small groups are temperamentally different from each other and from those who are inconsistent across contexts. Further, each type reveals its special characteristics in infancy.[86]

A similar degree of specificity is present in fish. A team of scientists observed the behavior of juvenile pumpkin seed sunfish when a red-tipped stick was moved toward them—a threatening event—and when a novel food was introduced into their foraging area. Some fish avoided the stick but approached the novel food, while others showed the opposite profile. Only a very small number of animals avoided both the stick and the food.[87] As with children, timidity or fearlessness can be context specific.

Healthy, alert four-month-old infants who are exposed to interesting visual, auditory, and olfactory stimuli display different patterns of reactivity. One group, about 20 percent, shows vigorous motor activity—thrashing of arms and legs—along with crying, suggesting that they are both easily aroused and distressed by the stimulation.[88] A larger group, about 40 percent, show very little motor activity and no distress, implying that they are not easily aroused by the same stimulation. These two types, called high and low reactive respectively, probably inherit different neurochemistries in the limbic structures that mediate avoidant reactions to novelty, especially the amygdala and its projections to motor areas, frontal lobes, hypothalamus, and autonomic nervous system.

When the high and low reactive infants were 14 months old and were presented with unfamiliar events, people, and rooms, the former were much more fearful than the latter. About 60 percent of the high reactives cried and became unusually shy and timid, while about 60 percent of the low reactives became fearless, spontaneous, and sociable. When these same children were observed at 21 months, only about one-third of the high reactives were still fearful and shy, and one-third of the low reactives were still fearless and sociable. When the children were 4½ years old, they were interviewed by an unfamiliar woman and later these children played with unfamiliar children. Now only 13 percent of those who had been high reactive infants maintained a consistently fearful-timid personality across all of the contexts at 14 and 21 months and 4½ years. These children are properly called "inhibited." However, not one high reactive infant displayed fearlessness and high sociability from 14 months through 4½ years—a profile characteristic of the "uninhibited" child.[89]

What term shall we use to describe the substantial group of high reactive infants who did not become consistently inhibited as older children? Remember, if one twin in a monozygotic pair develops psychotic symptoms and the other does not, we do not place them in the same psychiatric category, despite the fact that they have identical genes. The high reactive infants who did not become consistently inhibited may possess a potential to become timid and apprehensive when they become adolescents. Their timidity may be "in remission." When psychiatrists use this phrase to describe patients, they do not mean that the schizophrenic symptoms will never return but that patients in remission must be distinguished conceptually from those with symptoms. The quality of inhibition is formed from biology and a history of experience. It is not present at birth.

It is important to specify the child's age when assigning temperamental descriptors. Most four-year-olds who had been low reactive infants were very spontaneous with the unfamiliar examiner. They talked, smiled, laughed, and appeared relaxed and spirited. But a maturational change that occurs in all children at five to six years renders them more thoughtful about the meaning of social encounters and more acutely aware of the evaluations of adult interviewers. As a result, the majority of seven-year-olds, including low reactives, are more subdued with the unfamiliar adult than they were three years earlier. They talked later in the interview and smiled and laughed less often. However, this subdued behavior is characteristic of most seven-year-olds because of the maturation of the new cognitive competence. Thus the attribution "subdued with an unfamiliar adult" has one meaning when applied to four-year-olds but a different meaning when applied to seven-year-olds because the causes of the subdued mood are not the same. That is why the history of the person must always be a part of the meaning of any description.

We recently saw two seven-year-old boys who were very subdued with the female examiner. One had been a high reactive infant; the other low reactive. Neither boy spoke spontaneously, other than to give answers to the direct questions, and each smiled only once during the entire battery. But the boy who had been a high reactive infant did not look at the examiner initially, spoke in a very soft voice, was reflective on difficult tests, and had high blood pressure. The boy who had been a low reactive infant was relaxed, looked at the examiner frequently, was impulsive on the tests, and had low blood pressure. Although both boys were subdued with the examiner, the different temperaments they displayed as infants were revealed in other measurements.[90]

The same conclusion follows from a comparison of two groups of four-to-five-year-old children. One group had a parent who suffered from panic attacks, while the parents of the other group were free of psychiatric disorder. Although more of the former were quiet and serious with the unfamiliar examiner, a small number of children with healthy parents were emotionally subdued. If one focused only on their quiet manner with the examiner, these two groups appeared similar. But they differed on other characteristics. Those born to parents with panic attacks were more timid when they were brought to an unfamiliar room and, in addition, had a more reactive sympathetic nervous system. Presumably, they would have displayed different profiles had we observed them earlier.[91]

Peter Kosso provides a nice example of this controversy.[92] We call the color of aspen leaves in midsummer green but those in October yellow, because those are the colors we see. But the leaves belong to the same tree and therefore possess the same fundamental biology. Hence it would not be irrational to decide to call aspen leaves "grellow" all the time, implying that they are green during one season but yellow during another. Although there is a change in appearance, all of the leaves retain the unique genetic structure that is definitive of aspen trees. Adoption of that strategy would suggest that we call sociable children who had been high reactive infants "shynoshy," while high reactive infants who became shy would be called "shy" and sociable children who had not been high reactive would be called "noshy."

The decision as to what to call children who change their outward profile is a function of one's position on the debate between appearance and reality. Some scientists argue that we cannot ever know what actually occurs in nature. Bohr was skeptical about our ability to grasp whatever hidden whole lay behind what was observed, even though he agreed it was necessary to use words as conceptual aids to describe the invisible processes. But these words were conjectures to help understanding and communication. If a six-year-old is sociable and bold, we cannot state that he is inhibited simply because he began life as a high reactive infant.

Other scholars, for whom Einstein is the prototype, believe that one is obligated to try to infer the critical process, even though the events are invisible to machines and human senses. Einstein trusted the human mind's capability of capturing the events that lay behind the measurement. These scientists would argue that we do not violate any rules by speculating that sociable, bold children who had been high reactive infants are different from equally sociable children who were not high reactive. The former might retain a greater potential to become shy and timid in the future.

I side with Bohr. Rats freeze when they see a light that had previously signaled shock. Octogenarians say they are afraid of dying a slow death.

College students in a PET scanner show high levels of metabolic activity in the limbic system when they see a spider. Scientists who believe that the word fear accurately describes all of the above events should use that term. But they should not let themselves be lulled into believing that the same invisible processes occur in all of the above examples. To do so is to commit the error of awarding fear a Platonic reality—a thing in itself—that is a fiction. Hilary Putnam goes further when he says that when we talk of "Ding an sich," we do not know what we're talking about.[93] The immobile rat, the worried octogenarian, and the college student in the scanner are separate threads scientists try to interconnect into a stronger cable. At present the fragile threads that comprise concepts in the social sciences are far too separate. I suspect there will come a time when each of the threads, that is, each of the empirical instantiations of a concept, will intertwine. When that happens the meaning of the concept will reside in all of the threads, as is now true for the concept of species in biology. Hopefully, that happy time lies not too far distant for the ideas that sustain the behavioral sciences.

The meaning of a value on a single variable, for example, a velocity of 5 mph, is ambiguous without specification of the agent-object and the context. Is it a car on a beach or a cow in a pasture? Extremely anxious, quiet, tense children often have the same heart rate as fearless, spontaneous children when both are sitting quietly in a chair before any stressful procedure has been administered. However, after an hour of challenging tests, more children in the former group have a higher heart rate than the latter.

Stephen Stich offers an imaginative illustration of the contribution of the history of an event to its meaning.[94] Imagine a counterfeiter who had made a hundred dollar bill that was exactly like the one printed by the United States Engraving Office. However, their distinct origins render the meaning and value of the two bills very different. The same conclusion holds for a painting of the Seine by an artist who had simulated one of Monet's representations of the same scene.

The significant contribution of a person's history to the meaning of every descriptive term in psychology contrasts with its relative unimportance in physics and chemistry. All ounces of iron are the same no matter where they are found or refined. A moving magnet with a stationary conductor is regarded as equivalent to a stationary magnet with a moving conductor if the same current is generated. But the fact that an individual's (or animal's) prior history participates in a major way in its current functioning divides the life sciences from the physical sciences. Two male crayfish facing each other, who appear identical to an observer, react to the same injection of serotonin in different ways. One animal shows inhibition of the reflex flip of the tail while the other shows an enhanced tail reflex. The reasons for the opposed behavior is that in the past the former animal had been defeated by the latter. One must know the history of these animals in order to predict their current behavior.[95] One of Darwin's cogent intuitions was that the histories of two animal species are a better guide to their classification than their current similarity. Whales and sharks look alike but have very different phylogenetic histories; whales and mice appear different but have a more similar origin.

A group of one hundred adults whose answers on a personality questionnaire place all of them in the category extrovert are not the same because they have had different past histories which affect the meaning of this and all other descriptive categories in psychology. The distinction between what an entity is at the moment of observation and what it was in the past or what it might be at some future time is honored by all of the life sciences. Psychologists are unusual in their frequent failure to honor epigenetic stages. Psychological traits are not stable structures hidden deep in the person's core. Some qualities, like today's attire, can change tomorrow.

The first words chosen to name natural phenomena are always too general. Air, fire, water, and earth, which were conceived as essences, are not the four fundamental forms matter assumes. Darwin's concept of natural selection failed to distinguish between traits that persisted over generations because they were adaptive and traits that persisted simply because they were not maladaptive. Nor did Darwin award significance to the difference between a gradual extinction that was the result of the inheritance of maladaptive qualities and sudden extinction caused by an unusual ecological event, like a prolonged drought or a large asteroid striking the earth.

The first signs of erosion in the belief in unconstrained words for processes came during the early eighteenth century when students of medicine, a more inductive science than mechanics and astronomy, realized that all statements are probabilistic. Therefore, the relations between the observed signs, not the more interesting invisible events, comprised the information available to scholars for theory building. It became clear by the middle of the nineteenth century, however, that each method of observation yielded a different set of probabilities; hence the faith in Platonic abstractions was weakened.

That insight has not sufficiently permeated the philosophy of the behavioral sciences. Modern physicists appreciate that light can behave as a wave or a particle depending on the method of measurement. But some contemporary psychologists write as if that maxim did not apply to consciousness, intelligence, or fear.

This idea can be put in a different way. The sentences intended to describe nature are constructed from a set of more fundamental representations, only some of which are direct derivatives of perceived events. The student able to answer correctly the question, "What is rust?" but who has never seen a rusted piece of iron is qualitatively different (that is, less knowledgeable about rust) than one who also answered correctly but has seen some rusty nails, locks, pipes, and faucets. The latter knows the meaning of rust in a special way. Frank Jackson makes this point by asking us to imagine an expert on the physics of color who has lived her entire life in a world of black, white, and gray. She would learn something new and important the first time she saw a ripe tomato.[96]

Too many sentences describing psychological processes are not linked closely enough to measured events and, as a result, the concepts in the sentences are insufficiently constrained. Most concepts have two sets of relations—one is with other concepts, the other is with phenomena. The basis for the relation between one concept and another is usually a single shared feature; such a slender foundation is rarely true of the relation between a concept and a phenomenon. As a result, it is easy for a mind to create a network of related concepts, with each pair linked by only one common feature. Consider the concept of regulation, which is popular in personality and temperament research. This idea is linked to the concept of control of impulse; control of impulse is linked to the concept of coping; and coping is linked to adaptation. None of these ideas is constrained by agent or situation.

The influential theorist Jeffrey Gray writes that the brains of animals and humans possess a "behavioral approach system (BAS)" that organizes actions directed at gaining a desired event.[97] The concept of a single brain system for all desired states implies that the brains of rats, monkeys, and humans contain a set of circuits that organizes courting, mating, pursuit, hunting, eating, drinking, protection of infants, and preparation for sleep, even though these sequences differ in incentive, duration of the relevant act, and origin in the brain. Although lesion of a rat's olfactory system prevents mating, it has no effect on sleeping, drinking, or preparation for rest.

By contrast, the scientist whose mind automatically follows a route downward from concept to phenomenon imagines concrete contexts in which a particular class of agent is moving toward a desired object. This mind will not equate an infant's reaching for a toy with an adolescent embracing a love object. Neither would this mind equate the regulation of crying in a two-year-old child arriving at a day care center with the regulation of an act of vandalism toward a parked Mercedes Benz by an impoverished, angry adolescent.

Social scientists are fond of such unconstrained processes because they often begin the creative part of their research by generating hypotheses from abstract concepts, rather than from concepts that are closely tied to observed phenomena. I know psychologists who write about the heritability of IQ scores who have never administered or even watched anyone take an intelligence test. Some scientists who write about an infant's attachment to the mother have never observed an infant with a parent since a time, perhaps 25 years earlier, when they watched their infant sibling nurse. As a result, too much theory in the social sciences rests on sentences that are so extraordinarily permissive they invite broad generality. Social scientists fall in love with philosophically rich concepts rather than events. They treat single words for dynamic events as if they were full sentences, as if the single word "bite" communicated a perfectly clear, unambiguous meaning as to the agent, the object being bitten, the target, and the provocative situation.

I am not hostile to unifying principles and their necessity for the advancement of any science; psychology is no exception. Natural scientists justly celebrate the physicists' search for a grand unifying theory of the four fundamental forces in nature, while recognizing that the concepts of neutron, proton, and meson were invented to explain observed energy profiles. I celebrate all who search for these grand ideas. I am simply critical of the many currently popular synthetic concepts in the social sciences, and especially in psychology, that ignore stage of life, gender, species, and context.

Cultural anthropologists would be among the first to cry "Not guilty!" to the charge of overgeneralization. And indeed, the current mood among cultural anthropologists is particularistic and opposed to assuming that a fact true of one culture—for example, that Europeans and Americans classify emotions on the basis of their valence and intensity—is likely to be true for all cultures. However, students of culture prior to the 1960s were as friendly to highly abstract concepts as psychologists and sociologists are today.

The continued attraction to abstract attributes, like fearful, anxious, conscious, intelligent, or shy, derives its power from a historically popular premise in Western philosophy, which Bertrand Russell favored, that every object, and by inference every person, can be viewed in isolation as an entity with a set of essential properties that is not altered by the circumstances in which the object or person is observed.[98] A stone retains its shape and hardness whether on a path or at the bottom of a lake. A woman is assumed to carry her intelligence or timidity with her, wherever and whenever she may go.

It is necessary to distinguish, however, between words that describe the physical features of a single object, for example, the size, shape, and color of a stone, and words intended to represent abstract qualities. Although the shape, color, and size of a stone on a path do not change, the stone is simultaneously a member of a category called "potentially dangerous objects." If someone tripped on the stone or threw it at a window, it would become a dangerous object. But the quality of being "dangerous" is not obvious when the stone is lying on a path or at the bottom of a deep lake. Membership in the functional category "dangerous" changes with the context. That observation leads to a critical point.

All words for cognitive, emotional, and behavioral processes are functional categories, like potentially dangerous stones. Thus it is an error to write in ways that imply that intelligent or fearful are inherent qualities of a person that travel, unaltered, across locations and indefinitely long periods of time. Some children make rapid progress in learning to read, to write, or to multiply numbers. But the name for that quality, which many call "intelligent," is only accurate for children who have developed in particular environments and are behaving in defined situations.

One important reason why unconstrained concepts remain entrenched in the social sciences is that some scholars wish to believe that most psychological processes are identical across individuals with different biologies, histories, and present living circumstances. For example, they resist using different words to describe declarative memory in three-year-olds, twenty-year-olds, and aging adults. But it is possible, if we assume that familiarity with the information being retrieved influences the accuracy of recall, that the nature of declarative memory may not be the same in these three age groups. Consider a group of adults shown a series of mathematical equations, paintings, or titles of nineteenth-century novels. The person who is especially familiar with one of these domains will be able to cluster the items in that domain, based on conceptual similarities, and show excellent declarative memory. The student of mathematics might cluster the equations well; an artist might organize the paintings; and a student of English literature might cluster the titles of the novels. The retrieval process will be different for those who are more or less familiar with the information. Under these conditions the investigator should add a statement about the sophistication of the subjects.

Biologists are more sensitive to the fact that each process is linked to a specific set of entities. Natural scientists assume a privileged link between a process and a particular class of object. Biologists, chemists, and physicists, for example, habitually think in terms of an entity together with its functions, rather than a function divorced from a particular entity. Seventeenth-century chemists recognized the necessity of specifying both substances and conditions in order to predict the result of mixing two chemicals. No natural scientist regards radiation, precession, crossing over, or ionization as general processes that apply to diverse things in the world. Both lungs and blood vessels expand and contract, but because lungs and arteries are different in structure and function, biologists use "dilate and constrict" for the blood vessels but "expand and contract" for the lungs. They recognize the value of using exact language to distinguish among similar processes in different organs.

When biologists write about the concept "bleach," colleagues recognize that the term refers to a change in the pigment of receptor cells in the retina in response to photons of light. They would not use the word bleach to refer to any entity that suddenly becomes lighter in color. On occasion, biologists are guilty of using overly abstract terms, often borrowed from the social sciences, that do not specify species. Some lurid examples include kin-based altruism, reciprocal cooperation, and enslavement. These constructs are used as if it made no difference whether the animal was a bee, a bat, or a baboon. Under these conditions, biologists resemble those psychologists who apply terms like attached, ambivalent, fearful, or sociable to dyads that might include a boy and a girl, man and woman, mother and infant, or grandfather and grandson. This practice violates the principle that the basic structure in scientific description is a complete thought, not an isolated predicate.

Many philosophers, but especially Gottlob Frege, have insisted that a complete statement, with agent, verb, and target, is the meaningful element in scientific prose.[99] Because a part (for example, a word for a process) can never be equated with the whole in which it participates (the complete statement), there is always the danger of assuming, incorrectly, that a given process operates identically across different agents or contexts. It would be nice if words accommodated to our idealistic wishes, but usually they do not.

Frege argued further that scientific propositions consist of abstract functions along with a set of specific arguments. A function is a sentence of the type "X fears Y," where agents, targets, and contexts are unspecified. A function can assume very different meanings when the agents X and Y are specified and a number of different arguments are created. The meanings of the arguments "Boys fear authoritarian fathers," "Students fear examinations," "Women fear aging," and "Men fear war" have distinctly different meanings.

Psychology, sociology, and anthropology are not fundamentally different in their epistemology from biology, and the history of biology contains a lesson for these more youthful social sciences. Only chromosomes cross over; only germ cells undergo meiosis; only neurons synapse; only pigment cells in the retina bleach. But learn, communicate, kill, approach, avoid, regulate, and mate are possible in ants, frogs, lizards, birds, rats, cats, chimps, and humans. The physiological and psychological processes that are the referents for these predicates cannot be identical across such diverse species. If we wish to compose more meaningful sentences about behavior, we must specify the class of agent and the type of situation in which those and so many other psychological processes are engaged.

CHAPTER TWO

The Allure of Infant Determinism

How far forward can the deep past extend its hand? Physicists believe that the current temperature of the universe—about three degrees Kelvin—resulted inevitably from dissipation of the intense radiation created by the Big Bang. No other scientific discipline so confidently awards so much explanatory power to an initial event in the distant past.

There is far less agreement among psychologists regarding the primacy of early events. Consider a twenty-year-old in profound anguish over failing an examination, a forty-year-old who has been arrested by the police, or a sixty-year-old in a mood of suicidal depression. At what stage in development did the probability of each of these events rise significantly above chance, and what experiences created that higher probability?

Every society speculates about the causes of variation among its members. Some attribute special power to a person's date of birth or to sorcery. Other cultures award influence to more materialistic factors, like climate, diet, and the individual's biology. A much smaller number of societies, including our own, have decided that experiences during the early years (especially the biological mother's affectionate care and interactive play with her infant) are the most potent force in shaping a life.

European and American writers have been insistent, since the beginning of the eighteenth century, that the habits wrought by the events of infancy could not be abrogated. Rousseau hyperbolically asserted that mothers are responsible for the health of their society. "When mothers deign to nurse their own children, then will be a reform in morals . . . natural feeling will revive in every heart . . . When women become good mothers, men will be good husbands and fathers."[1] These views became especially popular during the opening decades of this century. One commentator wrote in 1929, "The powerful significance of the intellectual processes—perception, fantasy, thinking and their social results in science, art, and philosophy in the human being—have their first roots in the specifically human mental structures of the 3 month old child . . . Historically, all phenomena of adult mental life must be traceable to birth."[2]

Some self-appointed experts warned that even "public entertainments" were dangerous toxins to young minds. "It is not only the ignorant who take their babies to movie and picture shows or other entertainments, they may be found at concerts and lectures which draw their audiences from the most cultured. The baby may show no signs of restlessness and be as good as you please, or may make up for lost sleep by an extra nap the next day, and yet be harmed thereby. No serious immediate symptoms of nervous over-stimulation may appear, but someday the accounting must come—it may be 20 or 40 years later before it is paid in full, but paid in full it will be."[3]

The anthropologist Geoffrey Gorer, in presenting a consensual view of the basic postulates of the social sciences in the period following the end of the Second World War, stated, first, that all habits are established through the administration of rewards and punishments. His second principle affirmed the potency of early experience: "The habits established early in the life of the individual influence all subsequent learning and, therefore, the experiences of early childhood are of predominant importance."[4] Recent textbooks in child development continue to insist that parents "start by giving the infant as much predictability and social interaction as possible" in order to influence the child's future.[5] Two respected authors, Michael Lamb and Marc Bornstein, inform students, "Events in infancy are important because they initiate multiple processes of development . . . Infancy must have a manifest and inevitable impact on development . . . By studying infancy we learn about processes and experiences that have long-term implications for psychological development."[6]

Why have so many been persuaded of the permanent psychological power of the early years? One clue can be found in eighteenth-century Europe, where a growing number of wives of merchants and skilled artisans were gradually freed of the responsibility of gathering wood, picking berries, tending domestic animals, and weeding vegetable plots. Society assigned to these women, idled by historical change, the task of shaping the future of their infants. A perfectly nurtured child who married well or mastered the skills that led to a position of prestige in the larger community would enhance the family's status. As the children of the bourgeoisie lost their economic value, they became investments in the family's future, and parents began to view them as objects of sentiment and pleasure.

Eighteenth-century European society had become more mobile, and it was now possible for the son of a tailor or blacksmith to rise in the social hierarchy, and for the son of a squire or parson to fall. Change in social class became simultaneously a hope and a fear and therefore a source of uncertainty for families located on the middle, most vulnerable rungs of the class ladder. When a source of uncertainty permeates the consciousness of large segments of a society, some explanation will be invented that is both reasonable and suggests actions that can be taken to mute the uncomfortable feeling. The popular notion that certain parental behaviors guaranteed the development of character traits necessary for a successful future, and therefore protected the family against a descent in status, rationalized ritual practices that swept some of the worry away. But this idea meant that the complementary hypothesis must also be true: If mothers did not nurture their infants properly, their children would be vulnerable to a dull mind, a wild spirit, and a downward spiral. Thus, it was morally incumbent on parents to implement the best rearing practices as early as possible.

Somewhere in America today a mother-to-be is playing a cassette recording of a Beethoven sonata near her abdomen in the hope that her unborn child will become sensitized to good music. Another expectant woman is reading aloud from Keats or Dickens so that her fetus might catch enough words to place her ahead of her peers in kindergarten. Some mothers insist on being in skin contact with their newborn during the first postnatal hour to ensure an emotional bonding they believe is necessary for their child's long-term mental health. These parents, who have taken the writings of John Bowlby and Erik Erikson seriously, are convinced that their infant's future is controlled in a nontrivial way by the events of the first hours, weeks, and months of life.[7]

The rituals that flow from this conviction absorb anxiety like a sponge. If future happiness, talent, and success are formed in the first years of life, and if careful attention to this stage guarantees a sunburst of joyous outcomes, then parents who conscientiously perform their child-rearing duties have less reason to be apprehensive. The relatively uncritical acceptance of these assumptions requires a deep faith in an unbroken connectedness between past and present and a view of each life as a highway that connects the first day to the last. This view of development rests on the assumption that every experience produces a permanent physical change somewhere in the central nervous system, and therefore the earliest experiences provide the scaffolding for the child's future thought and behavior. Development becomes analogous to building a house: Just as the form and quality of the foundation determine the integrity of the subsequent frame, first experiences have an overwhelming priority in determining the form and quality of the mature adult's emotional and mental life. The fresh tape that is a metaphor for the infant brain is altered permanently by each experience, and these messages are preserved with fidelity for an indefinite period.

Other life scientists tell a different story, however. The evolutionists Niles Eldredge and Stephen Gould created a mild stir among some of their colleagues when they suggested that the emergence of a new species could occur in a relatively short period of time. The pace of evolution need not, as Darwin believed, mimic the production of eggs in a rural English county.[8] The transformation of a fertilized egg into the trunk and limbs of an embryo, the onset of a winter flu epidemic, and the paralysis following a massive cerebral stroke are discontinuous events that transform what was prior in a dramatic way.

New discoveries in genetics also challenge the premise of infant determinists. A pragmatic "waste not, want not" philosophy had been part of the geneticist's credo only twenty-five years ago. How could a mutation, biologists asked, not have some consequences, either for good or for ill? Yet we now know that most amino acid substitutions caused by mutations appear to have no consequences for the vitality or viability of the organism.[9] Similarly, psychological determinists have assumed that every kiss, hug, lullaby, or scolding alters the child's brain in ways that will influence his future. But if slight changes in synapses, like some amino acid substitutions, are without functional consequence, then every smile at an infant is not to be viewed as a bank deposit accumulating psychic dividends.

A faith in connectedness has been associated with a belief in critical periods in development. This concept, which was popular fifty years ago but lost some of its appeal, has begun to return in some quarters. The idea of a critical period has a clear meaning in animals. Imprinting in precocial birds provides an excellent example. There is an initial period after hatching when a duckling or gosling will follow the first moving object it sees, normally the mother. Several days later, following brain growth, the young bird avoids unfamiliar objects. As a result, it becomes imprinted on its mother or, if reared in a laboratory, on the first moving person or object it sees.[10] During a critical interval early in life, certain experiences can affect the animal's future behavior permanently.

The neuroscientists David Hubel and Torsten Wiesel discovered another dramatic example of a critical period, this time in the development of vision. In a series of experiments, the investigators closed one eye of newborn kittens, so that only one side of the visual cortex received visual stimulation. In a kitten whose eye is closed for a brief critical period between fourteen and 30 days, when the neurochemistry of the visual cortex is in a special state, the anatomy in that part of the brain is influenced permanently and the cat will be functionally blind in one eye. However, in a kitten whose eye is closed a month after birth, no change in the brain occurs and the animal's vision will be normal after the eye is opened. Hubel and Wiesel concluded that during a brief, critical interval, both sides of the visual cortex require equivalent visual stimulation. If it is denied, visual functioning is affected permanently.[11]

The notion of critical periods captured the imagination of many developmental psychologists, who assumed that there must be such periods in human development. Scientists speculated about critical periods in the acquisition of language and of attachment bonds to parents, the latter being regarded as analogous to imprinting in ducklings. Marshal Klaus and John Kennell claimed, over twenty-five years ago, that maternal bonding to the infant must occur during the first critical hours after birth if development is to proceed normally. That bold statement, which worried the many mothers who had missed this experience, was based on one study of twenty-eight poor, unmarried women—hardly a sample that warranted such a provocative conclusion.[12]

To the disappointment of many, it has proven difficult to find critical periods in human development that are as robust as the discoveries with ducklings and kittens. The orphans produced by World War II and the Korean conflict, who had fragile bonds to adults during their first years, developed well after adoption by nurturant foster parents.[13] In one study, a group of frightened, quiet two-to-four-year-olds who had been raised in an overcrowded institution with too few caretakers were enrolled in regular play sessions with adults and children. The veil of indifference lifted after less than two years, and the typical emotional vitality of four-year-olds emerged. One investigator, who was unprepared for such a dramatic change, wrote,

> We had not anticipated the older children who had suffered deprivations for periods of 2½ to 4 years to show swift response to treatment. That they did so amazed us. These inarticulate underdeveloped youngsters who had formed no relationships in their lives, who were aimless and without a capacity to concentrate on anything, had resembled a pack of animals more than a group of human beings . . . As we worked with the children, it became apparent that their inadequacy was not the result of damage but, rather, was due to a dearth of normal experiences without which development of human qualities is impossible. After a year of treatment,

many of these older children were showing a trusting dependency toward the staff of volunteers and . . . self-reliance in play and routines.[14]

These demonstrations of developmental malleability motivated psychologists to replace the term critical period with the more permissive notion of sensitive period. This concept implies that, for each important human function, an optimal time exists when certain experiences are the most beneficial. A child could develop a particular competence even if she missed the relevant experience, but the adult function might be compromised. The idea of a sensitive period has intuitive appeal and is almost impossible to disprove, and in the case of language may actually be valid. If a child is not exposed to any spoken language during the first three years of life, future linguistic competence will be impaired to some degree. While some evidence has been collected, this hypothesis is hard to prove with certainty, for a child who has heard no human speech at all during the first three years of life is difficult to find. And those who are discovered may be developmentally retarded in other ways, owing to the special circumstances that brought about the language deprivation.

The concept of critical periods is beginning to return to the field of education, but the reasons are more political than scientific. Many children of poor urban families arrive in school minimally prepared for academic instruction. Some have no knowledge of the alphabet; some have never been read a bedtime story. Many of these children have great difficulty learning to read, and those who fail to acquire reading skill by the fourth grade are at risk for becoming adolescent delinquents. Everyone agrees on the necessity of benevolent intervention long before these children enter school, and one obvious strategy is to persuade the mothers of these children to adopt the regular practices of middle-class parents, namely, playing with and talking to their infants, reading to their three-year-olds, and promoting the importance of success at academic tasks.[15]

But how does one persuade them? Should they be shamed for their past failures, in the hope that the resulting feelings will motivate the desired behavior? This approach is unattractive for several reasons. First, shame and guilt have lost a great deal of power in this century, in part because no uniform set of standards for behavior exists among Americans from diverse ethnic groups. Many Americans have become tolerant of individual preferences and are reluctant to condemn less typical family practices. Second, economically stressed mothers who feel oppressed by the majority society have become either angry, fatalistic, or both. It is not easy to generate guilt in a parent who is mad at the messenger or unconvinced that she can change her children's lives. Most important, the decision to generate shame or guilt implies that poor mothers are morally flawed. Most middle-class adults are understandably reluctant to blame these victims by suggesting that they did not care enough about their children's welfare.

Hence, a preferred, and more benign, approach acknowledges that poor mothers love their children but do not know the basic facts of human development. If they were aware of the importance of playing with, talking to, and reading to their children, they would implement these rituals at once. In order to make this message more urgent, educators have exploited the current prestige of the neurosciences and told parents that the first two years of life are a critical period in infant development; if parents do not provide proper stimulation during this time, their child will be harmed permanently.

This tactic was used in the cover story of the February 3, 1997, issue of *Time* magazine, which stated boldly that new synapses are established every time a parent looks down at the infant's face, moving the brain a bit closer to perfection. The article quoted a child psychologist: "Experience in the first year of life lays the basis for networks of neurons that enable us to be smart, creative, and adaptable in all the years that follow."[16] There is nothing novel in these declarations. A 1914 government pamphlet for mothers contained exactly the same warning with even less scientific evidence. "The first nervous impulses which pass through the baby's eyes, ears, fingers, or mouth to the tender brain makes a pathway for itself; the next time another impulse travels over the same path, it deepens the impression of the first."[17]

This advice—whether given in 1914 or 1997—is well intentioned. Infants who are played with regularly are cognitively advanced over those who are ignored. However, it is a bit dishonest to suggest to poor parents that playing with and talking to their infant will protect the child from future academic failure and guarantee life success. The quality of the school, the motivation of the teachers, the values of peers, the mores of the neighborhood, and the child's identification with his socioeconomic class will exert important influence during the childhood years. Yes, of course, parents should be affectionate, playful, and conversational with their infants, but there are no guarantees.

Every American infant born in 1998 will be ranked with over three million other children when that age cohort enters elementary school. From first grade through high school graduation, each child's relative ability on varied academic tasks, compared with all others in that large group, will shape his future in a major way. The experiences of infancy represent only one of many factors that will contribute to the adolescent's relative rank. The education and income of the parents, place of residence, peer group values, and quality of school attended are among the most important determinants of later academic success.

A famous longitudinal study of children born and reared on the Hawaiian island of Kauai revealed that about 15 percent of the sample had serious academic or conduct problems during adolescence. The best predictor of which children would develop these problems was the social class of their family—over 80 percent of the children with problems came from the poorest segment of the sample, and only one child from an upper-middle-class home developed a psychological problem.[18] It is considerably more expensive to improve the quality of housing, education, and health of the approximately one million children living in poverty in America today than to urge their mothers to kiss, talk to, and play with them more consistently. Although a change in maternal behavior in this direction will have benevolent effects, those effects will be slim compared with the effect of changing current social policies.

Consider a thought experiment. A group of five hundred uneducated mothers living in poverty talk to and play with their children four hours a day, while a group of five hundred college-trained professional mothers living in economic affluence talk and play with their infants only twenty minutes a day. I am certain that more children in the former group will fail to graduate from high school or will serve time in prison, while more of the latter group will go on to professional vocations. Should that prediction be correct, it does not imply that the early parental play had no benevolent effect; rather, the correct inference is that other conditions correlated with social class have greater influence on school attendance and vocational choice.

The concept of relative fitness in evolutionary biology assumes that the success of any one individual or species in a locale depends not only on its genes and biological–behavioral characteristics but also on the competences of the other individuals or species living in the same eco-logical niche with whom it competes. Dark-winged moths won out over light-winged ones in the industrial areas of England because their dark color protected them from predation from birds when they alighted on soot-darkened tree trunks. But in rural England, where there was no black soot on the bark of trees, the opposite survival pattern was seen.[19] Similarly, the probability of a child attaining a challenging vocation with dignity and economic security—the analogue of a moth avoiding predation—is enhanced more by rearing in a home with college-educated parents than in a home with parents who were high school dropouts, independent of the experiences of infancy.

Unfortunately every society needs a small number of chiefs but a great many warriors. I recall an anecdote about an older professor and a student who were running from a bear. The student yelled to the pro-fessor, who was a few feet in front of him, "The bear is going to catch us and we will be killed unless we run faster." The older man replied, "It is not necessary for me to run faster than the bear, only faster than you."

Attachment and Uncertainty

The current concern with an infant's attachment to its parent requires a strong faith in connectedness, sensitive periods, and the significance of early social bonds. Although modern Americans believe that a bond of love between an infant and its caretaker is absolutely necessary for healthy development, not every observer of children came to that strong conclusion. Ancient Greeks and Romans were more concerned with the quality of a nurse's milk than with her affection for the infant. Although Montaigne and Darwin wrote about the human infant, neither bothered to note that an emotional bond to the mother was of special significance. A fifteenth-century wealthy Florentine, Leon Battista Alberti, did not think it important whether a mother or a wet nurse cared for the infant, for it was the father's vigilance and display of proper behavior that determined whether the child would become a virtuous adult.[20]

The seventeenth-century Dutch minister John Robinson was certain that a child needed parental severity more than affection; therefore, fathers were a more significant influence on their children than mothers. "There is running in the breasts of most parents a strong stream of parental affection toward . . . their children . . . which is always dangerous and also harmful."[21] Francis Wayland, an early president of Brown University, published a psychological text in 1835 called *The Elements of Moral Science* which sold over 75,000 copies. The section devoted to the obligations of parents urged them to keep the infant alive, healthy, intellectually vital, and, above all, moral. Mr. Wayland never mentioned the obligation to love them.[22]

These beliefs by presumably intelligent, thoughtful commentators suggest that our contemporary preoccupation with the image of nursing mothers tenderly kissing their serene infants to communicate their love is a product of special historical conditions. One such condition is the anxiety among middle-class Americans created by the large number of working mothers. The idea of paid strangers caring for vulnerable infants deviates from the nature of family life during the first half of this century and violates the notion that infants ought to be—some would say have a right to be—cared for by their biological mothers. Some commentators believe that to do otherwise risks compromising a child's mental health. John Bowlby fed these anxieties in the 1960s: "Gnawing uncertainty about the accessibility of responsive attachment figures is a principal condition for the development of an unstable and anxious personality."[23] Bowlby's affirmation of the belief that the infant's secure attachment to the mother influenced the child's future seized the minds and hearts of parents and psychologists.

The swell of enthusiasm for attachment theory was also, in part, an understandable reaction to the excessive cruelties of the Second World War. The atrocities generated a desire among psychologists and psychiatrists for a conception of human nature with less dark, Freudian pessimism. Erik Erikson's creative intuition to replace Freud's oral stage with a stage of trust satisfied this hunger for a more humane, less selfish infant who needed and was receptive to parental love. However, economists and political scientists expressed their revulsion at wartime atrocities in exactly the opposite way. These scholars invented rational choice theory, which claimed that humans always acted to maximize their personal satisfaction. Thus, the Second World War forced Western intellectuals to confront the human capacity for cruelty. Psychologists defended against that raw fact by projecting trust and need for love onto the innocent infant; economists chose to intellectualize this sad insight by projecting selfishness onto adults.

Finally, the economically parasitic role of modern children renders them more needy of reassurance that they are loved than children who perform daily chores. The ten-year-old in a fifteenth-century farming village realized that he was an object of value because he could see that his work made a material contribution to the family's welfare. The ten-year-old son of a middle-class official in eighteenth-century London could not point to a plowed field or high wood pile as a sign of his worthiness and, being more uncertain of his value, was more dependent upon symbolic signs of affection that assured him of his beloved place in his parents' eyes.

Bowlby's decision to use the idea of security to describe the infant's relation to its caretaker was dictated by the same historical conditions that led the poet W. H. Auden to name our century the Age of Anxiety. After the need for food, warmth, sleep, and relief of pain is satisfied, uncertainty fixes the spot where the roving mind dwells. The major source of uncertainty in fifteenth-century European societies, and in many current Third World villages, was whether the infant would live. That worry is muted in industrialized cultures, which have safer water and effective vaccines, and has been replaced with worry over the child's psychological vitality.

A state of uncertainty—Benjamin Franklin used the word uneasiness—originates in unexpected or unfamiliar events that are not understood easily or immediately. A mother's continued presence in the home, loyal friends, trusted employers, and faithful spouses, which were more regular features of nineteenth-century life, lost some of their certainty during this century. Adults did not know whom to trust when they moved to new cities next to neighbors they might never meet. The additional threats of world wars, nuclear destruction, violence on the streets, and pollution of air, water, and food made the muting of adult uncertainty imperative. Bowlby sensed that the angst of his historical era was a rupture of family and social bonds, and he guessed that a child's secure attachment to a parent protected her from fear and inoculated her against future uneasiness. Seventeenth-century European parents also wanted their children to be able to cope with anxiety, but they were certain that forcing children to deal with difficulty was a better way to teach resilience than to shower them with affectionate care and to protect them from moments of worry.

Different sources of uncertainty became salient during the last half of this century. The cruelties of World War II and Vietnam, increased violence, and the willingness among a majority to accept hedonistic self-interest as an ethical posture have replaced "Man as Machine" with the more chilling metaphor of "Man as Gorilla." We would like to believe that the human wildness we are witnessing around us can be tamed with love, for we have given up the hope that empathy will be sufficient. The idea of attachment serves the same therapeutic function that the philosophy of holism did during the earlier decades of this century. That supposition does not mean that either idea is without validity. But it does mean that the popularity of the concept of attachment rests on much more than scientific evidence. It thrives on the deep assumption that humans require love more than any other resource and the illusion that we can prevent men from hacking others to death by loving them when they are young children. The Japanese rape of Nanking in 1937, the cultural revolution in the People's Republic of China in the late 1960s, the mass murders in Bosnia, and the butchery in Rwanda put a partial lie to that hope. I suspect that most of the men who committed those terrible atrocities had loving parents during their childhood years.

As I indicated in Chapter 1, unfamiliar or discrepant events share some elements with what one knows but are different enough to be alerting. During the Depression of the 1930s rich families were rare, and Hollywood took advantage of the natural curiosity about them by making films about the wealthy. During the last decade poor families of color have become a discrepant minority, and Hollywood makes films about these disadvantaged youth in order to attract viewers. The most acclaimed artists of any historical era are those who anticipated themes that were about to become nodes of uncertainty in the larger society. The mood of alienation in T. S. Eliot's *Wasteland*, which was enhanced among Europeans following the First World War, has become so prevalent that the poem has lost some of its initial power. An act of incest between a caring middle-class Caucasian father and his adolescent daughter would have threatened American audiences before the Second World War. But by 1984 the anxiety surrounding this theme had become tame enough to allow a major television network to attract millions of viewers to a one-hour drama called "Something about Amelia." And when *Lolita* was first published in Paris in 1955, it was banned in France the following year. When it was published in the United States in 1958, *The New York Times* reviewer found it repulsive. Forty-three years later *Lolita* became a Hollywood movie for the second time. Shakespeare is rarely boring because his plots deal with universally discrepant ideas—a jealousy that provokes strangling a beloved, incest, and treachery. Over time the mind/heart, like a butterfly skipping from flower to flower, finds a new atypicality which recruits attention and arouses feeling.

One of the new atypicalities is an interest in spirituality. I suspect that the recent interest in this idea among both scientists and the general public is due in part to a failure of most new facts to arouse a level of emotion that was more common a half century ago. Before the Second World War, and indisputably before the turn of the century, when there was no World Wide Web and far fewer PhDs, new facts of broad significance occurred with less frequency; hence each discovery had a greater potential to generate a moment of wonder, awe, or delight. The day after major newspapers reported to the world in 1919 that Arthur Eddington and his research team had discovered that light from the stars appeared to bend as it brushed the sun, affirming a critical prediction of relativity, Einstein became a world hero. The rate of occurrence of equally stunning facts has been far faster during the second half of this century. The contemporary public is barraged weekly with dramatic scientific discoveries, from the pictures of Mars' surface to cloned sheep. There are also retractions of older statements; cosmologists happily report that new evidence indicates that the universe is older than its oldest stars, whereas a few years ago they were embarrassed by data which suggested the opposite. Americans who remain hungry for more knowledge can surf the Web until fully sated. However, the appeal of a fresh fact is correlated with its capacity to generate a tiny jolt of emotion. The plenitude of new knowledge almost guarantees that, except for the small number of scholars working in the field of discovery, most new facts will not provoke much emotion in a majority of citizens. NASA's space missions have become almost routine, and it is unlikely that 5 percent of the public knows the name of anyone who was on the last Apollo mission to the moon. But people remain attracted to ideas that can arouse them. One reason for the new interest in human spirituality is that its source in intuition is radically different from the rational, densely factual nature of science and therefore generates feeling.

A second, independent historical change contributing to the new curiosity about the spiritual face of humanity is that many discoveries in molecular biology and neuroscience appear, on the surface, to mechanize human processes, like reproduction and consciousness, and to rob them of some of the mystery on which their emotional power rests. If a donor ovum from Mary Smith can be fertilized in a petri dish with a sperm from Richard Jones and then implanted in the uterus of surrogate mother Ruth Williams so that Richard Jones's wife can be a mother nine months later, the meaning of parenthood is changed sufficiently to make many citizens feel that the mystery of human existence is disappearing, and with it the feeling of *agape* that infuses the concept of humanness with a sacred quality. It is not surprising therefore that the community is eager for a return of a sense of specialness to human life and a bit of the awe that cannot be felt by surfing the Web. Lists of facts alone cannot generate the feeling that accompanies detection of an unexpected simplicity and the savoring of that aesthetically satisfying moment Einstein regarded as his greatest pleasure.

One unfortunate consequence of the rush of new facts is the temptation among a small number to hype an empirical discovery so that it might have a chance of being heard above the din. Darwin only had to whisper; contemporary scientists have to scream in order to be heard. The media, naturally friendly to exaggeration, have obliged by reporting that infants can do simple arithmetic, that taking risks is an inherited human trait, and that humans will soon be cloned. A second consequence of information glut is a more permissive attitude toward empirical truth. If the density of new facts has made each one less precious and, in addition, a trifle dehumanizing, then the accuracy or truthfulness of a scientific or historical discovery becomes a less significant feature. Surprisingly, some historians have decided that because it is not possible to know exactly what happened in the deep past, a little willful imagination does not violate any moral constraint, especially if the fictional additions make the text more interesting or resolve social tensions. These scholars would not tolerate an equally permissive posture by their surgeon, architect, or the pilot that flies them to a holiday in Europe, even though the functioning of every brain, roof support, and jet plane is surrounded by a halo of uncertainty.

The Measurement of Attachment

The gold standard for measuring the quality of attachment in one-to-two-year-old children—called the Strange Situation—is based on Bowlby's assumption that the caretaker's most critical function is to reduce the infant's fear. In this experimental procedure, a mother and child come to an unfamiliar laboratory room for an initial acclimation. The mother then leaves and returns over a series of three-minute episodes. If the child becomes mildly distressed when the mother leaves but is soothed easily when she returns, the child is said to be "securely attached." But if the child seems unconcerned with the mother's departure and, as a result, ignores her when she returns, or if the child becomes very distressed and is not easily soothed upon her return, the child is said to be "insecurely attached" and something is assumed to be wrong with the relationship.[24]

There are several reasons to question these conclusions. The first is that the original study which suggested a relation between maternal sensitivity and a secure attachment in the child was based on 23 infants, of whom only 7 were classified as insecurely attached. A second basis for doubt is that the attachment classifications are not very stable over intervals as short as six months. The third is that the claim fails the test of reasonableness. The mother and infant, who have been together for over a year, have experienced pain, pleasure, joy, and distress, and the infant's representations of and behavioral reactions to the mother must contain aspects of all these experiences. Is it reasonable to believe that a half-hour sample of behavior in an unfamiliar laboratory room could reveal the history of all these experiences with the mother? Could any thirty-minute observation uncover psychological products created from over six thousand hours of interaction between these partners?

But there are other problems. When a mother leaves her infant in an unfamiliar place, between about 15 and 20 percent are temperamentally biased to become extremely fearful when faced with this discrepancy, especially if a stranger is in the room. These excessively fearful infants are not easily soothed when the mother returns and are labeled insecurely attached, even though they may have had sensitive, predictable mothers. They are simply temperamentally prone to become very fearful when unfamiliar events occur. In Mary Ainsworth's original study, excessive irritability at home was the best predictor of a resistant-insecure attachment. Further, children who have been attending day care centers from an early age have become accustomed to their mothers leaving them in an unfamiliar place and are less likely to cry when the mother leaves. Because they are minimally fearful during the mother's brief absence, they continue to play when she returns. However, they, too, are called insecurely attached.

One investigator who observed mother–infant pairs in their homes during the first year found that the children's behavior in the Strange Situation—whether securely or insecurely attached—was not related to the mother's sensitivity but rather to the child's temperament. The extremely irritable, fearful infants were most likely to be classified as resistant-insecurely attached, while those who were easy to care for were more often classified as securely attached. Indeed, the best predictor of this type of attachment was the display of wariness to the stranger.[25]

Another reason for skepticism is that serious differences in forms of rearing do not always affect the child's behavior in the Strange Situation. About two-thirds of a sample of over one thousand children from ten different cities behaved in the Strange Situation as if they were securely attached. But, surprisingly, it made no difference whether these children were cared for at home, attended a day care center, or were sent to a relative for most of the day.[26] This result is glaringly inconsistent with the belief that this laboratory procedure measures the quality of a young child's emotional attachment to a mother who was or was not sensitive and predictable. Indeed, over half of a large number of studies conducted by scientists working in different cities found no significant relation between the sensitivity of the mother's care and the security of her child's attachment.[27]

Robert Le Vine, a cultural anthropologist, argues that the child's behavior in the Strange Situation can be the product of the socialization received during the prior months. For example, mothers living in a town in northern Germany, who love their infants, nevertheless believe that children must learn to be self-reliant—the word in German is *Selbständigkeit*—and they worry about spoiling them. (Sixteenth-century German parents held the same ethic, for ten- and eleven-year-old sons of wealthy families were often sent to apprentice in families living several hundred miles away in order to prepare them for life.)[28] The German mothers typically do not go into the bedroom when the infant wakes so that the child will learn to comfort herself. These mothers also leave their infants alone for an hour or two when they go shopping or do an errand; no one in the community criticizes this practice.

These experiences teach infants that catastrophe does not occur when the mother is absent; hence, most infants extinguish a tendency to cry when the mother is not present. It should not be surprising, therefore, that about one-half of these infants were classified as Type A-insecurely attached—whereas only 25 percent of middle-class American infants receive this classification. When we add the Type C-insecurely attached children to those in Type A, then two-thirds of German children in this town would be classified as insecurely attached, compared with one-third for the United States. It is unlikely that two-thirds of these German children are at risk for future anxiety or maladaptive symptoms because of insecure attachments. Hence, the claim that insecurely attached children are at psychological risk because they do not have sensitive mothers is an ethical judgment as to which maternal behaviors and infant reactions to parental absence are considered the most virtuous.[29]

There are many reasons, therefore, to question the claim that a one-year-old child's behavior in the Strange Situation captures accurately the complexity of the infant's emotional relationship to its parents over the prior twelve months. This skeptical conclusion leaves psychologists in the uncomfortable position of believing in the usefulness of the concept of attachment but of having no sensitive way to measure it. This state of affairs illustrates a truth that applies to all of the sciences; namely facts, theories, and procedures are inextricably bound together. Some one-to-two-year-old children do not cry when their mother leaves them and do not look at or approach the parent when she returns a few minutes later. That fact is subject to different interpretations. If the context is an unfamiliar laboratory, then the psychologists fond of attachment theory claim that the child's behavior reflects a history of insensitive parenting. That claim has meaning only when the observed behavior occurs as part of the technical procedure called the Strange Situation. If we changed the context of observation to the home or changed the theory so that it referred to the parental practices that lead a child to adapt to temporary separation, a different, equally reasonable, interpretation is possible.

Some psychologists have become persuaded that the nature of the infant's attachment is transformed over time into a set of beliefs, called a "working model," that can be detected by asking adults to reminisce about their childhood.[30] The belief that the coherence of a woman's narration of her childhood memories might contain transformations of experiences that occurred during her infancy, and that this narrative might, in turn, be a useful tool for determining how the woman herself would respond to her infant, has met minimal opposition because the concept of attachment has become so attractive. Yet no scientist would look for remnants of the one-word sentences of eighteenth-month-olds in the linguistic competence of adults. Nor would most psychologists claim that an adult's conception of friendship contained derivatives of their experiences in a day care center. Yet the reasonableness of these assumptions about working models often goes unquestioned. Few investigators have bothered to ask whether the mother's verbal sophistication, temperament, and ease or tension with an unfamiliar interviewer might influence the form of her narrative. These problems have been ignored because of the wish to believe that the quality of the mother's recall of her past provides a deep insight into her current personality and how she cares for her infant.

This speculative hypothesis demands, first, that the sentences spoken to an interviewer correspond closely to the psychological structures that are at the foundation of her personality. This assumption invites serious skepticism. Most sentences, spoken or written, are novel and constructed from components whose form still eludes us. The exceptions are well-rehearsed units like "Thank you" or "How are you?" as well as sentences that had been memorized like, "Four score and seven years ago." But most of the sentences that represent a person's memories of the past are novel creations. They did not exist before they were uttered and were patched together from psychological structures that do not resemble the structure of the spoken sentences. Further, it is well known that some adults possess a personality that exaggerates the stressful and dysphoric qualities of past experience. These dour melancholics will recall less satisfying childhoods but not necessarily because they actually had a less loving family.

The words alone, without information on tone of voice, facial expression, and bodily posture, do not possess a clear, unequivocal meaning.

That is why novelists always add this information. Imagine *Anna Karenina* as consisting only of a series of speeches by the characters. No printed text of a great play comes close to conveying the author's intention—that is why we go to the theater.

A person's narrative of her past does not always reveal the mental states that produced the story. Wittgenstein's two great insights were that there need not be a complex meaning behind every utterance nor a referent in experience for every sentence. Consider facial expressions as an analogy. A mother's frown intended to communicate disapproval of her child's actions is the product of changes in the neurons of the motor cortex which innervate the facial nerve which, in turn, produces a contraction of the facial muscles. The intention to communicate disapproval is missing from this description of the neuroanatomy and neurophysiology of the facial expression.

Similarly, it is not obviously true that the ideas which lie behind the sentences "My mother was loving" or "I was anxious as a child" are either memory traces from an earlier time or a reflection of the person's feelings at the moment. We acknowledge that seducers and politicians utter flattering sentences that are not faithful either to their beliefs or to their feelings. Kind parents will smile and praise a child who has failed a task several times, even though their initial impulse is to be critical and their mood is one of sadness.

We perceive an American flag fluttering in the wind as a unity, but neuroscientists have learned that the shape, color, and movement of the flag are initially processed in different parts of the brain. Similarly, the explicit meanings, implicit associations, and feelings that are linked to the words strung together in a sentence probably originate in different parts of the mind/brain. Sentences are opaque with respect to their psychological origins. When a 25-year-old woman says, "My mother was loyal to all of her family," the interviewer cannot know the feelings associated with that sentence nor the speaker's implicit associations with the term "loyal," nor even whether the phrase "all of the family" refers to the children and husband, or perhaps all of the mother's relatives. If the latter, the speaker may intend to say that her mother gave too much attention to her parents and siblings and not enough to her own children. Scientists who rely only on verbal evidence have been ingenuous in assuming, without supporting evidence, that the psychological meanings of sentences are transparent.

One of the few studies that actually followed a large group of white middle-class children from infancy to age eighteen supports this skepticism. One-year-old children were observed in the Strange Situation and classified as having either a secure or an insecure attachment to their parent. When these children were eighteen years old, they were asked to reminisce about their earlier lives, and these narratives were scored for the adolescent's working model. Two important results emerged. First, the child's security of attachment at one year did not reliably predict the quality of the eighteen-year-old narratives; securely attached adults were not especially likely to produce coherently organized memories of the past that were full of serenity, predictability, and care. However, if the parents had been divorced during later childhood—which occurred for 16 percent of the group—the adult narratives revealed insecurity, and the eighteen-year-olds described themselves as anxious. Thus, stressful experiences during later childhood were the primary determinants of the young adult's memories, not the security of their attachment at one year of age.[31]

The scholars who ask parents to talk about their past believe that these memories are correlated with psychological structures that control the parent's ministrations to her infant. This premise resembles the belief held by psychologists in the 1950s that a patient who perceived female genitals on Card 10 of the Rorschach ink blot test was a schizophrenic. The age, social class, ethnicity, temperament, and verbal sophistication of the parent are assumed, without evidence, to have minimal influence on the coherence of the mother's reminiscence—a flagrant display of unconstrained predicates. It brings to mind a Harvard student who in 1964 was seeking admission to a New York medical school and who told me that the faculty member interviewing him asked him to draw a person. He did not understand the reason for the request and asked himself what kind of drawing might impress the interviewer. He remembered from a freshman psychology course taken four years earlier a procedure called the Goodenough Draw-A-

Man Test. Unfortunately, he had forgotten that it was a test of children's intelligence, and was inappropriate for adults. He only remembered that the more items placed in a drawing, the more intelligent the person. Therefore the student put everything into the drawing—teeth, mustache, eyeglasses, belt buckle, suspenders, shoelaces—and did not understand why the interviewer looked so serious when he handed him the drawing. The student did not realize that the faculty member had administered the Machover Draw-A-Person Test, which assumed that the addition of many elements was indicative of a serious neurosis.

Some attachment theorists acknowledge that the state of being securely or insecurely attached in a one-year-old can be altered by subsequent experiences. Alan Sroufe notes: "We would not expect a child to be permanently scarred by early experiences or permanently protected from environmental assaults. Early experience can not be more important than later experience and life in a changing environment should alter the quality of a child's adaptation." But in another place, Sroufe and Elizabeth Carlson write that the different patterns of infant attachment can influence later self-regulation of emotion: "What is incorporated from the caregiving experiences are not specific behavioral features, but the quality and patterning of relationships, mediated by affect." "Attachment organization is . . . a system of internal structures . . . that emerge with development and provide the basis of personality functioning."[32] These last two statements retreat a bit from the belief in malleability implied in the first quotation. However, these inconsistencies are common in scientific fields, like psychology, that rest on weak evidence. Biologists at the turn of the century believed in both localization of brain function and holism.

The Difficulties of Rejecting Determinism

Sciences differ in the robustness of their most fundamental assumptions and empirically based principles. Physics is always held up as the model of good science. If the moon's position in the sky for the next seven nights deviated from its expected place, the universality of the inverse square law would be questioned. If water failed to boil after being placed on a hot fire for an hour, the gas laws would be reexamined. Hundreds of other imagined anomalies would threaten the foundations of the physical sciences if they were actually observed. Even in the life sciences, where fewer universal laws pertain, some events would shock all of us. If a cat gave birth to piglets, we would question the genetic principles of inheritance; if a person did not age, we would question the theory of cell metabolism.

When we ask the same question of psychology, however, we are embarrassed by the dearth of anomalies that would pose a threat to the field's fundamental principles. The concept of conditioning is among the most robust ideas in psychological science. Yet some animals do not condition easily, some habits cannot be conditioned, and the conditioning of motor behavior and heart rate does not follow the same time course. Thus, if a scientist discovered that a certain strain of mice could not be conditioned to freeze at the sound of a tone that was previously associated with shock, no one would reject the principles of conditioning. They would simply note an exception to the rule.

Many scientists would be surprised if someone reported that the occurrence of a particular reaction in a fetus predicted, better than chance, criminal behavior in adulthood. But that claim would not require questioning of any current assumptions. Unfortunately, neither would the opposite claim—that no fetal reaction predicted criminality. The challenge is to think of *any* human behavior that would force psychologists to question a current premise. I can think of very few, other than a small number of phenomena in human perception and memory. If this evaluation is correct, then psychology has a degree of immaturity that makes it easy for a theorist to declare that the events of the first year have a continuing influence on the child's future.

The absence of consensus on a small set of psychological outcomes we wish to explain makes it easy to award influence to early experience. Nineteenth-century naturalists agreed that it was important to understand the enormous variety among plants and animals. That was the problem Darwin tried to solve. No comparable agreement has been reached on the derivatives of early experience that should be given the highest priority. Are they specific cognitive abilities, psychiatric symptoms, fame, wealth, a good marriage, parenting success, a satisfying sex life, capacity for love, meaningful work, loyal friends, or simply a subjective feeling of well-being? The lack of accord among clinicians, humanists, or scientists as to which quality—or qualities—has the tightest link to specific early experiences makes either refuting the determinist's claim or proving it correct impossible. Psychologists are left in the unhappy position of suspecting that some parts of the adult profile are traceable to the early years but being unsure which aspects of that profile have the tightest connections to the past. The absence of specificity makes it easy to treat as true the vague claim, "Early experience affects the adult's future."

The most convincing evidence *in favor* of infant determinism comes from experiments with laboratory animals. If a newborn rat is taken from its mother for a few minutes each day for the first fourteen days, the hippocampus of the animal is altered permanently, and the adult is less easily stressed by new surroundings than rat pups who were left with their mother undisturbed.[33] In another experiment, scientists painted the teats of nursing rats with a distinct orange scent so that the infants would associate the scent with whatever state accompanied feeding. When these rats reached puberty and were placed with receptive females who had been painted with the same scent, they were sexually more aroused by these scented females than were males who had been nursed by unscented mothers.[34] Once again, early experience influenced the future in a measurable way.

However, these rats lived in cages in quiet laboratory rooms, with a regular supply of food and water and no predators. They were protected from the events that normally occur in the animal's natural habitat. If the rats had been returned to their natural environments, perhaps the products of their infant experience would not have been preserved; artificial conditions can create artificial facts.

Equally strong connections between the experiences of human infants and later outcomes are more difficult to demonstrate because children cannot be subjected to this degree of experimental control. Some natural experiments are suggestive, however. For example, many middle-class mothers living in parts of Holland follow their doctors' advice and place their tightly swaddled infants in bedrooms with closed doors and no toys because they believe that an austere environment creates good character. Although the one-year-olds reared under these conditions are a trifle less mature in the attainment of the milestones of infancy than children in other parts of the country who are not reared this way, by five years of age no psychological effect of the early experience can be found.[35]

A group of institutionalized infants in Iowa were cared for by over two dozen different adults in the first year of life before they were adopted. However, these children did not differ from normally reared children when both groups were assessed between eight and seventeen years of age. Further, if infants reared in an unstimulating institutionalized environment without a stable attachment figure were adopted before the second birthday, their future development appeared to be normal.

Similarly, some young children orphaned during the Second World War were adopted by middle-class Americans. When psychiatrists and psychologists assessed them several years after they had been living in their new families, most were free of anxiety and appeared to resemble normally reared American children. "The thing that is most impressive is that with only a few exceptions they do not seem to be suffering either from frozen affects or the indiscriminate friendliness that Bowlby describes . . . The relationships to their adopted families are genuinely affectionate . . . The present results indicate that for the child suffering extreme loss the chances for recovery are far better than had previously been expected."[36]

More recently, a group of children who had spent their first year in orphanages in Romania were adopted by nurturant British parents. When they arrived in London, they were emaciated and psychologically retarded, as one would expect, given their harsh experiences. However, when they were evaluated several years after their adoption, a majority, though not all, were similar in their intellectual profile to the average British child.[37]

Although the evidence does not support infant determinism, an appeal to reason is also persuasive. The thousands of infants who will be born today across the world will experience very different environments in their first two years. Some will be raised by surrogate caretakers on kibbutzim; some will be cared for by grandmothers or older sisters; some will attend day care centers; some will remain at home with their mothers. Some will have many toys; some will have none. Some will spend the first year in a dark, quiet hut wrapped in old rags; some will crawl in brightly lit rooms full of toys, picture books, and television images. But despite this extraordinary variation in early experience, excluding the small proportion with serious brain damage or a genetic defect, most will speak before they are two years old, become self-conscious by the third birthday, and be able to assume some family responsibilities by age seven. The psychological differences among these children are trivial when compared with the long list of similarities. The prevalence of serious mental disorders like schizophrenia and depression, as well as the less impairing anxiety disorders, is surprisingly similar around the world, even though children are being reared in different environments. This fact is not consistent with the awarding of significance to the first two years, at least for the development of these particular symptoms.

All animals possess a powerful, genetically based bias to develop the behaviors that are definitive of their species. It is difficult, although possible, to arrange early life conditions so that a bird will not sing its characteristic song or a monkey will fail to mate. Humans are prepared by their biology to form friendships, fall in love, cope with fear, and try, continually, to move toward their prized goals, despite early experiences that might make these attainments hard to accomplish. These urges are remarkably difficult to subdue.

The advocates of infant determinism, however, insist that a temporal sequence of developmental products, with relatively high transitional probabilities between stages, leads to a particular outcome in adolescence or adulthood. Attachment theorists maintain that an insecurely attached infant has a greater-than-chance probability of being a fearful three-year-old; and, in turn, a fearful three-year-old has a greater-than-chance probability of being a shy, timid seven-year-old. The implicit assumption is that the structures acquired in the first stage influence the subsequent ones. If the first phase were different, the outcome would necessarily be altered. However, for many sequences in nature, the first stage can be altered without necessarily changing the final result. A fertilized egg normally develops in the womb in which it was fertilized. But we know that if an egg is fertilized outside a uterus and implanted in a woman's body (and not always the body of the woman who supplied the egg), the outcome—a healthy fetus—is very similar to what it would have been if the first stage had been the traditional one.

Let us assume, for the moment, that the attachment theorists are correct in claiming that a mother who is insensitive to her infant's needs will produce an insecurely attached one-year-old. But it does not follow that the insecure attachment in the first year is responsible for a troublesome outcome in adolescence. Mothers who must work full-time to support their family, mothers who did not want the child, and mothers who are depressed should be less sensitive and therefore should create insecurely attached children. If the children born to these three different types of mothers remained in their natal homes, which is usually the case, each would continue to be exposed to a harassed, rejecting, or depressed parent, and the similarity of the continuing environments could produce an anxious, timid older child. But the culprit is a long, repeated history of experience, not simply the events of the first year.

The contents of the mind consist of perceptual representations of experience, which are easily altered by new events, and symbolic concepts, which are more difficult to change. Only one exposure to the beard of an uncle who did not have facial hair a month earlier can transform a four-year-old's perceptual representation of the older man. But her belief that snow is white cannot be changed easily by repeating one hundred times "Snow is red." Infants, unlike four-year-olds, have no symbolic concepts like "Snow is white." They possess only the perceptual representations that are vulnerable to alteration.[38]

Although very few prospective longitudinal studies have followed infants to adulthood, the few investigators who have done so failed to find convincing support for early determinism. One group of scientists followed 89 middle-class children living in southeastern Ohio. The infants and children were observed at home, in school, and in laboratory settings. The small number of adults who displayed serious psychological symptoms later in life did not show atypical behavior in the first two years. One girl who had a schizophrenic breakdown when she went to college could not be distinguished from others in the sample during the first three years of life.[39]

The best predictor of later psychological problems in a group of over six hundred children born on the island of Kauai and followed until they were over thirty years of age was continued residence in a family of poverty, combined with prematurity or other biological stress surrounding birth. But because even this combination was not very predictive of future symptoms, the authors wrote, "As we watched these children grow from babyhood to adulthood, we could not help but respect the self-righting tendencies within them that produced normal development under all but the most persistently adverse circumstances."[40]

A group of 42 adults had been reared in residential nurseries in Great Britain for their first two years. Some were adopted into relatively stable, nurturant homes after the second birthday, while others returned to their biological parents. As adolescents and young adults, the adopted children were less likely to display criminal behavior than those who had been returned to their biological parents. Because both groups of children had similar experiences during the first two years, it is fair to conclude that experiences after age two were more influential in producing the criminal behavior than events of the first two years.[41]

Equally convincing is a study of a large number of Swiss children born to unmarried, poorly educated immigrant parents. They spent their first year in an impoverished residential nursery where stimulation was minimal and caretakers were changed often—risk factors that should be associated with an insecure attachment and later psychological problems. The 137 children were studied again when they were fourteen years old. Although most of these adolescents had average intelligence and were popular with friends, an unexpectedly large number were extremely sensitive, dysphoric, or anxious, compared with most adolescents living in the same city. However, these affective symptoms were most frequent in those who had been physically abused or spent their postinfancy years with step-parents or biological parents who quarreled frequently. The children who had spent their first year in the same depriving nursery but had been sent later to benevolent homes did not show the dysphoria or anxiety that characterized the former group and were similar to the majority of Swiss children raised with nurturant parents from birth.[42]

Thus, the development of anxiety and depression in some of the adolescents was attributable to experiences that occurred *after* they had left the nursery, that is, after the period of infancy was over. This finding led the author to suggest that pessimism about a child's future because the first year was spent in a less than optimal environment is unwarranted. Even Freud had to recognize the resilience of "Little Hans"—the boy with a phobia of horses. Upon meeting Hans a dozen years later, Freud encountered a well-adjusted youth of nineteen years who suffered from neither excessive conflict nor inhibition.

Jean MacFarlane, who conducted a long-term longitudinal study of children born in Berkeley, California, realized that her predictions of adult personality from the child's characteristics were usually inaccurate. She concluded, "It seems clear that we overweighted the troublesome and the pathogenic aspects and underweighted elements that were maturity inducing . . . we had not sensed that continuous patterns would be modified or converted into almost the opposite characteristic."[43] The child psychiatrist Michael Rutter agrees: "The ill effects of early traumata are by no means inevitable or irrevocable . . . the evidence runs strongly counter to views that early experiences irrevocably change personal development."[44]

The Child's Interpretation of Experience

No scientist has demonstrated that particular experiences in the first two years produce a particular adult outcome in even, say, one-fifth of those exposed to that experience. Attendance at an infant day care center does not produce children who are very different from those raised at home, if the children come from the same social class and ethnic background. The few successful predictors of adult psychopathology are more closely associated with the child's biology and continued membership in a particular social class, rather than with specific early experiences. For example, Barbara Fish discovered a small number of infants who showed a rare profile of poor motor coordination and emotional lability early in the first year. A little less than one-half of these infants developed schizophrenia in early adulthood.[45] But this rare profile is probably attributable to the infant's inherent constitution rather than particular parental treatment. Even loss of both parents, which occurs in wartime, does not place a majority of orphans at risk for serious mental disorder or bias them to develop a particular personality.

Thus we must ask: What mechanisms might allow the experiences of early infancy to influence a person's future emotional and mental profile? One likely explanation is that early experiences establish expectations of nurture or neglect, as well as conditioned emotional reactions that appear to resemble, but are not identical to, adult states of fear, anger, apathy, and frustration on the one hand, or excitement and pleasure on the other. I do not doubt that such expectations and conditioned reactions are established. Infants who are tickled, played with, talked to, and smiled at are more alert, more vocal, and laugh more fully and frequently than infants who missed these pleasurable experiences. No one disputes that infant experiences have influence. What is controversial is the fixity of those first profiles. The proponents of connectedness believe that some of these early expectations and emotional reactions will be neither transformed nor eliminated by subsequent events. *That* is the debatable claim.

The scholars who are uncomfortable with the uncertainty that characterizes human development wish to eliminate it by placing much of the burden of the present on the deep past. The same solution was selected by seventeenth-century naturalists who did not understand how a newborn infant acquired its anatomy. They solved this problem by suggesting that all the organs were present in minuscule form in the original egg or sperm.

Some of the evidence provided by neuroscientists demonstrates impermanence. When rats that were normally reared in austere empty cages were transferred to spacious living areas with rope bridges and attractive objects, tiny spines on the dendrites of neurons in their brain began to grow. The more stimulating environment physically changed their brain. But these changes were not permanent. When the rats were put back in their austere cages, in time the extra spines regressed and their brain became similar to those of animals that had never experienced the enriched environment.[46] In another study, children with abnormally high blood levels of the amino acid phenylalanine at one year of age but low levels at age five performed on tests of cognitive abilities as if the high level during infancy was without long-term damaging consequences.[47] If material changes in the brain, created by experience or amino acid metabolites, are not always preserved, it is less likely that the changes wrought by tickling, playing, and smiling are preserved independent of the unpredictable life events that occur after the second birthday.

Attachment theorists contend that a one-year-old who has had a sensitive, loving, predictable mother over the first twelve months is likely to acquire a permanent expectation that adults will be available when the child becomes anxious. But in some isolated villages in Guatemala, most infants are nursed on demand and experience a series of homogeneously predictable days. However, the adults are suspicious, anxious, angry, and minimally trusting of others. How could such an unhappy profile emerge in these communities if the secure attachment of the first year had been preserved?

Many years ago I analyzed a rich corpus of longitudinal data on children from southern Ohio who were born between 1929 and 1939 and were followed from infancy to early adulthood.[48] Research staff visited the homes and observed the mothers' behavior with their children. Maternal behavior toward infants varied widely, but this variation did not predict variation in mood and behavior when these children became adults. The mothers' social class, rather than differences in their treatment of infants, was the critical factor in predicting academic success. College-educated mothers were more critical of their school-age daughters than sons; less-well-educated mothers were more critical of their sons than daughters. Yet both the sons and daughters of college-educated mothers performed better academically than either the sons or daughters of less-well-educated mothers.

The mothers were also judged for degree of protection of their children during the first three years of life. The variation among mothers in this quality was also dramatic, but it did not have obvious consequences for the adult's degree of dependence on spouse, lover, or family, and it did not predict school performance. Middle-class mothers protected their sons more often than working-class parents, and the former performed better in school. Middle-class mothers were less protective of their daughters than working-class mothers, and, again, the former did better in school. A host of experiences correlated with a family's social class, and not just the mothers' behavior, was a significant determinant of the child's later academic achievement.

An important reason why long-term preservation of early qualities is unlikely is the fact that the brain is still growing during the first two years of life. The frontal lobes, which evaluate information from the environment and the body, are especially immature during these early years. Emotional experiences are not evaluated fully, and many early memories can be lost. When asked to recall their earliest memory, most adults cannot retrieve anything that happened before they were three years old.[49]

In one study, mothers of three-month-old infants repeated a novel word to their infants several times a day for two weeks. When the investigator returned 24 hours after the mothers had stopped speaking the word and spoke the word to the infant, most of the babies showed a facial reaction suggesting that they recognized the word as familiar. But three days later all signs of recognition were gone. Without additional exposure to the word, the very young infants forgot it.[50] If young infants do not reexperience an event, it will be lost.[51] If a four-month-old is shown an attractive toy and ten seconds later is shown that toy alongside a novel one, the infant will look longer at the new toy, indicating that he remembered having seen the older one. But if we wait twenty minutes before showing the infant the novel object, he will not spend more time looking at the new toy, indicating that he failed to remember having seen the old toy twenty minutes earlier.

The most important argument against the doctrine of infant determinism flows from the hypothesis that infants, like adults, are influenced primarily by events that are different—or discrepant—from their usual experience, rather than by particular adult actions. Thus infants who are never kissed may not develop traits different from those who are kissed every hour, if all other aspects of their environments are identical. The kiss is most influential when it occurs irregularly or at unexpected times because the surprise facilitates the learning of emotional responses toward others. The infant fed every four hours by a mother who is following her doctor's orders—as was commonly recommended by pediatricians in the 1930s—will, when other things are equal, be no different from an infant who is fed whenever it cries. But the infant fed on an irregular schedule, sometimes when it cries but sometimes when it is quiet, will develop special habits.

Eight-month-olds are so sensitive to discrepancy they are surprised when, after listening to a continuous string of three nonsense words (each three syllables long) for only two minutes, the order of syllables in one of the words is altered—the infants who had been hearing "bidaku" for two minutes suddenly heard "kudabi."[52] Elegant studies of single neurons reveal that unfamiliar stimuli generate large increases in firing rates, which subsequently become greatly reduced as the stimulus becomes familiar.[53]

The altered features that render an event discrepant depend on the larger whole of which it is a part. Adding a dark spot to a human face makes it discrepant. However, adding the same dark spot to a tree trunk will not. The appearance of a triangle on a computer screen is only discrepant if it was preceded by a series of different geometric figures. Thus discrepancy is not a quality of any single event; it is always a quality that belongs to the relation between events. Humans continually evaluate the relation between an event that currently fills their perceptual space and what happened moments, weeks, or years earlier.

Discrepant events become critical in the third and fourth years, when children begin to interpret their experiences. One child may interpret harsh punishment for failing to clean his room as a sign of hostility from the parent, while another may interpret the same punishment as a sign of a caring parent who wants her to develop good habits. As part of the longitudinal study in Ohio mentioned above, I asked 25-year-old sub-

jects about their childhood memories with their families. A small number of adults who had unusually harsh parents (based on detailed observations in the home when these adults were younger) said that although
they remembered their parents as strict, they were glad they had chosen
that style of discipline. These adults believed that their current lives,
which were happy and full of purpose, were the result of their parents'
adoption of a strict disciplinary style.

Frank McCourt, the author of *Angela's Ashes*, recalls that he had three
fathers: the one who lit the fire and made hot tea on cold winter morn-
ings, the one who read stories to him at bedtime, and the one who came
home drunk on Friday evening, having spent all of his week's earnings
in pubs.[54] The young McCourt may have partially forgiven the father's
irresponsibility because he interpreted the tea and stories as meaning
that his father loved him. A parent must be unusually selfish or cruel before a child will come to the horrendous conclusion that his parent is
without virtue.

The Mehinaku Indians of Central Brazil, who are extremely indul-
gent with infants, treat disobedience by grabbing the child's wrist,
sloshing a dipper full of water on the legs, and vigorously scarifying the
calves and thighs with a fish tooth scraper while the child screams in
pain. However, because the punishment is predictable and perceived as
just, adults living in this community are neither more aggressive, con-
forming, nor anxious than those from cultures that do not follow such a
harsh practice.[55] Tutsi and Hutu parents are considerably gentler with
their children, yet these children became the adults who brutally murdered members of the other tribe.

Attempts to understand how the human mind is changed by experience have cycled between two extreme positions. At one end stands
John Locke, who made sensory experience the actor and the child's
mind a passive recorder of events with the minimal number of transformations necessary to make them assimilable. At the other end stands
Immanuel Kant, who made the person the actor and events a passive
gallery from which the mind chooses features to dwell upon. The mind
imposes serious transformations on targeted events before assigning
them to one or more symbolic categories.

John Watson and Sigmund Freud replaced Locke and Kant. The behaviorist Watson shrank mind to almost nothingness in the face of an imposing environment which, like a gigantic machine, stamped in habits that could not be resisted. The child who saw a smile on the parent's face when he picked up a spoon to eat his cereal should forevermore use his spoon whenever a cereal bowl appeared in front of him. Freud, following Kant, believed that the mind was inherently a tangle of desires and fears. Every parental response to the child must first traverse this dense jungle of thoughts and feelings before it can be assigned a meaning.

American psychiatrists and clinical psychologists were friendly to Freud until the 1960s, when several historical events dampened enthusiasm for his explanations. Although sexual ideas and behavior became more permissible, neurotic symptoms did not disappear, as Freud would have predicted. The absence of strong empirical support for psychoanalytic theory, despite several decades of research, made Freud far less attractive to the new cohort of students, and the Kantian argument began to lose favor. Furthermore, Western society became concerned with the consequences of experiences that were regarded as traumatic for all children (especially divorce, abuse, and surrogate care), all of which increased in frequency after World War II. Scientists assumed that these environmentally imposed experiences must have profound effects on most children, regardless of the symbolic transformations a particular child might perform on them.

Finally, the ascendance of molecular biology, which is loyal to positivistic standards, motivated developmentalists to use objective measurements that were free of ambiguity. Because investigators can be more certain about whether a divorce occurred than whether the child interpreted the divorce as threatening, the former became the primary variable of interest and the latter, which would have required a potentially unreliable inference, was ignored. These four independent factors came together to move developmental scholars back to John Locke's side of the ideological divide, even though all children do not interpret a divorce, surrogate care, or poverty in the same way.

I once interviewed a thirteen-year-old girl whom I first saw when she was two years old after the police had removed her from a bedroom where she had been kept since her birth. She was adopted by a nurturant family and was still living with them when I saw her as an adolescent. She remembered her home imprisonment, and when I asked her why her mother locked her in the bedroom, she replied that the mother was harassed because of several other children in the home and therefore locking her in the room made life easier for the mother. I detected no anger in her reply and even sensed a bit of sympathy for the harried parent. Similarly, many years ago, while watching a six-year-old boy being tested at the Johns Hopkins University in Baltimore, I saw his poor, uneducated mother slap him with force across the face when he failed a question. When the testing was over, I asked the mother why she had struck the boy so harshly. "I want him to grow up to be a good, smart boy," she replied, and added, "I got to teach him how to behave, he knows I love him."

When an adult friend was eleven years old, she left Latvia with her mother to avoid the Nazis. She lost her mother in Czechoslovakia and did not find her, in Germany, until a month later. Her memory of this experience was not replete with fear but rather with a feeling of excitement and confidence that she would find her mother eventually. Many examples of equally surprising constructions of events undermine the notion of a fixed relation between an event and an outcome. That conclusion does not mean that traumatic events are irrelevant or never have unfortunate consequences. But it does mean that the mind, like a skilled actress, always interprets the lines it is given.

Puritan parents in New England used very harsh socialization methods, yet most children developed adaptive personalities because, presumably, the children treated the punishments as appropriate reflections of their parents' concern for their developing character. Equally harsh punishment administered by a modern New England parent would be interpreted as unfair—or cruel—and would generate strong anger. John Stuart Mill described his father as aloof, stern, and lacking in affection, but, unlike a modern American son, he did not interpret those qualities as a sign of a lack of paternal love. "I was loyally devoted to him . . . I hesitate to pronounce whether I was more a loser or gainer by his severity."[56]

A Japanese physician and novelist recalled his feelings toward his father, who was a prominent doctor and poet. "My father was, above all, an awesome, frightening being. He was often enraged. When he became angry, it was with all of his physical and spiritual strength. Even when I overheard my father reprimand somebody in the next room, a cold shiver used to run down my spine, not to speak of the times when I was chastised . . . and yet, he was truly a support as I grew up."[57] George Bernard Shaw offers another example of the importance of a child's subjective interpretations. Shaw lived in poverty with an alcoholic father, an indifferent mother, and an awareness that school teachers regarded him as a poor student. Shaw's objective environment should have crushed him, if not as a child, then fifteen years later after his first novels were rejected by publishers. But he needed to do something important and must have believed that he could, for he persisted until fame was achieved. Perhaps his knowledge that a relative who had rescued his commander in battle two hundred years earlier was rewarded with a large land grant in Kilkenny persuaded the young Shaw that he was part of a virtuous, competent pedigree.[58] Often, such a belief is enough.

The practice of clitoridectomy or circumcision at adolescence provides an equally telling example. The youth in cultures where this ritual occurs interpret this painful procedure as permitting them the privileges of adult status. The same practice imposed on American or European children would be viewed as cruel or illegal. Inuit grandmothers living in Hudson Bay tease their grandchildren in ways that rarely occur in American homes. One grandmother suggested to her six-year-old granddaughter holding her infant brother in a parka to tip the infant out of the parka and let him fall to the ground. The girl understood that this remark was intended as a way to tease her.[59] American children would not understand such a request and would become anxious.

A small, isolated group in New Guinea believes that males are born sterile. Thus, all boys must acquire sperm if they are to father a child in the future. This culture invented a ritual to accomplish this goal. The preadolescent boys are brought to a clearing, away from the village, and the older men, playing flutes, dance around the young boys. From that time until they are late adolescents, the boys perform fellatio on older, unmarried adolescents in order to gain seed. When these young boys become sixteen or seventeen years old, this practice stops. The young boys do not interpret this behavior as a sign of homosexuality or sexual abuse but as a ritual that will allow them to become fathers.[60]

During the Cultural Revolution Chinese authorities often punished opponents by imprisoning them in a deep well, sometimes for periods longer than a year. Europeans have been cruel with their enemies, but they have less often used this form of punishment. The cultural difference is explicable if we recognize that the Chinese believe that emotionally close relationships with others are a sine qua non of being human. Hence, isolating a person from all social contact is an extremely painful, humiliating experience. The emphasis on individual autonomy in American and European society celebrates the ability to cope with life on one's own. The assumption that social isolation should be unbearable is less reasonable in our setting.

Millions of Chinese children during Mao's reign were in day care ten to twelve hours a day, seven days a week; I suspect that most of them interpreted that regimen as normative and did not conclude that their mothers did not love them. However, children living in communities where few infants are sent to day care centers might decide that their parents did not have sufficient affection for them to stay home during their early years. The child's interpretation, not the fact of having attended a day care center, is of greater force in shaping development. If the psychological effects of experience rest with the imposed interpretation, and not with the experience-qua-experience, particular events in the first two years will not have universal consequences because infants do not interpret their experience.

Imagine two spots of light, A and B, that objectively reflect equal amounts of light energy. If spot A is surrounded by a light gray background and spot B by a dark background, B will be perceived as lighter than A because of the contrast between the spot of light and its background. More surprising, if two surfaces are objectively the same shade of gray, one can be made to appear darker, lighter, or similar to the other by altering the other surfaces in the vicinity—that is, by changing the background context.[61] So too with children. The child's interpretations of an experience, say verbal chastisement for breaking a glass, will always depend on background conditions, especially attitudes toward the adult, expectations, and past experiences. An observer cannot know at the time an event occurs the symbolic construction the child will impose.

But these symbolic constructions of experiences are the most important determinants of a person's level of anxiety, depression, apathy, and anger. The Palestinian youths who throw stones at Israeli soldiers believe that the Israeli government has oppressed them unjustly. The causes of their violent actions are not traceable to the parental treatment they received in their first few years. Similarly, no happy African-American two-year-old knows about the pockets of racism in American society or the history of oppression blacks have suffered. The realization that there is prejudice will not take form until that child is five or six years old. Moreover, evaluations of racism in our society by minority children are context-dependent: the belief that the majority society will not permit them success is held more strongly by native born minority members than by the children of immigrants.

Each person's principal motives are derived from the chronic uncertainties of the first dozen or so years of life, not just the first year or two. These emotionally laden ideas emerge from recognition of a difference between a perceived state and a construction that represents the ideal. Detecting a difference between two events—ideas are events—is one of the best-honed talents of our species. Some children are not sure a parent values them. Others doubt their acceptability to peers. Still others are uncertain over their family's economic security or their physical attractiveness, social class position, ability to resist domination, or virtue. Although many children live with more than one of these worries, one often dominates the list. The six-year-old who believes that his peers do not like him experiences a moment of uncertainty when he realizes the difference between what is and what he wishes to be true. A regular repetition of these uncertainties, day after day, can create a permanent vulnerability to this feeling, like setting the trigger of a gun to fire at the slightest pressure. The important point is that these uncertainties do not emerge until late childhood. None is possible in infancy.

A fundamental reason why many Americans, both psychologists and laypeople, have become attached to the notion of infant determinism is that we have no trouble imagining how a parent's behavior might affect the child. We have seen children cry following a punishment, smile after a kiss, obey a gentle request, but disobey a harsh one. A host of similar exchanges between parents and children are easy to imagine, and therefore we assume, without evidence, the fixity of the psychological products of those exchanges.

By contrast, the child's interpretation of the interaction, which is the more critical event, is more difficult to imagine. The tendency to award significance to perceptually salient events often leads to mistaken inferences regarding cause and effect. This fact is nicely illustrated in the investigations with infant rat pups that were mentioned above. When scientists took newborn rats away from their nursing mother for a few minutes each day over the first two weeks of life, these pups—when they became adults—showed less emotionality in a novel situation than adult animals that had been reared normally as infants. Other scientists discovered later that the rat pups separated from the mother underwent a permanent change in brain physiology. The hippocampus of these animals had a larger number of receptors for glucocorticoids than normally reared animals. This finding produced such stunning support for the role of infant experience that it was written into almost every textbook in psychology as proving that the early stress of separation from the mother had a permanent effect on developing newborns, possibly including humans.

But to the surprise of many, later studies revealed that the primary cause of the altered hippocampus was not the stress induced in the pups by being removed from the mother but the tendency of the mother to lick and groom the pup more vigorously than normal after it was returned to her. The cause of this maternal behavior was the rat pup's cooler temperature, which aroused the mother. The vigorous tactile stimulation increased brain serotonin in the infant, which led in turn to an increased number of glucocorticoid receptors in the hippocampus, which led in turn to decreased activity in the hypothalamic nuclei that produce glucocorticoids. As a result of this sequence, the adult rats were less emotional when placed in an unfamiliar environment than rats that had been licked and groomed by their mother less often. The vigorous tactile stimulation of the infant pup, not the stress of being removed from the mother, produced the altered brain anatomy and special adult behavior.[62]

This scientific story illustrates how easy it is to attribute causal influence to the most obvious events and how difficult it is to imagine the subtle, or often invisible, ones that are of greater priority. Many psychologists and psychiatrists had assumed that the small number of infants who refuse to eat and who begin to lose weight are reacting to the rejecting mood of their mother. It now appears, however, that their failure to thrive is due to factors in the child that no one had thought possible, particularly poor coordination of the muscles involved in swallowing, an easy gag reflex, or an impairment in the sensory processes related to taste.

An equally dramatic illustration is the 1830 debate between two of the most eminent French biologists, Étienne Geoffroy Saint-Hilaire and Georges Cuvier. Geoffroy suggested that all animals shared a basic body plan, even though this concept is not so evident when one compares bees and bears. Cuvier satirized this speculative idea, reminding Geoffroy that it lacked firm facts. But recent discoveries, 150 years after their debates, vindicate Geoffroy, for it appears that a set of genes called HOX that determine an animal's basic body plan have been preserved from bees to bears to baboons.[63]

Thirty years after the Cuvier–Geoffroy debates, Darwin recognized that the most vulnerable aspect of his theoretical argument was that no one had discovered in the geological record the many intermediate forms, say between fish and frogs, that the idea of slow, gradual evolution demanded. Darwin appreciated that, without this missing evidence, it was difficult for most naturalists to imagine how one species could give rise to another over the course of many thousands of generations. "The mind cannot possibly grasp the full meaning of the term of a hundred million years; it cannot add up and perceive the full effects of many slight variations accumulated during an almost infinite number of generations."[64]

We regard Newton as a genius because he guessed correctly that unseen gravitational forces hold planets in their orbits. One of Einstein's insights was to realize that, when light is directed at a metal surface, the energy of the electrons emitted is not a function of the intensity of the light, which is obvious, but of the light's frequency, which in some ranges is invisible. One reason it took so long for viruses and bacteria to be discovered was that they were not easily visualized by scientists prior to the second half of the nineteenth century. Acceptance of the hypothesis that some illnesses are the result of invisible infectious agents had to wait until Pasteur treated sheep with a vaccine against anthrax and successfully protected them from the disease.

Most physicists working in the early 1930s preferred the visualizability of Schrodinger's wave equations to Heisenberg's nonvisualizable mathematical solutions to subatomic phenomena. But physicists today acknowledge that Heisenberg's equations, which have no instantiation in everyday experience, explain quantum phenomena more completely. Ptolemy's conception of a moving sun and a stationary earth was more appealing to intuition than the heliocentric views of Kepler and Galileo, which deny that each day the sun moves slowly across the sky.

Most of the important explanatory ideas in biology, physics, and neuroscience—the DNA helix, meson, and chemical synapse—were not possible during the nineteenth century despite considerable brooding on evolution, matter, and the brain by brilliant scholars. These fruitful concepts were too different from what was known, and they remained hidden from the mind's guesses about underlying mechanisms. Psychologists award slaps, chastisements, hugs, and kisses considerable formative power because they are perceptually salient events. But I suspect that the child's private interpretations of these events represent the more significant influence. Pavlov would have been annoyed by this position, for he wrote in the *Lectures on Conditioned Reflexes* that we will gain "extraordinary control over human behavior when the . . . human mind will contemplate itself not from within but from without."[65]

If the child's private interpretations of experience, which are unavailable to observers and vulnerable to change, turn out to be the most important factors in development, a tape recorder is a poor metaphor for development. It tempts us to believe that no experience is ever lost and that the mind retains, for an indefinite time, faithful representations of what was perceived. I have often had the experience of watching a movie I saw 35 or 40 years ago and having no recognition memory for any of the scenes. I felt as if I had never seen that film before. The magnetic material on a tape records a Bach cello suite in just one way. But children's minds are not tape recorders; they derive different meanings, often unconsciously, from their encounters. Because that process remains both mysterious and nonvisualizable, we dismiss its potency.

This contrast between the formative power inherent in environmental events and the mind's constructions of those events is an instance of a larger debate that occurs in other sciences. Immunologists, for example, are now considering the possibility that the quality of being a foreign molecule in the body is not inherent in the molecule's chemical structure but in the body's reaction to the molecule. That is, the physiological context contributes to the likelihood that the immune system will treat a particular substance as foreign.[66]

The suggestion that the child's interpretation of experience is the key to the formation of character and personality is analogous to Whitehead's insistence that the idea underlying each symbol is the basis for its importance. A parent's frown, which is simply a change in the muscles of the face, derives its power from the fact that children interpret the expression as symbolic of disapproval. As we watch parents playing with their infants, it may seem obvious that the child is being shaped by adult behaviors; in this frame, the parents' behaviors are the stable referent through which the child moves. But that image neglects the many times that parents punish and children do not conform, or the times when parents reward civility but children are rude. In this frame, the child's mind is the stable place around which the outside world moves.

Even if some of the infants' emotional reactions to others were preserved for a decade or so, those who favor infant determinism would have to argue that subsequent experiences could not transform these first emotions. Such a claim seems extraordinary. Each day therapists help adult patients extinguish fearful reactions to snakes and to bridges. Most adults experience the gradual loss, over time, of strong emotional reactions, perhaps fear of an animal, sadness over the death of a parent, anger at a rival, or intense sexual arousal at the sight or thought of another. It strains credulity to argue that infants are exceptions to this universal aspect of human nature and do not lose emotional reactions acquired during the first two years of life. Between six and ten months almost every infant develops a reaction of fear to some strangers which is strong in some infants and weaker in others. An infant who sees a grandparent infrequently may show intense fear during this brief developmental stage. However, a year later the fear has vanished due to cognitive maturation and pleasant interactions with the adult. Nothing in the behavior of the four-year-old hints at any preservation of the earlier fear.

We can put this matter in a somewhat different way by reflecting on the vulnerability to revision of four basic classes of representations humans create. The smallest class, and probably the one least amenable to change, refers to logical structures that permit a person to argue coherently and to detect flaws in the reasoning of others. For example, a five-year-old believes that an object cannot simultaneously be two different things or be in two different states. A sad infant cannot be happy, even though she might become so after she stops crying. This logical belief is difficult to change and is not present in the first year of life.

A second class of representations that is difficult to change are the implicit, or tacit, semantic associations prevalent among most members of a culture. American children possess an implicit association between the concept "female" and the concept "natural." Most Americans and Europeans have strong semantic associations among the concepts devil, sin, male, and bad as well as among angel, kindness, female, and good. Mexicans have a strong association among sun, male, and strength; Hindus show strong semantic links among the terms meat, hot, and sexual desire. Dylan Thomas's famous line "And death shall have no dominion" is effective poetically because all readers recognize the overpowering force of the idea of death. Playwrights, poets, novelists, and advertisers rely on these implicit semantic structures to influence our emotions and preferences. Few, if any, of these semantic networks are present during the first two years of life.

A third kind of structure consists of the affective reactions to the meaning of particular events—for example, a feeling of sadness on learning of the death of a friend, disgust at hearing of a brutal rape, and pride when a son or daughter has won a prize. None of these three classes of representations is present in the first two years of life. Each requires the cognitive growth that occurs during the preschool years.

The fourth class of representations refers to knowledge about events in the world, including facts that describe cause–effect relations. This realm of knowledge begins to grow as soon as the child is born, but these structures are the most vulnerable to change. Indeed, that expectation is a scientific maxim. Most factual beliefs of two-year-olds are vulnerable to alteration through new experiences. The child learns, for example, that some foods he loves are not healthy, some activities he enjoys are dangerous, and some speech is prohibited in certain settings. Thus, the representations acquired in the first two years are the very ones most vulnerable to alteration, while those that are more resistant to change are acquired after infancy is over.

Some of the psychological products of the first two years might be preserved, but only if the environment sustained the behavior, not because the original reaction was destined to remain stable. Infants living in poverty have more frequent colds and bouts of diarrhea than those living in affluent homes. Adults who were raised in poverty and remained impoverished are more likely to have strokes, heart attacks, tuberculosis, and sexually transmitted diseases and to die earlier than those who have enjoyed middle-class affluence.[67] But the causes of the higher rates of adult morbidity and earlier mortality among the poor are not the result of more colds and diarrhea in the first two years of life. Rather, they are due to the continuity, over many years, of poor diet, greater life stress, and less adequate medical care. Those who favor infant determinism do not award sufficient power to the events of later childhood and adolescence, many of which are correlated with social class.

One of the few robust facts in the social sciences is that a person's social class predicts the probability of school failure, violent crime, choice of vocation, and physical and mental symptoms. Most children born to parents with less than a high school education experience socialization regimens that are different from those living with parents who have a college degree, and some scientists have assumed that the differences in behavior between adults from two social classes are, in the main, the product of their environments during the first two years. Children who have neglecting or indifferent parents are likely to fail in school and to develop impairing symptoms during later childhood. But most of these children remained in their home settings or were sent to foster families not committed to their growth. If an adult has impairing symptoms, it is more reasonable to attribute them to the continuous influence of an adverse environment than to conclude that the symptoms represent the untouched traces of early neglect. Pediatricians from cities with high levels of air pollution realize that the asthmatic symptoms they treat do not represent inherently stable qualities in the child but are a reaction to the toxic ecology in which their patients live.

Although the evolution of *Homo sapiens* required the appearance of fish hundreds of millions of years earlier, an explanation of the rise of *Homo sapiens* which begins "Once there were fish" is not very informative. Statements that ascribe adult behavior to the experiences of infancy are equally uninformative. Moreover, the infant determinists' contention that an original cause in the deep past exerts its influence indefinitely has moral connotations.

Every society needs some transcendental themes to which its citizens can be loyal. God, the beauty of knowledge, and the sanctity of faithful, romantic love were, in the past, among the most revered ideas in American society. Unfortunately, the facts of modern life have made it difficult for many to remain unquestionably loyal to those ethical standards. The sacredness of the mother–infant bond and therefore the psychological significance of the attachment of a baby to its mother are among the sturdiest of our dwindling set of unsullied ethical beliefs. Worry over the large number of mothers who place their infants in surrogate care and, in that action, violate the natural bond between the biological mother and her infant is widespread. If infants were able to flourish when cared for by any concerned adult, making the biological mother expendable, one of our few remaining moral imperatives would have become a conventional belief.

An uncritical acceptance of a strong form of infant determinism fills the understandable need to simplify the complexity of each individual's developmental itinerary. The extraordinary variation in adult psychological profiles remains mysterious; hence, we are vulnerable to accepting premature answers that remove some of the uncertainty. The ancient Mesopotamians found the regular changes in the moon's appearance a mystery. Because the 28-day lunar cycle seemed to consist of four perceptually distinct shapes, each appearing roughly every seven days, the number seven was regarded as sacred and was honored by the Hebrew Sabbath and the accompanying rituals that were not to be violated.[68]

Science has removed so much of the mystery from celestial events, birth, illness, and death, we might ask what natural events are able to generate a feeling of mystery in modern citizens. What remains mysterious, I believe, are the dramatic differences in talent, mental health, and capacities for intense love, sadness, joy, or hatred. Our wisest commentators are puzzled, for example, by the high rates of adolescent crime, suicide, and school failure, as well as the behavior of mothers like Susan Smith, who drowned her children in a lake. Early experience, which awards a profound formative power to mothers as they care for their infants, is one popular explanation for these sad outcomes. A mother who violates the imperative to love her infant and, as a result, produces an insecurely attached child is like a person who violates the Sabbath rituals.

American society has awarded women a dignity that surpasses that found in most countries of the world. Carl Degler has suggested that one reason for this ethos was the mutual interdependence of nineteenth-century husbands and wives as they settled the land west of the Appalachians. As a result, a woman's love for her husband and children was given extraordinary healing qualities.[69] The conviction that the conscientious love of mothers toward their infants has consequences that extend far into the future requires the converse assumption that an infant deprived of this resource will necessarily be less potent.

But the doctrine of infant determinism ignores the many powerful influences that affect the profile of adolescents and young adults after the second birthday. These include the influence of older and younger siblings, emotional identifications with family, class, and ethnic group, and major historical events that affect an entire society. I now consider each of these influences in detail.

Birth Order, Identification, and Historical Era

The child's birth rank in the family, especially if the age spread between the child and the next elder or younger sibling is less than four years, affects a small number of psychological qualities.[70] The most robust is the attitude toward legitimate authority. First-born children—about 40 percent of Americans—are more likely to hold a benevolent, respectful view of authority. Later-borns are more likely to form a skeptical, occasionally cynical, conception. As a consequence, the eldest in a family is most disposed to adopt the parents' values. If these values are also endorsed by the majority culture, the first-born will be more receptive than the later born to a continued loyalty to the dominant standards of the society.

First-borns from middle-class American homes obtain better grades and are more often valedictorians of their high school class, gifted in some domain of talent, and listed in *Who's Who* in America.[71] They are also more likely than later-borns to select the professions of law, medicine, and business, each of which is regarded as socially desirable by middle-class family, friends, and mentors. This vocational choice is reasonable for those whose posture toward legitimate authority is "What is it you wish me to do?" More later-borns, by contrast, choose vocations with less social consensus on prestige, such as acting, writing, singing, or photography—vocations that are less often embedded in a hierarchy of organization linked to differential status.[72]

The different constructions created by children in different birth positions help to explain why later-borns find it a bit easier to resist the social pressures to conform to the expectations of parents and teachers. Consider, as a hypothetical example, two middle-class boys born to well-educated, reasonably nurturant, affectionate, and just parents. The child's initial conception of adult authority is based on the categorization of the parents, who, to the first-born eight-year-year old, seem to possess desirable characteristics, especially the psychological power the child would like to command. If the parents praise conformity to their values and punish deviations, it will be difficult for the first-born to escape these imperatives and reject the ethic of civility and achievement.[73]

However, the five-year-old with an eight-year-old sibling lives in a different world. Although the older brother is perceived by the younger as a minor authority, he is far less nurturant than the parents. He teases the later-born, seizes his toys, and reminds the younger sibling of his relative impotence. These daily events affect the later-born's conception of those who are older. They can generate a low but chronic level of resentment toward those with authority and lead the later-born to conclude, partly on realistic grounds, that, relative to the older sibling, he is less talented at many of the skills the family values. Unfortunately, five-year-olds are not mature enough to rationalize the difference in strength and skill as a function of age. Thus, the later-born is more vulnerable to doubt about the self than is the older sibling.

The parents contribute to this dynamic by awarding some privileges to the first that are denied to the later-born, including greater freedom, later bedtime, and, at birthdays, more expensive gifts. To the later-born, parents appear to be unjust and thus to have feet of clay; hence, the imperative to conform to their requests and to adopt their values is felt with less urgency.

Finally, the later-born is often restricted in the choice of skill to actualize because of a desire to be better than the first-born in some domain. If the first-born has chosen academic mastery as a major area of achievement, the later-born, recognizing that he reads less perfectly than his older brother, may be motivated to reject academics and become an athlete. If the first-born is skilled in baseball, the later-born may reject baseball in favor of soccer. And if the first-born plays the clarinet well, the later-born may become a drummer.

In order to develop a profile that is distinct from, but as competent as, that of the first-born, the later-born must select from what is left. It is not surprising, therefore, that later-borns are less strongly motivated for academic mastery, more often arrested for antisocial behavior, and, if they become scientists, more likely to agree with radically new theoretical conceptions that upset the cherished positions of the scientific authorities in the domain of discovery.

Frank Sulloway has accumulated stunning proof of this last claim. Most first-born naturalists who commented on evolution between 1860 and 1875 rejected Darwin's revolutionary ideas, while later-borns were three times more likely than first-borns to endorse them.[74] Both Charles Darwin and Alfred Russel Wallace, co-developers of the theory of evolution through natural selection, were later-borns. The ideological independence of the later-born is contained in a remark in Darwin's autobiography. "As far as I can judge, I am not apt to follow blindly the level of other men . . . This has naturally led me to distrust greatly deductive reasoning in the mixed sciences."[75]

Later-borns were twice as likely as first-borns, across 28 different innovative scientific ideas, to support a novel conceptual advance over the status quo. It is unlikely that this result is the product of different patterns of infant care or security of attachment. The baby in the family often experiences less critical, more permissive parents, which should have engendered a more, rather than a less, secure infancy. In a study of a large sample of middle-class children living in two-parent families, I did not find any important differences in behavior, mood, or physiology between first- and later-born two-year-olds.

The consequences of birth order are relevant to the debate on connectedness because the different constructions of first and later-borns are absent in the first two years of life. The cognitive immaturity of the two-year-old prevents him from inferring that he is less adequate than his older sibling. The important psychological consequences of birth order must wait until children can appreciate their relation to a sibling and brood about the difference in parental attitudes toward each member of the family.

Scientific advances are marked by insightful hunches, often from a small number of facts, as to the mechanisms underlying the phenomenon. For example, the physicists' strong belief in the Big Bang rests on the implications of three observations: (1) the redshift of starlight, interpreted as meaning that the galaxies are receding from one another at a velocity proportional to their distance and that the universe is expanding, as one would expect from an initial mega-explosion; (2) the background cosmic temperature of three degrees Kelvin, which agrees with the predicted rate of cooling of the universe if an original Big Bang had occurred; and (3) the preponderance of the lighter elements hydrogen and helium in the cosmos, whose proportions (nearly 75 and 25 percent, respectively, of the universe's mass) are close to the theoretical values predicted on the presumption of an original explosion. These three facts sustain a commitment to the notion of the Big Bang.

Similarly, Darwin's hypothesis of evolution through natural selection rested on three observations: (1) that, in the Galapagos, animals of one species living on contiguous islands with similar vegetation possessed different anatomical features; (2) that the characteristics of a species can be altered through selective breeding, as demonstrated by the artificial selection practiced by animal breeders; and (3) that species produce many more offspring than the resources in their environment can support (an idea Darwin borrowed from Malthus). From these facts Darwin inferred that competition among individuals for limited resources leads to the "natural selection" of adaptive characteristics. Over time, with the aid of geographical isolation, this process causes new species to evolve.

The validity of the idea that social-class or ethnic-group identification can be an important influence on psychological development after infancy is also based on three observations: (1) that the ethical values held by most adolescents are more similar to those of their parents and other familiar adults whom they respect than to randomly selected adults in the society; (2) that children and adults experience emotions, such as pride or shame, when learning about the experiences of another person or group with whom they believe they share features; (3) that the intensity of these vicarious emotions is correlated with the distinctiveness of the shared qualities. The childhood shame Frank McCourt felt when he found his father drunk in a local bar is one example of identification. The exalted mood among American Jews following Israel's victory in the Seven Day War provides another. These three facts invite speculation as to the psychological process responsible for these phenomena—identification is the term used most often to name this process.

The human brain prepares young children to seek and to detect similarities among an array of objects or events. Most two-year-olds presented with four red cubes and four yellow spheres will touch, in sequence, the objects with the same color and shape. Many two-year-old children call the first horse they see "doggie" because the larger animal shares distinctive features with the many dogs they have observed. But the two-year-old is not mature enough to construct a category based on similarities in behaviors, beliefs, and moods. Children must be at least five years old in order to compare the similarities between themselves and others on these qualities and to infer that some of the qualities of the other are applicable to the self.

For example, most five-year-old girls believe that they share more features with their mothers than with their fathers, and therefore a five-year-old girl who sees her mother become frightened by a thunderstorm may infer that a fear of storms is one of her own characteristics as well. On the other hand, a girl who perceives her mother to be fearless, forceful with the father, and popular with friends will be tempted to assume that she, too, possesses some form of these desirable qualities. This happier inference is more difficult because the five-year-old rarely feels fearless and courageous. It is easier for the child to assume that she shares features with a fearful parent than with a bold one. However, that bias will change later.

The child's identification with her gender can be symbolically creative. The categories male and female are associated in the mind of both child and adult with other concepts that superficially appear unrelated to gender. By seven to eight years of age, the concept "female" is linked unconsciously to the concept "natural." All cultures regard giving birth to and caring for young infants as prototypically natural events. Hence, the concept female should be semantically closer to the concept nature than the concept male. This deduction was affirmed in a study of seven-year-old American children.

During the first session the psychologist sensitized the children to the contrast between natural and manufactured objects by showing them pictures of both categories and asking them to guess which of two nonsense words (gip or lum) was the best name for each category. The children solved this problem quickly and in a few minutes were calling all the natural pictures one word and all the manufactured objects the other one. One week later the psychologist returned and told the children they would play the same game but with different pictures and different nonsense words (dep and tas). Initially the pictures were of male and female objects, like a pipe, a man's suit, a purse, and a woman's shoe. When the children were performing correctly, the psychologist inserted new pictures of natural and manufactured objects. Both boys and girls applied the word symbolic of female to the pictures of natural items (plant, seashell, cloud, tree, lake, robin, leaf) and the word symbolic of male to the manufactured objects (street sign, sailboat, television set, pen, desk, bottle, and clock). Ninety-one percent of the children called the plant a female object and ninety-one percent called the street sign male.[76] This interesting fact implies that girls believe that they are symbolically closer to a category representing natural phenomena than boys. Perhaps one reason why Pythagoreans regarded the number two as female and the number three as male is that more natural events occur in pairs than trios.

Identification is not just a cognitive belief. An identification requires both a belief in shared features and the experience of vicarious emotions. Every category that a person believes is applicable to self does not have to be linked to an emotion. When the child assumes that her membership in a category cannot be easily changed—this belief is most obvious for gender—she may experience a vicarious emotion when desirable or undesirable events happen to the person with whom category membership is shared. If a girl experiences pride when the father praises the mother, tension when the mother is threatened, or sadness when the mother cries, we can infer that an identification with the mother has been established. But the young child's emotional reaction is limited to individual persons rather than to groups of people. The five-year-old girl does not experience vicarious emotion when an unfamiliar girl is praised because the abstract category "female" has not yet become a basis for identification.

Humans award special salience to categories defined by uncommon features. That is one reason why dinosaurs, turtles, elephants, and snakes are so interesting to children. It also explains why humans often regard objects that have a distinctive feature as dangerous and therefore to be shunned. Mary Douglas has suggested that the ancient Hebrew prohibition against eating clams and oysters might have been based, in part, on the fact that most edible species from the sea with which the Hebrews were familiar had scales. Similarly, the prohibition on eating pork might have been supported, in part, by the fact that the pig is an unusual animal. Although it has a cloven hoof, it is not a ruminant. That discrepancy could have been interpreted as signifying danger and therefore something to avoid. Red hair was uncommon in medieval Europe, and many Europeans believed that a red-haired person was conceived because the mother had intercourse during her menses—presumed to be a violation of natural law.[77]

The more distinctive the features that are shared between child and parent, the stronger the identification. A father who is both tall and thin and, in addition, has red hair and freckles will engender a stronger identification in a son who has these four features than in a son who is short, chubby, brown-haired, and without freckles.

The distinctive qualities that most often engender identification during childhood are rendered more salient through the evaluation of rewards or punishments to members belonging to the category. Gender, ethnicity, and religion, but not speed of walking or the color of one's eyes, fit these criteria. Children as young as five years believe that racial characteristics are permanent.[78] Members of minority groups in every society are more strongly identified with their group than with those who belong to majority groups, especially if the former has some distinctive feature. That is why whites in South Africa are more strongly identified with their ethnic group than are whites in England or the United States. The distinctive facial features, food prohibitions, and religious rituals of Jews in Central Europe during the Middle Ages and the Renaissance guaranteed a strong identification with that category.

A basic principle in human perception is that the mind is attracted to any place in an array where a locus of difference is detected. We notice a single yellow flower on an expansive green lawn; a leaf on the clean deck of a house; a Western European face among a sea of Japanese in a Kyoto suburb. That is why it is impossible to prevent a child from categorizing the self with respect to gender and, when his ethnic group is physically distinctive, with respect to ethnicity. The child cannot avoid concluding that a distinctive feature signals something meaningful.

A second robust perceptual principle is that elements that are proximal to each other, that are continuous, or that have a common fate seem to cohere to define a unitary object. Coherence among physical elements of an object is analogous to consistency among the symbolic meanings ascribed to categories. If a child in Montana classifies herself as Vietnamese, conceptual consistency demands that she behave in ways that are in accord with her understanding of the stereotype for Vietnamese children. To fail to do so is to violate the principle of consistency and, as a result, to feel uncertain. Adolescents award a reality to categories of people that is as firm as the one they award to objects. If a rock suddenly changed color or lost its hardness, observers would be surprised and feel uncertain. Similarly, an adolescent who believes he belongs to the conjunctive categories Hispanic, Catholic, and male will experience uncertainty if he behaves in ways that violate the features of that trio of categories. He does not have the freedom to decide whether he will accept or refuse the implications of that category assignment. Human perceptual and conceptual systems share an imperative to attend to nodes of difference and to honor coherence and consistency.

The enhanced intellectual maturity of adolescents makes it possible for more abstract features, like religion and social class, to become the basis for category membership. Many Muslim and Christian adolescents in Sarajevo identify with the religion of their families, even though few, if any, physical features distinguish the two groups. Adults may decide that a childhood identification generates anxiety and may attempt to change their category membership. Some Jews change their last name, some Mexicans try to lighten their skin, as Richard Rodriguez notes in his moving memoir, and some African Americans straighten their hair.[79] However, attempts to dilute an ethnic identification can generate guilt because the person believes that the original category is the true one. Attempts to alter it are interpreted as acts of disloyalty to the other members of the category and can have some of the same emotional consequences that follow abandoning one's family.

Some American youth of color who identify with their ethnic category, especially those who are born in the United States, believe that whites are morally tainted because of their prejudice, greed, and hypocrisy and therefore are not desirable role models. Too often, one of the sad consequences of this belief is an unwillingness to work diligently at school because middle-class whites, who may be regarded as the enemy, want them to master academic skills, go to college, and become professionals. Their ethnic identification can thwart the actions that are likely to benefit the African-American or Hispanic-American adolescent in the long run.

The media, unwittingly, contribute to the reluctance of some African- and Hispanic-American youth to adopt the values of the white majority. Television and movies emphasize the distinctiveness of each ethnic group and the prejudicial attitudes held by whites. America in 1900 was over 90 percent white and Christian. Today, less than two-thirds belong to both of these categories and the remaining Americans belong to a large number of ethnic and religious groups. Thus, the category "American" has become fuzzy, and identification with it more problematic. Indeed, many Mexican immigrants who have lived in America for two or more decades continue to believe they are here temporarily and that eventually they will return to their native country. The Dominicans have a saying for this: "Un pie aquí, un pie allá" (One foot here, one foot there).

The features that define social class, as distinct from ethnicity, are both less salient and less stable. The signs children use to construct this category include features of residence, neighborhood, and material possessions such as the car their parents drive or the number of computer games they own. Most seven-year-olds have no trouble distinguishing drawings of homes that represent poor and wealthy families, but parents do not usually remind their children of their social class, and no special rituals or holidays define class membership. Thus, a child's discovery of his social class is conceptually difficult, less uniform, and more diffuse and does not form before six or seven years of age or even later. Frank Manuel points out that Karl Marx wanted to make class a more important psychological category for identification than ethnicity or religion.[80] The nonviolent collapse of communism in the Soviet Union, in contrast with the civil unrest in Bosnia, Ireland, Israel, and Rwanda, proves how difficult it is to reverse these priorities.

The number of poor families in a city or town affects identification with class. A state of poverty is most distinctive in societies where many are affluent, as is true for most modern Western states. But in many isolated villages with less than a thousand people, located in rural areas of underdeveloped countries, over 90 percent of the residents are poor in an absolute sense. However, there is less crime and less hopelessness because the people are less conscious of the difference between their economic state and that of those who live in large cities hundreds of miles away. No uniform psychological outcomes flow from absolute poverty, but many predictable, undesirable outcomes flow from a belief in one's relative poverty.

Many Americans believe that hard work and intelligence are all that are needed to gain the wealth that has become, in this century, a primary feature of personal worth. Consequently, class has a greater potential for shame in the United States than it does in many countries of the world. Ten-year-olds who identify with their poor families are vulnerable to feelings of shame or impotence if they wonder whether their parents are lazy or incompetent. Character, whether actualized as honesty, perseverance, or loyalty, has been pushed aside by the ethically neutral and more easily measured dimension of material wealth. The advantage of this change in values is that it makes it theoretically possible for all American citizens, no matter what their ethnic, national, or religious origin, to attain signs of higher status. But the price of this change in social accounting is narcissism, selfishness, disloyalty, and a readiness for shame that is hard to rationalize among those who are poor.

John Updike has confessed that he feels nervous and occasionally stutters when in the presence of Boston Brahmins. Updike's identification with his working-class origins has remained with him.[81] The British literary critic Frank Kermode, also born to poor parents, admits to feeling like an outsider: "Looking the part while not being quite equal to it seems to be something I do rather well."[82] In his preface to

Philosophical Explanations, Robert Nozick, a distinguished American philosopher from an immigrant background, questioned his right to address profound themes of human concern. "Isn't it ludicrous for someone just one generation from the shtetl, a pisher from Brownsville and East Flatbush in Brooklyn, even to touch on the topics of the monumental thinkers?"[83] It is unlikely that Montaigne, Kant, Russell, or Whitehead entertained such doubts.

Identification with a less-advantaged social class, on the other hand, can provide protection against shame or guilt if the adolescent generates reasons for the family's class position that remove some of the responsibility. These protective beliefs include the notion that the rich are corrupt and morally flawed, that secure jobs in a competitive, capitalist society are scarce, and that employers are prejudiced against the poor. Each of these interpretations permits the adolescent identified with a disadvantaged class to mute some dysphoria. But these protections are becoming more difficult to exploit as American society tries to eliminate prejudice and provide more opportunities for the poor. As the psychological protection is torn away, adolescents from poor families confront their status without healing rationalizations. Possibly for the first time in American history, being poor is treated by many youth as a serious stigma.

Because identification with a poor family can generate shame, guilt, and anger, it can also create physiological stress, which may contribute to the poorer health of the economically disadvantaged. Although the poor have less easy access to good medical care, experts do not believe this is the only reason for their higher rates of morbidity, from arthritis to heart disease to gall stones. Perhaps the emotional states created by the chronic identification contribute to the vulnerability to illness.

A parent's social class can affect her preferred socialization practices with her child. In the 1980s, working-class and middle-class parents in one study heard a tape-recording of a brief essay that compared the value of a restrictive compared with a permissive strategy of socialization. Each parent was told that they would have to remember as much of the essay as possible as soon as it was over. The working-class mothers recalled more of the essay stating that excessive restrictiveness was bad for children for it could make them excessively fearful. The recall of the middle-class mothers elaborated the idea that permissiveness would place their child at risk for delinquency and poor school grades.[84] What accounts for this difference?

Working-class American mothers, anxious over their less-secure economic position, do not want their children to be afraid to take risks, for that trait might put them at an economic disadvantage. Hence, they favor a more permissive regimen. Middle-class mothers, on the other hand, have become more apprehensive about their children not performing well in school or being tempted by asocial friends. Hence, they favor the more restrictive argument. Ever since the end of World War II, middle-class mothers have been more restrictive and working-class mothers less, a reversal of the practices of these two classes of mothers during the first decades of this century.

The development of children from different social classes is analogous to that of a young embryonic cell whose fate is determined by its spatial position. Whether a particular cell eventually becomes tendon or cartilage is a function of where it is in the developing embryo and which cells are next to it. Similarly, the psychological profile of the adolescent is determined in a major way by the family's place in the class hierarchy of the society. But identification with that category does not occur until years after the period of infancy is over.

Geographical boundaries that prevent interbreeding among members of a species are a major factor in the formation of new species because as smaller subsets of a species breed among themselves their distinctive characteristics are enhanced. Ernst Mayr is credited with the clearest statement of this important principle of geographic speciation.[85] It is likely that different social classes, like mountain ranges that separate animals of the same species from one another, place children with similar characteristics in families, neighborhoods, and schools that promote different values and opportunities, and present different contingencies. Marriages between upper-middle-class and working-class partners are unusual; most adults marry within their socioeconomic class or marry someone in a neighboring class. Thus, by seven years of age or earlier, children from working-class and upper-middle-class families have diverged into psychologically distinctive groups and by adolescence possess different views of self and society.

As with the influence of birth order, identification with an ethnic or social class develops after five or six years of age. Thus, an infant born to a poor Hispanic family of caring parents is not protected indefinitely from the self-doubt that can follow an identification with a disadvantaged class or victimized ethnic group. The African-American novelist John Wideman has a younger brother who is serving a life sentence for murder. The younger brother most likely experienced the same parental care his older brother enjoyed, but he was an adolescent in Pittsburgh during the 1960s when black anger at American racist attitudes exploded, and that experience probably influenced his behavior.[86] Parental nurture is not a guarantee of an accomplished, serene adulthood.

An infant born to a less caring upper-middle-class white family might be able to mute some of the psychological burden the experiences of infancy produced when he recognizes his privileged status. George Homans, an influential Harvard sociologist, noted in a memoir written shortly before his death that he coped with his intense childhood anxiety over his poor school grades and unpopularity with peers by reminding himself that he could trace his pedigree back to John Adams.[87] Darwin's description of his father glows with awe for his parent's intelligence, sympathy, generosity, kindness, and business sense. It is a paean of praise. Charles knew about the power of inheritance from his acquaintance with animal breeders and perhaps felt that his own cognitive abilities had been with him from birth.

I suspect that every child is emotionally moved by stories of heroic family members who possessed qualities symbolic of strength, bravery, compassion, or unusual intelligence. Jewish parents who were oppressed during the Spanish Inquisition probably told their children that although their lives were uncertain, they could trace their religious identity to the patriarchs celebrated in the Hebrew Bible. Frank McCourt's chronically unemployed father reminded him that, as a son of Ireland, he possessed the courage of those who came before him. These family myths can help children cope with fear, anxiety, shame, or guilt. But myths become effective only after six or seven years of age, when cognitive development permits the child to appreciate their meaning.

Finally, the historical era during which the adolescent years are spent can have a profound influence on adult values. Although the years from five to eight are important for establishing identifications, eight-year-olds are too young to understand the deep premises of their society. Religious piety permeated every part of life in seventeenth-century New England. The children living in this era could not have known that the devil was a premise and not a fact. The important advances in intellectual capacity that emerge at thirteen to fifteen years motivate youth to brood about their beliefs because their experiences are often not plumb with their childhood ideas. The adolescent wonders why, if God exists, do so many people suffer? Why, if sexual stimulation is pleasant, is it wrong to masturbate? However, at unpredictable times, historical events like a war or economic depression provoke changes in ideology as the adolescent contrasts the beliefs held prior to the event with those generated by the new social conditions. Adolescents, who are beginning to synthesize the assumptions they will rely on for the rest of their lives, are unusually receptive to historical events that challenge existing beliefs.

Consider a sixteen-year-old in Moscow in 1970 who accepted a frugal, restricted, but ordered life without street crime or local corruption in return for secure employment and state-supported education and health. A sixteen-year-old living in Moscow in 1998 confronts an inconsistency between that older conception and the increasing gap in wealth, rampant crime, and the necessity of a bribe to obtain an automobile license. Those glaring refutations of the adolescent's prior understanding generate the cynical premise that most people are selfish and the state is more corrupt and less potent than they had believed. The adolescents who accept this view are affected in a nontrivial way. When the millions of Russian adolescents who are crystallizing these skeptical ideas assume positions of responsibility in a decade or two, they will bring this harsh philosophy to their daily assignments.

Contemporary youth in Sarajevo have witnessed cruelties that will make deep skeptics of their generation. It will make little difference to an eighteen-year-old in Sarajevo whether she had a caring or an indifferent mother if she has lived through rape, artillery shells, and the senseless death of friends and family. But her skeptical attitude was absent during her first two years of life.

The economic depression in America that lasted from 1930 to 1940 left about one-third of American families chronically anxious over their economic security. Children were reminded daily that they should be careful with their clothes, and mothers skimped on meals while fathers drove rusted cars. Five-year-olds were not mature enough to sense the family's anxiety, but the adolescents, who were reminded day after day of the economic edge the family occupied, acquired a worry over money that lasted a lifetime. A large proportion of Americans who were adolescents during those years and are now in their seventh decade saved more money than the generation before or after them and conducted their lives with a continuous, gnawing concern over financial loss.[88]

One of the best examples of history's influence involves the ideological changes that occurred in Central Europe as the nineteenth century came to a close. When Max Weber was twenty years old, in 1894, the liberal tradition in Germany was in decline, the increased bureaucratization of citizens was eroding the spirit of individualism, and Marx's ideas were challenging the virtue of a capitalistic ethos.[89] When these new ideas met Weber's creative mind, the influential book *The Protestant Ethic and the Spirit of Capitalism* was born. The false idealism, hyperbole in language, surface superficialities, and denial of corruption that became obvious at the end of the Habsburg dynasty were best appreciated by late adolescents and young adults who, released from the older premises, were free to construct a new philosophy. It was not an accident that Wittgenstein, Freud, and Mahler were young adults living in Central Europe during this transitional era.

As a young man, Samuel Beckett witnessed the anarchy that tore through Ireland in the early decades of this century. He probably exploited his childhood memory of the senseless violence of the Easter uprising when he had one of the tramps in *Waiting for Godot* say, "This is becoming really insignificant," and let the other reply, "Not enough."

These events, like a blizzard across New England, can change a generation's views. The protest against the Vietnam War at the end of the

1960s turned large numbers of privileged adolescents against the values of established authority. College students seized administration buildings or shared sexual partners in unheated communal homes. High school youths defiantly left their classrooms to march in protest of the war, and they got away with it. It is heady for a sixteen-year-old to defy the rules of authority and escape punishment. For many youths, such experiences eroded a tendency to worry over coming to work at ten o'clock in the morning instead of nine and leaving at four instead of five. Many of these middle-class youths thumbed their noses at authority because they happened to be born during a thin slice of time when segments of American society were uncertain as to which actions were legitimate. When history tears a hole in the fabric of consensual assumptions, the mind flies through it into a space free of hoary myth to invent a new conception of self, ethics, and society.

The consequences of sibling order, identification, and historical era, each of which affects behavior and belief in profound ways, have little or no relevance during the first two years of life. But each can produce sharp discontinuities in development and transform the connections between infancy and adulthood. That is why William Greenough, a leading neuroscientist, wrote, "To focus upon the first three years and to downplay the later years is not warranted, by either human behavioral or neuroscience research."[90]

Thus, it is useful to ask why the idea of infant determinism resists criticism so effectively. I suspect that the major reason for its vitality is that it generates a feeling of correctness that is derived from our moral values. The persuasive power of ideas in mathematics, physics, and to some degree chemistry lies with the aesthetic nature of the explanatory argument. A set of equations that describes an aspect of nature with simplicity, elegance, and wide generalizability is able to produce a subtle emotion—a "shuddering"—in those who understand the mathematics. Dirac insisted that the beauty of an equation was a better sign of its correctness than its correspondence with empirical evidence. Ideas without beauty, he believed, were probably wrong. Psychology, sociology, and anthropology are not even close to generating formal knowledge that could lead most to say "That idea is beautiful." However, social scientists, too, are affected by, and most likely to adopt, explanations that generate emotion. But the usual basis for the emotional reaction is its link to an ethical premise rather than its formal elegance.

A majority of Americans and Europeans hold the ethical belief that a mother's care for her infant is inherently better than the care given by any other adult. The image of a mother taking her infant to a daycare center seems to many to violate a natural law. As a result, when scholars say it is best if mothers take care of their own infants, most have the intuition that they are speaking the truth. When we add the attractiveness of the assumptions of connectedness and of material changes in the infant's brain etched by experience, the conclusion that the mother's care for and stimulation of her child in the first few years must set the course of development for good or ill is almost impossible to resist. That idea generates a feeling of correctness as strong as the one Copernicus felt when he reflected on the loveliness of the circular orbits of planets.

But, sadly, the gut feeling that an idea is right is a poor guide to truth. Kepler's equations, which posited elliptical orbits, not circular ones, came closer to nature's plan. The equations of quantum electrodynamics, which Einstein regarded as ugly, have turned out to be correct—at least for now. It would be pleasing if a mother's care of her infant in the first two years set the child's future in a significant way. But I am afraid that, like Copernicus's beautifully circular orbits, this emotionally satisfying hypothesis strays too far from the facts.

A second reason why so many people prefer to believe in infant determinism is that it ignores the power of social class membership. Though a child's social class is the best predictor of future vocation, academic accomplishments, and psychiatric health, Americans wish to believe that their society is open and egalitarian, without rigid class boundaries. To acknowledge the power of class is to question this ethical canon.

Third, the doctrine of infant determinism minimizes the role of chance, an idea Americans find agreeable. And fourth, determinism is materialistic, for it assumes that the changes in the brain created by the first experiences do not fade. And finally, the private interpretations that older children impose on experience are hard to imagine. Even though every parent sees remarkable changes in the behavior of their children over the first dozen years and therefore should be opposed to the doctrine of infant determinism, these factors frustrate that insight.

The common theme that unites the three forces of birth order, identification with ethnic or social-class groups, and historical period is the disposition to detect and interpret discrepancy. Later-borns cannot help recognizing and interpreting the differences in strength and ability between themselves and their older siblings, nor can they ignore the different ways parents react to each child in the family. Similarly, children in a particular class or ethnic group brood about the differences between themselves and others and often conclude that the category of the other is inappropriate for them. Adolescents exposed to war, depression, and revolution cannot escape trying to understand the inconsistency between their understanding of the past and the present. The resolution often requires a rejection of some or all of the older assumptions.

Sometimes a single event can provoke a dramatically new view of self or other in an adolescent. In Arthur Miller's play *Death of a Salesman*, Biff's personality changes in a major way when he discovers his father, whom he admired, with a prostitute. Miller used this scene to remind us that, on occasion, some aspects of our understanding of the past can be erased in a moment. Had Darwin's uncle not volunteered to drive thirty miles to persuade Charles's father to let him go on the *Beagle* voyage, the young Darwin would have missed the sculpting experience of his life. Those who insist that some psychological structures acquired in the first two years are protected from later events hold a truly unusual view of nature that insists too strongly on a coherent, connected story.

Modern societies are fond of the notion of continuity. The biological version of this idea holds that each new animal species carries most of the structures and functions of the ancestral form from which it sprang; hence, the differences between related species are minimal. The psychological meaning of continuity is that each new stage of development carries with it most of the structures and dispositions acquired in the prior stage. Hence, explanations that trace some aspects of the present to an original cause exert a strong attraction.

But biologists also acknowledge the emergence of novel structures and functions. The tiny bones in the human middle ear that make hearing possible are derived from a set of bones that first appeared millions of years ago in very early mammals as a hinge between the jaw and the skull. The vertebral column, the lung, and internal fertilization were novel evolutionary events, just as inference, reflective thought, guilt, and jealousy in humans are novel developmental events. These facts challenge a dogmatic commitment to a continuist philosophy and enlarge the gap between past and present to reveal a large circle of light where change is constructed.

Imagine a contest in which one experienced psychologist is given an accurate description of one hundred children at two years of age that includes the children's experiences with their parents, their temperament, language skills, attachment patterns, and style of behavior with others, but nothing else. Another psychologist is told the gender, social class, ethnicity, and birth order of each person but is given no information on their early experiences nor what they were like when they were two years old. Each psychologist has to predict the profile of cognitive skills, personality, uncertainties, job satisfaction, and marital status at age 25. I am certain that the second psychologist will do far better than the first because the information she has changes less dramatically over the course of childhood.

The longitudinal studies of children affirm this prediction. The social class of a child's family is a better predictor of an adult's vocation and personal traits than the child's psychological profile at age two. I suspect that predicting adult moods, symptoms, personality, and talents from the profile on the second birthday is as impossible as predicting earthquakes. Geologists are coming to believe that whether a particular disturbance in the earth's mantle will grow into a large earthquake depends on so many details of physical conditions in large areas that individual earthquakes are probably inherently unpredictable.[91]

That fact does not mean that the events of the first two years are without any force. It only means that a fearful, quiet, tense two-year-old who has had an uncertain environment remains malleable should benevolent changes occur, and a laughing, securely attached, smart two-year-old is not protected from angst should her life turn harsh. Both science and autobiography affirm that a capacity for change is as essential to human development as it is to the evolution of new species. The events of the opening years do start an infant down a particular path, but it is a path with an extraordinarily large number of intersections.

CHAPTER THREE

The Pleasure Principle

When a person consciously selects one act over another—going skiing for the weekend rather than traveling to visit an old friend who is very ill—what goal does she seek? Two distinctly different psychological states have been nominated. Some scholars have argued that the primary aim is attainment of a conscious feeling of pleasure that originates in changes in one or more of the sensory modalities—sometimes an increase in excitation, as in taste and touch, sometimes a decrease in excitation, as in pain.[1]

The second, qualitatively different, goal has its origin in thought rather than sensation. The desired state is a conceptual consonance between an idea, called a standard, and the chosen action. When that consonance occurs, the person momentarily experiences a pleasant feeling because his behavior is in accord with a standard he has categorized as good. Surprisingly, no word in English names this feeling with precision; virtue comes close. People eat cake for the sensory delight of its taste, but on occasion will refuse cake in order to remain loyal to a standard that urges avoidance of too many calories.[2]

The state created by excitation of the senses has a quality and duration that no one would confuse with the one created by the recognition that a particular action, thought, or feeling matches a representation the person has classified as good. Darwin recognized this critical differ-ence. On May 5, 1839, he wrote in one of his notebooks that humans feel they ought to follow certain lines of conduct and must learn that "it is his interest to follow it . . . By interest I do not mean any calculated pleasure but the satisfaction of the mind." He had acknowledged nine months earlier that happiness consists of doing good and being perfect.[3]

The differences between the pleasures of sensory experience and those of consonance with a standard bear on a persistent philosophical debate over the bases for holding a belief. When a belief refers to an event in nature, the favored justification is scientific evidence that threads its way back to sensory experience. But the justification for those beliefs that are also ethical standards is often an emotionally tinged intuition that cannot be as easily traced to sensory experience.

Economists ignore the distinction between the pleasure of sense and the pleasure of virtue because it resists quantification. They simply de-clare, without the support of deep argument, that all economic deci-sions are based on a wish to maximize satisfaction. They leave to the community the difficult task of figuring out the meanings of "satisfac-tion." The evolution, development, incentives, brain profiles, and psy-chological states that define the satisfactions of sense compared with the attainment of virtue are so distinct it is a serious conceptual error to claim that humans are driven by a unitary desire to maximize pleasure. No single biological state defines pleasure because it is, finally, a judg-ment.

Laboratory investigations affirm that the meaning of pleasure is am-biguous even in animals. Research on the so-called pleasure centers in the brain, first discovered by James Olds and Peter Milner, assumes that the mammalian brain contains sets of neurons which, when excited, create a state of sensory pleasure. Rats will press a lever continually if this action is followed by electrical stimulation of the medial forebrain bundle, one of the brain's pleasure centers. But, surprisingly, they will ignore the lever when they are returned to the experimental chamber after only an hour away from it. If the stimulation had been so rich with sensory delight, one would think that the rats would rush immediately to the lever and begin pressing with fervor. Recent evidence suggests that the electrical stimulation may simply draw the animal's attention to the lever and make it more salient, rather than produce a tiny jolt of sensory pleasure. Perhaps that is why Charles Gallistel, in agreement with the Greek cynics, suggests that "pleasure is not an experience in its own right."[4]

The philosopher Alasdair MacIntyre reminds us that "if someone suggests to us, in the spirit of Bentham and Mill, that we should guide our own choices by the prospects of our own future pleasure or happiness, the appropriate retort is to inquire: 'But which pleasure, which happiness ought to guide me?' For there are too many different kinds of enjoyable activity, too many different modes in which happiness is achieved . . . Different pleasures and different happinesses are to a large degree incommensurable: there are no scales of quality or quantity on which to weigh them. Consequently, appeal to the criteria of pleasure will not tell me whether to drink or swim and appeal to those of happiness cannot decide for me between a life of a monk and that of a soldier."[5]

The claim that human behavior is often in the service of enhancing a feeling of virtue is supported by the mundane observation that children and adults spend a great deal of time testing their competence. I watched my five-year-old granddaughter fill a bucket from an outdoor spigot, pour the water from the bucket into a sprinkler, and then sprinkle the nearby grass. After carefully repeating this arduous sequence five times without getting herself or the house wet, her serious face was replaced with a broad smile as she exclaimed, "Isn't this fun!" Freud would not have awarded my granddaughter's moment of pride an independent status, believing that she smiled because she was sublimating her repressed libidinal instincts.

Children build sand castles and adults climb rugged mountains because implementing actions that are guided by an idea of perfection is as much a biologically prepared disposition as are the pursuit of sweet tastes and the avoidance of bodily pain. After we have protected ourselves from actual or possible harm, the affirmation of virtue takes precedence over the search for sensory pleasure most of every day. The pursuit and eventual capture of power, status, wealth, romance, and ten-year-old brandy, which contemporary Western society treats as sensory pleasures, can be strategies to affirm one's virtue. In societies where frugality is prized, as in Puritan New England, individuals hide their wealth. In contemporary America, where wealth has become an unconflicted sign of virtue, one feels obligated to display it. A winter holiday in the Caribbean serves a motive to do what one ought to do as frequently as it serves the wish to avoid blizzards. "I am doing what I should be doing" is often the silent voice behind the louder declaration, "I am doing what I enjoy." What looks like a search for sensory pleasure can sometimes disguise a search for virtue. Indeed, the advice "live for the moment" is interpreted as a moral imperative by those who are unsure what they should be doing after breakfast. The congestion, noise, unshaded heat, and aridity of Las Vegas are not very conducive to sensory pleasure. The popularity of this city therefore must be based in part on the ethical belief that one ought to sample new experiences. This imperative, which is an integral part of the American canon, renders a visit to what used to be called sin city an ethical act.

Defenders of capitalism in the seventeenth and eighteenth centuries claimed that a passionate involvement in making money would not only replace aggression, gluttony, and whoring but would also constrain the arbitrary despotism of rulers and bring civility to society.[6] Listen to John D. Rockefeller in a 1905 interview: "I believe the power to make money is a gift from God ... It is my duty to make money." Getting rich was a moral enterprise. But the increasing misery and anomie among urban peasants created by unbridled capitalism prompted many to reevaluate the ethical halo surrounding this goal. During the second half of this century, legal restraints imposed on robber barons, combined with the absence of other attractive virtues to celebrate, have restored virtue to the accumulation of wealth.

Our government's attempt to bring small businesses to ghettos in order to reduce crime by providing work opportunities for welfare recipients is a modern example of Adam Smith's argument that work makes people better citizens. However, this strategy can be successful only if the poor agree that work makes them feel more virtuous. Smith would have been puzzled by the shameless announcement of poverty by homeless adults begging money from clients entering a bank. He was certain that everyone would be mortified by such a confession of distress.[7]

Montesquieu and Smith were right about the basis for nascent capitalism, but not because a desire for money replaced the desire for idleness, gluttony, or plunder. Rather, it was because gaining wealth had acquired moral authority. A merchant who prices his goods so low that his profit is minimal will feel uneasy because he is not acting in accord with what he should be doing. Few, if any, life goals escape a moral gloss. Cynical essays in *The New Yorker* implying that anyone who places faith in the honesty of politicians is a fool are declaring that a skeptical suspicion of rhetoric is a morally praiseworthy attitude.

Although the content of every set of moral standards is tied to time and place, the desire to believe that self is ethically worthy, like the ability to understand language, is universal. Humans are the only species that applies a symbolic evaluation of good or bad to actions, thoughts, feelings, and personal characteristics and tries continually to choose acts that make it easier to regard the self as good. Both Darwin and Linnaeus, the great taxonomist, recognized this truth. Darwin wrote: "I fully subscribe to the judgment of those writers who maintain that of all the differences between man and the lower animals, the moral sense or conscience is by far the most important." Linnaeus struggled with how to classify humans but finally recognized that their moral sense made them unique: "I well know what a splendidly great difference there is between a man and a bestia when I look at them from a point of view of morality."[8] The ancient distinction between body and soul acknowledged this uniquely human quality. Unfortunately, the conceptual mistake of treating the origin of the soul as qualitatively different from that of the body blocked a fuller understanding of human nature. A moral motive and its attendant emotions are as obvious a product of biological evolution as digestion and respiration.

Some anthropologists define culture as a group that shares moral values. The fact that every society has a moral code implies that a concern with good and bad is a biologically prepared characteristic. The specific content of that code is influenced by historical, religious, and economic factors. Although some cultures forbid eating pigs while others forbid eating cows, all cultures have taboos which, when violated, render the agent less virtuous. A childless woman in the People's Republic of China who has lost her husband attains virtue if she commits suicide as a way to publicize her faithfulness.[9] The pair of statements the ancient Greeks inscribed at the oracle in Delphi—*Know thyself* and *Nothing in excess*—were moral commands, not mathematical axioms. The ancient Greeks valued rational control of natural impulse, especially the lust of Eros. A youth who let his tutor embrace him, or permitted intercrural intercourse, violated no moral precept. But if the same youth became aroused by the embrace or permitted the older man anal penetration, he would have violated a community ethic and would have felt ashamed.[10]

The experiences of the anthropologist Richard Shweder in a temple town in India demonstrate the power of cultural taboos, even for adults who were not raised with those beliefs. Shweder and his American wife had invited some members of the community for dinner. Because the three guests were of different status, it was important to serve food that all could eat without sanction. One permissible food was a dish of rice and vegetables that had been placed in a temple as a gift to one of the gods. The anthropologist went to the temple and asked the Brahman priest for food from which a god had already removed the spirit. The dinner was successful but there was considerable rice left after the guests had departed. Shweder's wife diced some chicken into the bowl and served it. Shweder confessed that he suddenly felt revulsion because the presence of the chicken violated a local taboo. He was unable to eat it.

Shweder and his colleagues have suggested that most moral standards can be grouped into one of three large categories. The first, most prevalent in America and Europe, awards sanctity to individual autonomy. No one should infringe on another person's liberty. A second class awards sanctity to the social web in which each person lives and urges loyalty and nurturance to kin, friends, and community. The third category prohibits the violation of natural or divine order; the desecration of a human body and incest are obvious examples.[11]

The specific ethics of a community often change with time. Few contemporary American fathers would follow the seventeenth-century practice of urging their nine-year-old daughters to be meek, modest, silent, and frugal.[12] Thomas Hobbes, who thought morality should aid civility, asserted that seventeenth-century citizens should give up some of their autonomy to a sovereign. John Rawls, writing over three hundred years later, believed that a communitarian concern for the economically disadvantaged should take precedence. This last view is free of Leibniz's elitist implication that only the wise can know who should be cared for. Most moralists writing at the end of the twentieth century urge only tolerance, which is an easier stance to adopt because it does not require empathy or compassion.[13]

My purpose here is not prescriptive. I am not concerned primarily with defending particular intentions, feelings, or actions as most worthy, even though human biology makes a small number of standards easy to acquire. Rather, my intent is to explore the psychology of the human agent and the universal desire to regard self as good and, as a consequence, to think and act in ways that support rather than disconfirm that evaluation. I wish to explore the notion that what is moral has always been a pervasive human preoccupation, while refraining from judgments of good, better, best. I am even tempted to suggest that the continuous seeking of evidence to prove one's virtue is, like Darwin's notion of natural selection, the most potent condition sculpting each person's traits over their lifetime.

The evolution of *Homo sapiens* was marked by the emergence, between the second and third birthdays, of an appreciation of the symbolic categories good and bad which children subsequently apply to the self's actions, thoughts, and feelings. Any information that humans interpret as signifying that they are good or bad has emotional salience. The act *qua* act is far less important than its symbolic evaluation. Killing in self-defense is acceptable; the same act by a robber on a dark night is not. Unlike any other animal, humans continually judge the moral implications of their wishes, behaviors, and feelings.

Experiences that escape this moral scrutiny are difficult to imagine. The historian Hayden White notes that reconstructing the history of any part of the past without moralizing is next to impossible.[14] Novels, critical reviews, plays, autobiographies, historical treatises, and most essays in social science journals implicitly assume that certain states of affairs are good and others are bad.

Those who believe that sensory pleasure is at the root of all morality usually argue, as behaviorists did fifty years ago, that the child experiences a reduction in fear, and therefore an increase in sensory pleasure, when she conforms to adult requests. In time, adherence to family and community standards becomes a habit. This argument is deeply flawed. Many white children born in the rural American South after 1950 lived their first dozen years with affectionate parents who held racist beliefs. In the 1960s and 1970s, when they became adolescents, a majority risked the uncomfortable feeling that follows parental criticism when they rejected their parents' prejudices and adopted more tolerant beliefs. These adolescents were sensitive to the larger culture's definition of the attitudes that brought a sense of virtue. For the same reason, some young adults from affluent families, who could begin lucrative careers in business, law, or medicine in comfortable urban offices, volunteer to work in poor rural villages in Latin America, India, Indonesia, or Africa.

The traditional argument that moral standards are derived from sensory pleasure or the reduction of pain cannot explain the universal fact that people become angry when they see others violate standards they believe are right. Why do we become upset when we see a stranger lie to a tourist or push ahead in a queue when our own lives are unaffected by those rude acts? One explanation is that these asocial acts by one stranger to another provoke bystanders to question the correctness of their own moral beliefs. Because these beliefs are central to each day's decisions and conduct, their violation, even by a stranger, threatens the rational foundation of the observer's ethical code. Not even the cleverest ape could be conditioned to become angry upon seeing one animal steal food from another. Surprise or fear, perhaps, but anger is impossible. The popular writings of Camus and Sartre capture the combination of angst and anger that postwar Europeans felt when they realized that if there was no firm basis for any particular moral evaluation, life was absurd. Although evolutionary biologists insist that the appearance of humans was due to a quirky role of the genetic dice, our species refuses to act as if good and evil are arbitrary choices bereft of natural significance.

The Continuist Premise

Although many philosophers have acknowledged the power of a moral motive, and many playwrights and novelists have made it the central theme of their greatest works, most social scientists and biologists have been less willing to award it an ascendant influence. Ethical truths, as the philosopher Robert Nozick notes, seem to have no place within the contemporary scientific picture of the world.[15]

The pervasive influence of evolutionary theory is one reason for the relative neglect of moral motives and emotions in the biological and social sciences. Most natural scientists, even if they had not read him, would have agreed with T. H. Huxley that no clear line of demarcation between animals and humans exists, and therefore they were unwilling to ascribe to humans any qualities that would render them biologically distinctive.[16] As Darwin's ideas became ascendant during the last decade of the nineteenth century, scientists began to study animals in order to illuminate the human condition, on the assumption that no human psychological function was seriously discontinuous with those possessed by at least one animal species.

In *Beyond the Pleasure Principle*, for example, Freud insisted that the human desire to perfect a talent does not require any process not present in animals. This statement is not even true for human sexuality. But whereas a year in the life of a chimpanzee is composed of the natural cycles of light and dark, rain and sun, eating and rest, fighting and grooming, copulating and nursing, a year in the life of a human is composed of actions intended to maintain family integrity, actualize talents, seek status, and decide which thoughts, actions, and people are good and which bad. Moral preoccupations and the parsing of experience into symbolic categories are dominant features of human existence. I suspect that the experiential envelope of mountain sheep and elephants, despite their distinctive ecologies, might be more similar to one another than those of humans and apes.

Darwin wrote *Descent of Man* a decade after *Origin of Species*, in part, to explain how human morality, which did not seem to him to be particularly adaptive for the individual, might have evolved from animal behavior. Darwin's hunch was that conscience was a derivative of the social behavior of mammals, even though he had written in his notebook thirty years earlier that the origin of the social instincts in man and animals must be considered separately. Hominid evolution added to this social instinct the ability to think about past, present, and future and as a result to experience a conflict between acting on present desires and anticipating the consequences of one's actions for others as well as self. When humans have a choice as to which behavior to display, it is helpful to have a rule to guide selection. Moral standards solve the problem of choice by weighting one action as more virtuous than another.

Rather than make guilt and shame critical to human conscience, Darwin, reflecting the prejudices of his era, nominated language and reason as seminal features in morality. A similar prejudice led Aquinas to insist that reason was the foundation of morality, and Kant to reject feelings as the basis for justifying one's standards. Kant did not believe that such an unpredictable process should be the basis for socially appropriate behavior. People should tell the truth, Kant argued, regardless of how they felt, because they had an obligation to do so.

But I suspect, with Huxley, that feelings are more critical to human morality than language and reason. Each family of animals inherits a special constellation of talents that awards it advantage in its niche. Most birds fly with grace and speed but locomote clumsily on sand. Humans inherited arms and hands well suited to making and throwing spears to kill large animals but far less adequate for strangling them to death. Humans, like chimps, are social animals that use facial expressions and language to serve a species-defining affiliative motive. It is not obvious, however, why reason would serve the retention of social bonds more effectively than shame or guilt.

I suspect that the decision by many European philosophers to base morality on language and reason, rather than feelings, was that evaluating the correctness, coherence, and logical consistency of an argument is relatively easy. Because emotions evade these judgments, most Western philosophers have tried to persuade us that our choices are overdetermined by rational processes. This bias against feelings is absent in many other cultural traditions, and was not shared by John Dewey, who acknowledged that the essence of human experience is the filtering of recollections through a "mesh of imagination so as to suit the demands of the emotions."[17] At the end of the film *The Return of Martin Guerre*, an imposter who claimed he was the husband returning to a wife he had abandoned years earlier is found guilty and hanged. The priest who played a key role in the trial asks the wife why she accepted this man into her bed when she knew he was not her husband. The wife replies, "We were good together."

Although Freud was friendly to a continuist argument and wrote about the importance of smell in both animal and human sexuality, his major concepts could not be applied to any species but our own. The ideas of ego, superego, defense, repression, and oral-anal-phallic fixations have no obvious analogues in monkeys. Similarly, the concepts and procedures that define most current investigations of human personality and development are appropriate only for humans.

Even though many scientists pay lip service to the continuist premise, their daily work is not constrained by that idea. Most psychologists offer homage to the assumption that human behavior is an evolutionary derivative of tendencies that can be observed in monkeys, while they write about characteristics absent in animals, like deductive reasoning, long-term planning, learning disorders, extroversion, obsessions, schizophrenia, and anorexia. This state of affairs is reminiscent of Cranly's advice to Stephen Daedalus in *A Portrait of the Artist as a Young Man*. Cranly tells Stephen that even though he has lost his faith in the symbolic meaning of the Easter Mass, he should attend anyway, because it would make his mother happy.

The invention of powerful methods to study the psychological derivatives of genes and brain physiology in animals emboldened biologists to insist on the validity of the continuist premise implicit in Darwinian theory.[18] The stringent positivist standards in the biological disciplines require a degree of experimental control that can only be achieved with animals. As a result, investigations of fear, perception, memory, and conditioning, all of which can be studied in animals, take precedence over the study of moral motives and emotions, which have no obvious analogue in animals. There can be no mouse model for human pride, shame, or guilt.

Thus, scientists who study behavior are caught on the horns of a dilemma. On the one hand, professional success is more likely if strong experimental methods are used. On the other hand, some of the phenomena discovered with these elegant methods are not very relevant to an understanding of human ethical choice. This issue was the focus of serious debate among American students of animal behavior in the first decade of this century, and of a 1992 editorial in *Science* which questioned the use of inbred strains of rats to determine the carcinogenic potential of particular foods for humans.[19]

Words like cooperate, communicate, steal, murder, and selfish were invented millennia ago to describe human behavior, and the sense and referential meanings of these words are appropriate only to humans. The fact that two monkeys behave as if they are cooperative, simply because both animals benefit from the interaction, is of scientific interest and invites study and explanation. But it is not at all obvious that this behavior possesses the defining features of human cooperation, namely, the agent's simultaneous awareness of both the need of the other and of his ability and obligation to help. A honey bee is not being "cooperative" with a plant when it carries the plant's pollen to another flower. A single, objective similarity between cooperative, aggressive, or selfish behavior in humans and an action in another animal species is extremely easy to detect. But if the psychological foundations of the animal and human behaviors are different, we should reflect carefully before using the same word.

Evolutionary biologists freely borrow terms that were intended to describe human behavior and apply them to animals. I suspect, however, that they would be peeved if students of human behavior called a rhesus female who had copulated with four males in an hour unfaithful. When a husband throws a knife at his wife, we call that act aggressive. But we do not do so when a six-month-old infant throws the same object at his mother because we recognize that an intention to hurt was absent in the latter case. The vast majority of animal species—perhaps all—have no conscious intentions. For that reason, it is misleading and theoretically regressive to describe the animal behavior with words which have intentionality as a primary feature. Otherwise, our hypersexed rhesus female is, indeed, a tart.

This issue is yet another instance of the tension that exists in all sciences between an emphasis on qualitative differences among phenomena and shared features that imply continuity. Some scholars are splitters who prefer analysis; lumpers seek unity. Aristotle, who was fascinated by the uniquenesses he observed in the living world, was a splitter; Galileo, who searched successfully for universal laws in the physical world, was a lumper. The founders of immunology also waged this battle.[20] Robert Koch, the father of bacteriology, was impressed with the structural differences he saw among varied strains of bacteria that caused very different diseases. Karl Landsteiner, on the other hand, working in the early twentieth century, favored continuity among strains because he quantified the magnitude of antibody reactions produced by different bacterial groups. Rats, cats, apes, and humans do share many important structures and functions that imply considerable continuity in evolution, but that fact does not mean that some species cannot possess one or more qualitatively distinct functions that do not share obvious features with their phylogenetic relatives.

The contemporary search for early signs of a conscience in primates could take a lesson from nineteenth-century discussions on the origin of vertebrates. Some naturalists saw similarities between spiders and the first animal with a backbone; others saw stronger similarities with starfish. But all agreed that the first chordates were seriously divergent from both spiders and starfish. Although a frog's legs are derivatives of the pectoral fins of fish, the two body parts obviously differ in structure and function. The same is true for human conscience. An appreciation of right and wrong and its attendant feelings probably have a distant origin in the monkey's continual vigilance toward the actions, expressions, and vocal calls of others. But the human moral sense is, like frog legs, so dramatically different from the phylogenetically older competence it is an error to regard one as an obvious derivative of the other. The human sensitivity to changes in the face and gesture of another may be on a continuum with a disposition present in our primate ancestors. But the human moral motive is qualitatively distinct because it contains symbolic and emotional elements that are not present in any primate.

Many writers follow Darwin and place the origins of human conscience in social exchange, insisting that no individual acts unless he stands to gain some external prize.[21] That principle may be true for animals; it is not always true for humans. The symbolic private assurance that one is virtuous—given by the self to the self—is an attractive prize humans seek. That urge is absent in the most cooperative nonhuman species.

Because all theories imply more than is known, it is not surprising that over a century after *On the Origin of Species* challenged the biblical dogma that humans were unique, we have to be reminded of those human qualities, maintained by natural selection, that are not found in other animals. A moral motive, which represents a sharp break with our phylogenetic past, is not simply a complex version of worker bees helping the hive survive or a chimp standing quietly, head bowed, over a dead member of the troop. The reluctance to acknowledge the uniqueness of the human moral motive is a bit odd because biologists acknowledge unique traits in a large number of species. The spinning of webs by spiders, echolocation in bats, and imprinting in precocial birds are restricted to a particular genus or species. Unique characteristics are totally consistent with Darwinian theory.

Nonetheless, there remains an inexplicably stubborn resistance to treating any human quality as unique. If a linguist claims that only humans have a language with a grammar, some scientist will reply that chimpanzees can be taught to communicate with pieces of plastic. Jane Goodall's discovery that chimpanzees use tools is celebrated because of the pleasing implication that my use of a hammer to hang my granddaughter's recent artwork on the wall is not fundamentally different from a chimpanzee's use of a twig to ferret out termites. The modern synthesis in evolutionary biology does not demand that every feature which defines a particular phylum, order, family, genus, or species have a homologous structure or function in a related taxon. The chick embryo provided unique insights into embryological development that were not possible through the study of frog larvae.[22] Echolocation in bats has no strict homologue in beavers; the distribution of work in a beehive has no homologue in a beaver colony; and the construction of spider webs has no homologue in crabs.

Scientists work on animal models to study alcoholism, anxiety, dyslexia, depression, and aggression using invasive techniques that cannot be implemented with children or adults. One popular example is the study of an infant monkey's reaction to separation from its mother, or from other monkeys, on the assumption that the state produced by separation is analogous to the anxiety children experience when exposed to a variety of stressors. The rationale behind this careful work requires some faith that the investigator will uncover facts that will inform the human condition; its value would be compromised somewhat if the various forms of human anxiety were not analogous to the state created in an infant monkey separated from its mother. Yet that possibility cannot be dismissed.

Infant monkeys reared only with plastic horses wrapped in fur became attached to them and behaved like infants who had been raised with living dogs. This surprising result prompted the investigators to conclude, "The differential effects of living with inanimate attachment figures on the attachment process per se are less distinct and consequential for rhesus monkeys than are the influences on the development of individuals' responsiveness to the environment."[23] Human infants raised in a room with only a plastic toy would develop profoundly abnormal social behavior.

Children evaluate separation from a parent, and their judgment includes the relevance of that separation for the child's sense of virtue. Consider a thought experiment: Two five-year-olds from different homes are sent to foster homes. In one case, the parents died in an auto accident, while in the other case the parents got a divorce and neither one wanted the child. If all other things are equal, the emotional health of the child from the divorced family will be at much greater risk than that of the orphan because of the implications the child would draw from parental rejection. Monkeys, by contrast, would suffer from only the loss of the parent; they would not be able to symbolically evaluate the causes of that loss. Hence, separation from a parent has more uniform consequences in monkeys than in humans.

It is not obvious that any animal is a useful model for understanding human guilt and shame. The best way to understand dominance hierarchies in monkeys is to study monkeys; the best way to understand the human moral motive and its accompanying emotions is to study humans—there can be no shortcuts. I do not suggest that research on animals has no value. Animal research has given us a clearer understanding of our circadian rhythms and the genetic bases for many diseases. Animals and humans do share many features. But they do not share all of them. The domains with the least commonality involve intentions, values, and behaviors associated with anxiety, shame, guilt, and pride. The animal evidence does little to inform these human states. An editorial in *The Economist*, commenting on recent advances in evolutionary biology, criticized the imperialistic attitude held by some who insist that animal behavior can explain most human action: "Darwinism is good," the writer noted, "but not that good."[24]

The concern with human morality cycles with the level of civility in the society. The brutish character of Europe in the seventeenth century prompted Hobbes to defend a strong central authority in order to control human greed, aggression, and murder. The English had become a bit gentler by the early decades of the nineteenth century, when John Stuart Mill urged the moral priority of personal liberty. In the view of many, American society during the last third of this century has reached a new low of incivility; we have experienced levels of dishonesty, fraud, narcissism, and senseless violence that threaten the average citizen. In response, some scientists, who as a group usually find philosophy boring, have turned their interest to morality in order to reassure us that a motive to be good is not an acquired trait which has to be taught anew to every generation but is an intrinsic component of our species. These include Richard Alexander, E. O. Wilson, Frans de Waal, James Q. Wilson, and Ernst Mayr.[25]

De Waal presents rich anecdotes of chimpanzee behavior to persuade readers that these attractive animals possess rules and punish fellow chimpanzees who break them. De Waal concedes, however, that he has never seen a guilty chimpanzee. He never will see one, because guilt requires an agent to know, simultaneously, that a voluntary act has hurt another and that he could have suppressed it. There is a possibility that chimpanzees can recognize another animal in distress and perhaps appreciate, in a primitive way, that an action they initiated caused the distress. But as Yerkes and Koehler realized seventy years ago, chimpanzees cannot reflect on that sequence and conclude that events could have been otherwise.[26] Guilt requires the ability to infer the state of others, to reflect on a past action, to compare the products of that reflection with acquired standards, to realize that a particular action that violated a standard could have been inhibited and, finally, to evaluate the self as a consequence of that violation. Guilt is not a possible state for chimpanzees.

Indeed, these animals are unable to make much simpler inferences. For example, they do not assume that a blind-folded adult cannot see their actions.[27] Further, no scientist has ever observed a chimp in its natural habitat point to a distant object when another chimp was nearby, suggesting that they do not infer that another individual can learn something from their actions. Moreover, chimps who see a person point to a place where a desirable object has just been hidden fail to conclude that they should reach to that location. Two-year-old humans make that inference at once.[28]

More convincing is an experiment in which a small and a large amount of a tasty food are placed in front of a chimpanzee. If he grabs the smaller one first, he will be given the larger one, but if he grabs the larger one first, he is not allowed to eat anything. Chimpanzees have a difficult time learning what they should do to get the larger amount of food.[29] A three-year-old child learns the correct response to this simple problem in a minute or two because she figures out the novel rule that the examiner is using. The abilities to infer the intentions, thoughts, and feelings of another—animal or human—are unique innovations in the hominid line that were denied to chimps and the common ancestor we shared with them.

Those who argue that the origins of human ethics can be detected in animal behaviors fail to tell us which species we should select as a guide. Gibbons pair bond but chimps do not. Rhesus live in troops while orangutans are solitary. Thus, it is not clear whether humans are predisposed to be faithful to their mate or promiscuous, social or solitary. Nevertheless, we are eager to read books about an ethical sense in our hairy kin because they assure us that conformity to social rules is not an arbitrary posture that we can dismiss easily. The animal observations are interpreted to imply that the human respect for rules is such a fundamental feature of our evolution that it is sensible, and not odd, that each of us prefers to obey the law and feels a bit apprehensive if we do not. The media remind us daily of deceitful politicians, dishonest scientists, murderous schoolmistresses, fraudulent physicians, embezzling bankers, and mathematicians who send bombs in the mail. Are we who are law abiding a strange, deviant group who do not know that our natural inclination is to lie, cheat, and kill? De Waal reassures us, correctly, that the lawbreakers, not we, are the freaks. When we arrive at work on time, pay bills, and help old people cross the street, we are being neither deviant nor stodgy but loyal to our primate nature. That soothing message temporarily quiets our doubts and permits us to continue our ethical ways with the assurance that there is justice in the world and that too much self-interest will exact a price.[30]

The contemporary mood of uncertainty over a biologically prepared moral sense, which Plato would not have understood, has rendered those who seriously violate social rules titillating. Humans are aroused by and interested in ideas and events that are moderate transformations of what is familiar. In a society where most people believe that the majority are law abiding and not planning robbery, rape, murder, or child abuse, reflection on these asocial acts elicits some anxiety and we do not dwell long on these ideas. Hollywood does not make expensive movies about cannibalism or a father sodomizing his son because those scenes would bother most Americans. But dishonesty, torture, murder, arrogance, deceit, and narcissism, which are always with us, are being cleansed of some of their earlier moral revulsion. The prevalence of these behaviors has permitted Americans to think about these acts and to pass from a state of aversion, terror, or disgust to one of curious interest. These themes now sit in a narrow space characterized by uncertainty. They titillate us in the same way that films filled with carnal sex did in the 1960s.

The happy prediction is that we will in time become bored with these ideas because they will have exhausted their novelty. Indeed, as honesty, politeness, and control of anger become less familiar in urban America, they may become the major themes of our plays, books, and movies because they will possess the same degree of strangeness that senseless violence does today. Perhaps the current popularity of movies based on the novels of Jane Austen and Henry James, as well as television dramas about angels, are early signs of the accuracy of this prediction.

The Emergence of a Moral Sense

The human capacity for a moral motive and its associated emotions took from our primate ancestry a keen sensitivity to the voice, face, and actions of others but added five unique abilities: (1) to infer the thoughts and feelings of others, (2) to be self-aware, (3) to apply the categories good and bad to events and to self, (4) to reflect on past actions, and (5) to know that a particular act could have been suppressed. The combination of these five talents created a novel system that first emerges in children in the second year and matures during the decade that follows.

Adults living in diverse isolated societies recognize that as children reach the end of the second year they know that some actions will provoke adult disapproval. Some cultures interpret this new stage as the result of a cognitive advance that permits two-year-olds to understand the meaning of right and wrong. Parents in these societies will tell informants that the child's new knowledge was a developmental inevitability that did not require direct teaching. It is likely that the human mind is prepared to learn words which name the feelings that form the foundations of the symbolic categories good and bad. This competence is similar to the three-month-old's perceptual bias to look longer at objects in motion, designs with a circular shape, a sharp contour, and the color red, and to listen more attentively to intermittent rather than continuous sounds and to consonant rather than dissonant melodies.

This suggestion that human morality is a biologically prepared competence is analogous to the position of some mathematicians and philosophers that the concept of number and the rules of arithmetic are not arbitrary inventions and therefore are intuitively easy to grasp. The opposing position, called formalism, claims that mathematics is simply one set of rules that humans invented and passed along to their children, and that other rules could have been generated and applied successfully to the physical world. Some ethicists argue that the knowledge that destroying another's property is morally wrong is universal. Others insist that this ethic, and a host of others, are cultural inventions and it would be easy to teach children that destruction of property is a perfectly acceptable behavior.

The first signs of a moral competence can be observed in every home with children. A two-year-old looks warily toward a parent after spilling juice on the floor. The child's face and posture announce that she has committed an act that violates what she knows to be proper. One-year-olds who spill juice do not show this anticipation of parental disapproval, even though their parents have chastised them for this act. One-year-olds have had many opportunities to learn that acts which destroy the integrity of property are unacceptable, but their cognitive abilities are simply not mature enough to connect the symbolic meaning of their action with adult disapproval. Something happens in the mind/brain of children in the second year to make them sensitive to the propriety of their behavior. I suspect that the psychological changes that occur between one and two years of age are as profound as those that occurred when the hominid line split off from its closest primate ancestors.

All animals are biologically prepared to react in specific ways to particular events. Humans, like other primates, are prepared to be exceptionally sensitive to subtle changes in the face, voice, and gestures of others. The child is especially sensitive to the parents' face and voice. During most of the day, the mother's face is emotionally neutral and the voice has a similar rhythm, timbre, and loudness. Most two-year-olds have acquired a firm representation of the facial and vocal pattern that occurs when a parent talks to them. But occasionally the mother's face assumes an expression of disapproval and her voice rises in intensity as she says, "No, don't do that." That discrepant event is not immediately understandable and creates uncertainty.

A two-year-old has just pulled a tablecloth from the kitchen table and brought to the floor two full glasses of milk. The parent responds with an explosive, "No, I told you to be careful." The child is surprised by the parent's reaction because he does not initially connect it to his prior behavior. If the child does not understand the parental response within a second or two, he will experience a temporary state of fear. It will not take many similar experiences to teach the two-year-old to connect his prior action with the surprising parental reaction and a feeling of uncertainty when he thinks of committing the act. Once that association has been learned, the thought of a similar behavioral violation becomes a conditioned incentive for a state of uncertainty. Adam Smith thought that this special form of worry over other people's evaluations remained the foundation of adult morality.

Two problems remain. Why does it take almost two years for this competence to emerge? And why does a child begin to impose a good/bad evaluation not only on acts that have been punished directly but also on behaviors that have not yet been chastised? John Locke's view that all morality has to be taught is wrong.

Although the one-year-old has experienced the changes in face and voice that communicate parental displeasure, she is not mature enough to infer that breaking objects, dirtying clothes, and yelling at the dinner table, although followed by disapproval, belong to a unified category of "bad acts." In order to infer the category of improper or bad acts, the child has to discover the connections among three different events— her actions, the outcomes of those actions, and especially the parent's subsequent reactions to the child. Creation of this category is delayed because the ability to make inferences based on a temporal sequence of complex events is fragile in the first year. The young mind is simply not mature enough to discover the sophisticated concept "punishable behavior."

This new maturational competence, however, does not explain why children impose a symbolic good/bad label on punished actions, usually aggression toward others, destruction of property, persistent disobedience, and chronic failure to keep the body clean. An answer to that question requires more speculation. A state of uncertainty to discrepant events that cannot be understood is a biologically prepared reaction that invites a name when, toward the end of the second year, children become aware of their feelings. When the feeling of uncertainty pierces awareness, the child is motivated to name it. The symbolic label the child applies is probably very close in sense meaning to the adult understanding of the word "bad." By the second birthday, many children categorize as bad those acts that are followed by signs of adult disapproval.

Children also create representations of the normal appearances of objects and notice those that deviate from normal. A child who sees a broken toy assumes that an action by another must have caused the flaw. Because breaking a toy is bad, the broken toy itself is also bad. For the same reason, a pile of salt on the table and a shirt with no buttons are bad. The referent for the concept bad, therefore, is a large family of events whose primary features are the child's feeling of uncertainty in the face of adult disapproval, discrepant experiences that cannot be understood, physical pain, loss of some object or person to which the child is attached, frustration, and anticipation of harm. The feelings created by these varied events are discernibly different. No two-year-old confuses the feeling of frustration over losing a toy to an older child with a stomach cramp, a stern warning, or a shirt with no buttons. But because the child wishes to avoid each of these feelings, all are instances of the child's new category "bad."

Similarly, a family of feelings represents the complementary category "good." These include events that generate pleasant sensations of taste, touch, and smell; praise from adults; objects or people to which the child is attached; attainment of a goal following effort; and assimilation of a discrepant event. Each of these experiences produces a distinctive feeling, but all share the fact that children wish to attain them, and therefore any instance of this category is regarded as "good."

No particular feeling is the primary basis for the categories good or bad, and no one feeling state represents the average of all of them. There are only particular emotional referents for each member of the two categories. This state of affairs is not different from our understanding of the symbolic category "strong." People are strong if they can lift heavy objects; ideas are strong if they can evoke an emotion; trees are strong if they cannot be moved easily; and tastes are strong if they are intense. People, ideas, trees, and tastes are strong in their own way. The concepts good and bad, which emerge in the second year, are similar inventions.

The ability to empathize with another who is in distress, which also emerges in the second year, has direct relevance for morality. Two boys, almost sixteen months old, were fighting over a toy. When one began to cry, the other released the toy; but when the boy with the toy continued to cry, the other ran to another room, retrieved the crying child's favorite toy, and gave it to him. This sequence required the inference that the crying child was distressed and could be consoled. The chimps of the Gombe National Park, by contrast, reacted to a chimp paralyzed by polio with fear and later with attack. Two-year-old children have a capacity to infer the thoughts and feelings of another and will show signs of tension if another person is hurt, or may offer penance if they caused another's distress. As a result, an intention to hurt another leads to an anticipation of the unpleasant feelings the other might experience and (more often than not) to suppression of the asocial act. This developmental fact is not completely consistent with the view, popular among philosophers like David Hume and biologists like Jacques Monod, that moral values cannot be derived from objective knowledge.[31] The appearance of empathy in all children by the end of the second year implies that two-year-olds are prepared by their biology to regard hurting others as bad—that is, a moral violation.

Most two-year-olds are also aware of the fact that they are individuals with particular characteristics, feelings, and intentions. When this aspect of self-awareness appears, children apply the labels good and bad to self, as they have been doing for objects and acts during the past six months. If self is a bad object, the child is vulnerable to the same feeling states that are linked to actions classified as bad. When the child recognizes that she is an object for which one of these descriptors is apt, she will try to avoid accruing more evidence that might suggest that bad is an appropriate adjective for her. She begins to understand that when she is bad, she produces unpleasant feelings in others in the same way that bad objects or events produce unpleasant feelings in herself, and she concludes that, as a consequence, others will avoid her.

That insight is a seminal origin of the moral motive, although it will not be the only basis for morality in later years. A desire to avoid, or to deny, the labeling of self as bad increases in intensity as the child matures; in time, it will take precedence over fear of disapproval or punishment as the primary governor of behavior. Freud recognized the importance of this advance but was unwilling to compromise the theoretical relation of id to ego. Hence, he declared simply that the superego—which for Freud represented the ego's resistance to committing acts that would lead the person to regard the self as bad—emerges in all children as a byproduct of growth.

Most four-year-old children hesitated when asked to spill juice on a laboratory table, indicating they were aware that this act was a violation of a standard they learned at home. One-year-olds did not hesitate. Four-year-olds were also asked to tear up a full-color photograph of a woman who said to the child, "This is my favorite picture. Tear up my favorite picture." A few children gave the picture back to the examiner, saying, "No, it's your favorite picture." These children could not be certain they would not be chastised for disobeying the examiner's request—they had conformed to a series of requests for several minutes. But these children treated the request to tear up the photo as too serious a violation of their understanding of what was right and therefore risked disapproval by refusing to comply. The children wished to avoid the subjective uncertainty that would follow if they obeyed the examiner's request.[32]

Although three-year-olds are aware that objects, events, acts, and the self can be good or bad, they remain protected from the feeling of guilt that follows recognition that they could have suppressed the act that violated a personal standard. That insight must await a later advance in cognitive growth. Children under five years of age have difficulty controlling their actions. When children of different ages were asked to say "night" when they saw a picture of a sun and "day" when they saw a picture of a moon, the three-to-four-year-olds had great difficulty inhibiting the natural tendency to say "night" to the moon and "day" to the sun. By contrast, six-to-seven-year-olds found this task extremely easy.[33] If four-year-olds cannot control many of their simple actions, they are unlikely to assume blame for most of their mistakes.

The two-year-old knows that breaking a vase is wrong but has no conception that the act which broke the vase could have been avoided. The six-year-old, however, can rerun the behavioral sequence mentally and decide whether the damage could have been prevented. If he believes he could have avoided the accident, he is likely to experience guilt.[34] The father of a shy five-year-old who was aware that her parents wanted her to control her timidity reported that when both of them were walking on an unfamiliar street, the child said to her father: "Let's pretend you are a stranger and I will walk ahead of you. I have to practice being brave." The cognitive sophistication that permits the six-year-old to conclude that if he had not run in the living room, the vase would not have been broken and therefore he is responsible for the accident involves the ability to integrate past, present, and future in a seamless structure. This talent, which Piaget called reversibility, is the heart of the developmental stage he called concrete operations.

Positing a biological foundation for the human moral sense does not imply that one particular ethical system is more natural than another, any more than positing a biological foundation for language implies a preference for one grammar. A concern with right and wrong is an easy classification for children to learn because of the fundamental nature of the human brain, but the specific actions that are deemed moral vary with cultural conditions that lie beyond the genome's reach. Trust, mistrust, brutal honesty, polite civility, defending family honor, and turning the other cheek have been promoted at different times as compelling moral arguments. Although the range of moral choices is limited by our biological nature, the ethical possibilities are greater than many suppose. The writer Louis Menand reminds us that we have to figure out for ourselves what we ought and ought not to do: "Go ahead, ask your genes what to do. You might as well be asking Zeus."[35]

Identification, Self-Esteem, and Virtue

Although shame and guilt are biologically prepared, developmentally timed emotions, there is considerable variation, across individuals and cultures, in the frequency and intensity of these states. The majority of modern Europeans and North Americans believe that their status, accomplishments, and wealth are mainly a function of their personal efforts. As a result, failure to attain the social position, talent, or material prosperity they had set as life goals renders them vulnerable to shame or guilt. By contrast, the majority of peasants in small, medieval European villages assumed that their social and economic status was determined by relatively rigid class boundaries; hence, they had less reason to feel guilty over their adult status. The burden of guilt is also lighter among adults living in cultures that believe in sorcery, witches, or demons.

Feelings of guilt can also be enhanced by identification with one's family or social group. If a child is identified with a parent who has done something bad—for example, the mother was criticized by a neighbor for being cruel to a puppy—the child is tempted to conclude that she too possesses an undesirable quality. If, in addition, the child experiences vicariously the emotion that is appropriate for the parent, this conclusion will be more painful.

As American society has become more tolerant of minority ethnic and religious groups, these social categories have lost some of the stigma attached to them before World War II, and other social categories have assumed an enhanced significance. The state of being poor, which is a distinctive feature in America, possesses more psychological relevance for today's children than it did during the Depression of the 1930s, when one third of Americans were poor and the gap in wealth between the top and bottom third of the population was much smaller. The twelve-year-old living in a family of poverty, aware of the implications of his economic status, is tempted to infer that his family possesses undesirable qualities that prevent it from attaining greater affluence. If a child of poverty is fortunate enough to have some protective category, the shame can be diluted. Frank McCourt recalled that his impoverished Irish family was forced to rely on charity to survive. But McCourt also remembered his father reminding him that his pedigree consisted of courageous, God-fearing Irish Catholic men who fought honorably against the British in defense of Ireland's freedom. Too many poor American children can use neither religious, national, nor ethnic pride to dilute the embarrassment that poverty creates. Although it may help the adolescent to shift some of the blame for his family's poverty to the broader society, many adolescents growing up in poverty are unable to escape entirely from feeling demeaned, frustrated, and envious of the more affluent middle-class majority.

Economically stressed African Americans live with two potential sources of vulnerability—being poor and being black. When Michael Jordan is hailed as one of the country's most talented athletes, African-American children experience a moment of pride. But when the media publicize an African-American man imprisoned for a brutal murder, the sense of virtue among some African-American children can suffer. The comparable consequences for white children are considerably less intense. Although it helps the black adolescent's sense of virtue to shift some of the basis for the stigma of poverty to the broader society, it is difficult to shift completely. Hence, many feel anger at a white middle-class majority who are perceived as the cause of a state that is simultaneously frustrating and demeaning. The anger of some African-Americans and the anxiety and counterhostility of some whites represent America's most serious problems. They are affecting our politics, educational institutions, and national mood, and must be repaired.

The absence of widespread moral outrage among the middle class over the impaired health and psychological state of so many poor children, and their reluctance to demand public support for benevolent interventions, are puzzling. If humans have a moral sense, why do the majority not feel sufficiently guilty over this state of affairs to demand change? One reason is that a majority of Americans also hold an ethical standard which demands that every adult who is cognitively competent be responsible for his or her actions. If an individual does not act responsibly when he has the choice, then, as Plato argued, he is morally flawed. A seventy-year-old patient with Alzheimer's disease is clearly not responsible for that affliction; therefore, the community is willing to spend public funds to help. Americans are a trifle more ambivalent about ten-year-olds who cannot read, but most citizens give these children the benefit of the doubt and support the cost of remedial educational efforts. But a mother who fails to nurture her child and to socialize civil habits is placed in a different category, regardless of her economic circumstances. Most Americans believe that she had a choice, blame her failure of will, and therefore are unwilling to aid her.

Because community empathy for these children depends on the truth of that conclusion, it is important to ask: Are most mothers living in poverty who do not have a high school diploma capable of exercising their will and of nurturing and socializing their children in ways that will aid their psychological growth? Although the scientific answer to that question is still uncertain, many citizens in our society have concluded that the answer is yes. Sadly, that moral judgment, not material stinginess, mutes a natural sympathy for the children of the poor.

Many teachers believe that children who are aggressive, emotionally labile, or frightened behave this way because of low self-esteem. The concept of self-esteem was invented as a way to explain a person's confidence, or lack of it, in approaching and coping with each day's challenges. The idea implies that each individual unconsciously computes an average of the distance between each of their important qualities and the associated ideal. Self-esteem is supposed to represent that average. There is, however, a more accurate way to describe some of the children who are angry, emotionally labile, or anxious than to say their self-esteem is low. Many of these individuals recognize, unconsciously, that they have failed to attain the qualities they regard as good. Their flawed sense of virtue motivates the public traits that are the defining features of low self-esteem.

A serious problem with the concept of self-esteem is the belief that individuals are aware of this quality; hence, their answers to direct questions are assumed to be accurate. The most popular approach to measuring self-esteem is to ask people about their personal qualities. However, some children with life histories suggesting that they should have low self-esteem (for example, adolescent boys who have no friends and are failing in school) vehemently deny that ascription when asked directly.

Although the concept of self-esteem has minimal theoretical value, it does have some pragmatic utility. It avoids reference to a person's failure to live up to their own or community standards and implies instead that uncertainty, anxiety, and shame are the products of how a person has been treated by others. Low self-esteem, it is believed, is caused by the critical actions of others rather than the child's evaluation of his moral lapses. If children are members of minority groups, the implication is that the prejudices of the majority produced their uneasy state.

A second practical reason for retaining the concept of self-esteem is that it offers the hope for benevolent change. It is grounded in the belief that large numbers of anxious, failing, timid, or angry children and adolescents can be helped with a proper dose of benign experiences. A focus on self-esteem allows American social scientists to place the origins of a person's traits in the actions of others and to argue that we can change the individual by altering his or her social conditions. Teachers retain the faith that, regardless of a person's past, we should never close down the possibility of a better future. They point to Lincoln's poverty, Roosevelt's polio, and Helen Keller's sensory impairments. If these individuals could overcome the burdens of their past, anyone can.

Bodily Tone and Virtue

The quality of a person's bodily tone, which is influenced by inherited temperamental characteristics, is a more subtle process that can influence a person's sense of virtue. The spontaneous activity in muscles, heart, arteries, gut, and skin is transmitted from body to brain. The sensory information generated by these bodily targets passes first through the medulla, where neurons with opioid receptors can mute the intensity of the signal. This information is sent to the amygdala and from there to a part of the frontal lobe called the ventromedial prefrontal cortex. If the information pierces consciousness, it motivates an interpretation of the change in feeling. When the ventromedial prefrontal cortex is damaged or removed for medical reasons, the heart no longer informs the head of its moral imperatives, and behavior may lose its prior civility. There is reason to suspect that the right hemisphere is more sensitive to this bodily information than the left, and anxious adults are more accurate than most in detecting the number of heart beats in a given time interval.[36]

The popular, and intuitively reasonable, view of the relation between thought and guilt is that a person reflects on an act (or idea) that is a violation of a standard and, as a consequence, experiences a moment of guilt or shame. The corollary is that those who feel more chronic, or more intense, guilt must have violated personal standards more often, either in deed or mind. This interpretation matches our subjective experience—guilt can follow a misdeed within seconds—and therefore has tempted theorists to treat it as the only sequence. However, a serious problem with this view is that many civil, loyal, and law-abiding individuals feel chronic guilt, while many who are rude, hostile, and aggressive appear to feel no guilt whatsoever.

A speculative, but interesting, hypothesis is that individuals who possess a bodily tone which causes them to feel irritability, tension, apprehension, anxiety, vigilance, or uneasiness frequently will be motivated to understand why they feel this way. A frequent first guess about the source of their uneasiness, especially in our society, is that they probably violated one of their ethical standards. The person wonders if she was rude to a friend, told a white lie, harbored a prejudice, or realized, once again, that she has not made enough of her life. The list of possible moral lapses is so long that few people will have trouble finding some ethical flaw to explain the unwelcome feeling and, as a consequence, will experience a moment of guilt. However, the fortunate adults who inherit a less dysphoric bodily tone, or one subdued in intensity, will have less reason to brood about their brief fall from grace and, as a result, should carry a lighter burden of guilt and a surer sense of their virtue. So, too, will those from cultures who attribute power to witches and sorcerers or to climate and diet.

Depression is often accompanied by conscious feelings of guilt for failing to live up to one's standard of virtue. But because most depressed patients do not violate personal standards more often or more seriously than healthier adults, it is possible that the brain physiology that contributed in a causal way to the depressed mood also produced the dysphoric bodily tone. The patient, seeking to understand the dysphoria, attributes it to past sins—disloyalty, infidelity, less-than-perfect performance on a task, failure to gain a sign of status, or rejection because one did not meet another's expectations. These moral lapses are committed by everyone, but only a very small number become depressed. Hence, an important origin for the guilt that precedes some bouts of depression may be the dysphoric body tone, rather than serious moral errors.[37]

This argument bears a resemblance to the view of emotions put forward by William James and Carl Lange, who independently arrived at the hypothesis that each person uses sensory feedback from their body to decide what emotion they are feeling.[38] Students are given the example of the hiker who sees a bear, runs, and interprets the feedback from his flight to conclude that he is afraid. James and Lange may have made an error of omission by not applying this constructive idea to the emotion of guilt. A state of depression need not always be the result of serious violations of personal standards but, on occasion, is created from a search for the cause of chronic dysphoric feelings. The search can lead to the conclusion that the unhappy mood is due to failure to live up to a personal standard.

I am not suggesting that this sequence occurs in all, or even in most, cases of depression. For some patients, the sequence is, first, a profound loss or failure followed by a depression. We do not know at present what proportion of patients belong to each of these different etiological groups. The acute depression that lasts a few months is more often due to loss or failure, while the chronically depressed person is more likely to belong to the former group, as Burton implied over three hundred years ago in his classic *Anatomy of Melancholy*. This suggestion remains speculative because of the lack of sensitive methods to measure quality of bodily tone. But the belief that genes control the development of the embryo was also speculative in 1900. Biologists had to wait almost eighty years for the invention of methods that would affirm the validity of that idea.

Many inhibited children, who avoid unfamiliar people and situations, reported as adolescents that their greatest fear was to be criticized by others. These children, many of whom possessed high sympathetic tone, often displayed extreme emotional reactions when criticized by parents for minor misbehavior. The bodily tone of these children may have been similar to that of an eighteenth-century American girl, Mary Summer, who kept a thorough record of her misdeeds. During one summer month she misplaced her sister's sash, spilled cream on the floor, spoke in haste to her younger sister, left a hairbrush on the chair, failed to be diligent in school, did not use her time well, and lost her needle through carelessness.[39]

Recall Cranly telling Stephen Dedalus that he should ignore the fact that he had lost his faith in Catholicism and perform his Easter duty to please his mother. Readers may wonder why Stephen, whom Joyce describes as a sensitive youth, vulnerable to fears and dysphoric bodily sensations, is incapable of following his friend's advice. Why is Stephen so troubled by his inability to attend mass? If Stephen is a fictional example of the class of person who interprets a dysphoric internal tone as the consequence of a moral violation, he is wise to suppress behaviors that might provide additional proof of his moral failure. If he goes to Easter service as a nonbeliever, he will have violated his standard on hypocrisy and he will be vulnerable to additional guilt. Stephen confesses to Cranly his many fears—dogs, horses, thunderstorms—but "I fear more the chemical action which would be set up in my soul by a false homage to a symbol behind which are massed twenty centuries of authority and veneration." Stephen's way of protecting himself from additional guilt is to analyze his beliefs to assure himself that each is rational.[40]

Ludwig Wittgenstein shared Stephen's imperative for ruthless self-honesty. Wittgenstein was a painfully shy child who experienced almost pathological tension in uncongenial settings, and he became a melancholic adult who tried unsuccessfully to rid himself of a dysphoria that caused him intense suffering. Guilt over his inability to conquer this mood through will power alone, shame over his family's denial of a Jewish relative, doubt over his intellectual talent, and regret over the fact that he struck one of his pupils may have motivated him to give away most of the money inherited from his affluent family.

The Jews in history, he wrote in his notebooks, "are experienced as a sort of disease . . . and no one wants to put a disease on the same level as normal life." "I am too soft, too weak, and so too lazy to achieve anything significant." "It came into my head today as I was thinking about my philosophical work and saying to myself, I destroy, I destroy, I destroy." "I believe that my originality is an originality belonging to the soil rather than to the seed." On the first day of April 1942, when he was 53 years old, he confessed, "It is as though I had before me nothing but a long stretch of living death. I cannot imagine any future for me other than a ghastly one. Friendless and joyless."[41]

The Nobel poet Czesław Miłosz may also have experienced frequent bouts of dysphoria which he interpreted as the consequences of violations of his standards on moral courage. Miłosz wrote a diary in his seventy-seventh year titled *The Year of the Hunter*. One entry reads, "The polite boy inside me was pious, diligent, superstitious, conservative, always on the side of authority, and against anarchy. I was unable to reach the core of my repressions and to use them masterfully . . . Instead of saying, 'Yes, that's me, that's the way I am and that's that,' I felt ashamed of my lack of virtue."[42] Many writers are no more courageous than Miłosz, but because of a different temperament, they are not plagued by an uncertain virtue.

Leo Tolstoy, who continually berated himself for his vanity, idleness, and earlier exploitation of women, may also have lived with a chronically dysphoric tone. He suffered from insomnia, irritability, and a variety of physical complaints, which probably contributed to the mood he attributed to the prior day's failure to write, lack of empathy for a peasant's misfortune, and lust for fame. The diary he began in his eighteenth year opens with a criticism of self that he maintained for the rest of his life: "I've come to see clearly that the disorderly life which the majority of fashionable people take to be a consequence of youth is nothing other than the consequence of the early corruption of the soul." On some days, the psychic pain was acute: "I am a worthless, pathetic, unnecessary creature." Even after the public acclaim of his novels, he continued, in his seventh decade, to criticize himself: "What a worthless creature I must be. I can't tear apart all of these nasty cobwebs which hold me fast. And not because I haven't the strength, but because I'm morally unable to . . . The main thing is that I'm no good."[43]

The diary of Athol Fugard, a South African playwright who probably held the same standards on honesty and idleness as Tolstoy, lacks the moral angst that permeates Tolstoy's entries. Fugard rarely mentioned feelings of guilt in his 230 pages of confession; he attributed his moments of anguish to lack of money or a writing block.[44] I suspect that Fugard was blessed with a temperament very different from that inherited by Wittgenstein, Miłosz, and Tolstoy.

Evolution, Fear, and Guilt

Over the course of evolution, the central nucleus of the amygdala—an important structure in the acquisition of fear—became progressively smaller, while the basolateral nucleus and prefrontal cortex became larger and the connections between them elaborated. As these evolutionary changes in brain anatomy occurred, it is likely that fear of attack and of physical harm, which seem to be primary states for monkeys and chimps, became subordinated to shame or guilt. Perhaps that is why Hippocrates, Galen, and Burton chose the term melancholia rather than anxiety to label the syndrome that most often disrupts human serenity. Perhaps, too, that is why some fifteenth-century women accused of being witches confessed their guilt and why passengers in a sinking ship who believe they are about to die relive their past sins.

Evolution might have awarded humans an extreme degree of vigilance or apprehension in the presence of strangers—as is true of monkeys—but it did not. Rather, guilt over hurting others became an essential part of the human repertoire, perhaps because we are one of the few species able to kill large numbers of our own kind at any time during the year. Some protection against that chronically dangerous disposition would be adaptive.

An American officer with twenty years of military service suggested that soldiers have a natural inhibition to killing the enemy in a face-to-face encounter. "There is within most men an intense resistance to killing their fellow man. A resistance so strong that . . . soldiers on the battlefield will die before they can overcome it."[45] "The killer must suppress any dissonant thought that he has done anything wrong . . . his mental health is totally invested in believing that what he has done is good and right."

For every Vietnamese killed by an American soldier, 50,000 bullets were fired. Approximately 90 percent of the muskets found on the battlefield at Gettysburg were loaded but not fired, and only 20 percent of World War II soldiers in combat fired at the enemy; most fired in the air or not at all. William Manchester, a Marine in World War II, recalls how he felt after killing a Japanese soldier: "I can remember whispering foolishly, 'I'm sorry', and just throwing up . . . it was a betrayal of what I've been taught since a child."[46] When the killing occurs at a distance with artillery or high-altitude carpet bombing, soldiers are protected from seeing their victims and, as a result, feel less guilt. That is probably why hoods are placed on victims before they are executed.

The primary cause of psychiatric breakdown in wartime—called post-traumatic stress disorder or PTSD—is less often a fear of being killed than guilt over being disloyal to comrades, surviving a battle in which friends died, participating in or observing an atrocity, or killing an enemy whose face one can see. Israeli soldiers with PTSD were more likely to suffer from depression than anxiety, indicating that guilt rather than fear was the basis for their distress.[47]

Women who have been raped are more likely to develop PTSD than women of the same age and social class who have been robbed at gunpoint or threatened with death. A rape victim who wonders if any aspect of her behavior invited the attack will be more vulnerable to guilt than one who is robbed, attacked by an animal, or is a passenger in an automobile accident.[48] Nathan McCall, in his memoir *Makes Me Wanna Holler*, recalls his empathy for a girl who was being raped by a group of adolescents. Eventually it was his turn. "After a few miserable minutes, I got up and signaled for the next man to take his turn . . . I walked over to a corner and somebody whispered 'That shit is good, ain't it?' I said, 'Yea, man, that shit is good.' Actually I felt sick and unclean."[49]

In the fall of 1991 a man crashed his pickup truck into a cafeteria in a small Texas town at lunch time and started gunning down patrons at point-blank range. After murdering 23 people, he killed himself. One year later psychiatrists interviewed 136 survivors of this traumatic incident. One in six was suffering from PTSD, but these adults had displayed symptoms of anxiety or depression prior to the trauma. Those who had been psychologically healthy before the horrific event were free of symptoms, suggesting that a frightening experience does not usually produce PTSD. Perhaps that is why less than one third of Israeli citizens developed chronic or serious anxiety during the first few months of 1991 when Iraq threatened to send missiles to Israeli cities.[50]

I suspect that the current preoccupation with fear of being raped, robbed, stabbed, or killed is fueled by current world events. When sexual motives were partially freed of repression by historical conditions in the nineteenth century, Freud awarded sexuality a privileged position and argued that it had its roots in primate biology. Today, the butchery in Bosnia and Rwanda, the unprovoked murders in urban ghettos, and the bombings on London and Belfast streets make us uneasy. Scholars explain our feelings of anxiety by awarding fear of attack a position of priority in the human psyche. Some primatologists have even suggested that the reason why human social bonds are strong is that they protect us from a primordial fear of attack inherited from our primate kin. However, the feelings and physiology created by expectation of an aggressive attack are very different from the self-blame that follows violation of a moral standard on stealing from a friend. Anyone who collapsed the two feeling states into one overarching category would probably treat as similar a starving refugee and a monk on a hunger strike who is protesting religious persecution.

The pop-psychology view of human motivation is that our animal heritage imposes on us an irresistible need for power, fame, sex, and property and an easy access to anger. If these motives are part of our evolution, the argument goes, they should be treated as acceptable. This distortion of Darwin's views ignores the fact that humans are also equally capable of empathy, shame, and guilt. Indeed, some Israeli journalists criticized the Israeli media during the Gulf War for suggesting to the public that it was perfectly natural to care about only oneself rather than one's neighbors when Iraqi missiles landed on Tel-Aviv. One angry commentator suggested that Israel needed more moral philosophers and fewer psychologists.[51] What is historically new but not unique about current Western society is that the single-minded seeking of power, prestige, wealth, and sexual delight, which earlier centuries had criticized as moral flaws, has become for many a modern ethical code that enjoys the privilege of being treated as "good." It is ironic that one of the unanticipated consequences of the creative advances in modern biology is the rationalization of motives that are, when carried to the extreme, self-destructive.

Scholars from Aristotle to Kant held that every person has the ability to exercise rational control of their desires through a reliance on will. Although nineteenth-century writers acknowledged that our species shares characteristics with primates, only humans were thought to be in command of an ability to choose between morally proper and improper behavior. But the century that followed *On the Origin of Species* produced an increasing number of scientists who rejected that argument in favor of the view that humans were no more than hairless gorillas.

The appeal of this argument rests in part on our need to rationalize the conditions of our daily lives. The ethics of a society must bend a little to accommodate to the behaviors most people are forced to display. If not, each person will be vulnerable to terrible tensions during every day. A majority of Americans who live and work in metropolitan areas deal with strangers who they suspect will exploit or frustrate them. These strangers block access at crowded intersections, blow cigarette smoke in their direction in restaurants, and push ahead in long queues. Each person must have rapid access to moral outrage if he is to resist exploitation and to protect his property and dignity. Television dramas depict how easy anger wells up and forces otherwise reasonable people to behave in ways they will regret, even though they will eventually be forgiven if their intentions were not irredeemably evil.

In order to rationalize the blizzard of cruelty, greed, rudeness, and dishonesty in contemporary society, we have come to believe that it is not always possible or adaptive to control anger, cupidity, rivalry, and jealousy. This rationalization mutes feelings of guilt and dilutes a continuing sense of personal responsibility for hurting others. Although the population density in Japan is far greater than in the United States, the Japanese believe that each person is able to control his anger, and the differential frequency of violence in the two countries is enormous. The United States reports about five times as many violent crimes per capita as does Japan. Apparently, if humans believe they can contain their impulses, they do so.

The belief that anger, jealousy, self-interest, and competitiveness should not be suppressed because they are natural emotions has advantages in a society in which a large number of strangers must compete for a small number of positions of dignity, status, and economic security. Under these conditions it helps to be self-interested, and it is disadvantageous to be too cooperative, too loyal, too altruistic, or too reluctant to protest unjust advantage taken by another. In the film *El Norte*, a young Guatemalan who fled his Indian village for a job in a Los Angeles restaurant is advised by a Mexican coworker that in America people look out for themselves first. But rather than acknowledge that the structure of our society forces each of us to adopt self-interest as the first rule, many Americans find it more attractive to believe that this mood, along with jealousy, sexual exploitation, hatred, and violence, is an inevitable remnant of our animal heritage—and one we must learn to accept.

A rash of books published over the last twenty years has claimed—directly or indirectly—that human selfishness is to be expected, given our evolutionary history. After pointing to examples of selfish behavior in a variety of animal species, the writers imply (as if describing the animal behaviors were sufficient) that because self-interested behavior is seen throughout nature perhaps humans need not feel so ashamed of their narcissism and greed. The appeal of this argument resembles the seventeenth-century belief that a very tiny person lay quietly in each egg. The early naturalists had been puzzled by the enigma of the fully formed newborn and posited a solution that was easy to imagine. Contemporary scientists are equally frustrated by the extraordinary variety in human social behavior. They have tried to solve this problem by arguing that our troublesome tendencies were present in our phylogenetic past—a form of behavioral preformationism. The flaws in this argument are obvious.

Anyone with a modest knowledge of animal behavior and only minimal inferential skill can find examples of animal behavior to support almost any ethical message desired. Those who wish to sanctify the institution of marriage can point to the pair bonding of gibbons; those who think infidelity is more natural can point to chimpanzees. If you believe that people are naturally sociable, point to baboons; if you think they are solitary, point to orangutans. If you believe sex should replace fighting, point to bonobo chimpanzees. If you want mothers to care for infants, point to rhesus monkeys; if you prefer the father to be the primary caretaker, point to titi monkeys. If you believe that surrogate care is closer to nature, point to lionesses. If you are certain that men should dominate harems of beautiful women, point to elephant seals; if you believe women should be in positions of dominance, point to elephants. Nature has enough diversity to fit almost any ethical taste.

Most individuals need some help in rationalizing the fact that they are forced by social conditions to violate in excess one or more of their ethical standards. When the availability of contraceptives made sexual behavior outside of marriage safer, Americans and Europeans wanted to hear that illicit sexual liaisons were not morally reprehensible. Freud heard their plea and naturalized sex. When Americans were revolted by the horrific atrocities of Japanese and German soldiers during World War II and wondered whether there was any humanity left in our species, Erik Erikson reminded them that the infant's basic nature was to trust and to love.

Today the competitive nature of industrialized societies favors excessive self-interest over loyalty, and some scientists, helped by clever journalists, imply that we need not feel excessive shame or guilt over these narcissistic urges, for the same behaviors are observed every day in the animal kingdom. Even Adam Smith is being resurrected to make the argument more palatable. Out of self-interest, Smith noted, harmonious societies grow. Even though second marriages with stepchildren exist in no species but our own, some evolutionary scholars have suggested that the abuse of stepchildren is partly due to our evolutionary past. The behavior of bees is most often cited as evidence for a broadly based urge to be kind only to those who share our genes. These writers ignore the fact that the vast majority of stepchildren are treated with affection. More important, these writers are unperturbed by the fact that the relation between an adult and a stepchild has no analogue in monkeys, chimps, or gorillas. The more correct Darwinian inference for this social fact is that humans are qualitatively different from their ancestors, for they are the only primate to give benevolent care to juveniles who are not genetically related to them. The logic of evolutionary psychology—that what exists was probably biologically advantageous at some point in our primate history—cannot explain the small number of cases of stepchild abuse, any more than it can explain other infrequent human phenomena such as sky diving, masochism, suicide, and hyperactivity.

The phrases "selfish genes" and "inclusive fitness" have the misleading implication that proximal causes are less interesting and less important than evolutionary ones. But my understanding of why an eighteen-year-old girl in Bangkok, working as a streetwalker, sends her earnings to the parents who sold her into prostitution is not enhanced very much by being told that she does so to maximize the reproductive fitness of those who share her genes.

It is an error to assume that any human ethic is a clear derivative of some class of animal behavior. During the first three decades of this century, eugenicists argued that the facts of evolution have ethical implications; in this case their motive was to prevent the reproduction of those who had inferior talents or dangerous habits. Today, evolutionary arguments are used to cleanse greed, promiscuity, and the abuse of stepchildren of moral taint. Although this stance is more liberal, that does not mean it is more likely to be correct. The concern with right and wrong, the control of guilt, and the desire to feel virtuous are, like the appearance of milk in mammalian mothers, a unique event that was discontinuous with what was prior. It is not possible to find in fish, frogs, lizards, or birds a basis for the fact that mammalian mothers evolved organs that produce milk to nurse their young.

The continual desire to regard the self as good is a unique feature of *Homo sapiens*. Although it has a firm foundation in the human genome, it is not an obvious derivative of the competences of apes and monkeys. Should this claim prove to be valid, the use of animal behavior to explain human selfishness or altruism is a just-so story.

Each person holds a number of ethical beliefs that permit him to decide, without too much delay, which action to implement when he has a choice. However, most of us would be silent if asked to provide the foundation for those beliefs. The inability to justify our deepest moral standards with more than "It feels right" is a source of unease. As a result, any person or group that announces it can supply an answer to the query "Why do I believe this to be right?" is celebrated. The church was an effective source of justification for Europeans for over fifteen hundred years, until science began to compete for that role and eventually became a primary arbiter. Many contemporary citizens expect the facts of nature, as interpreted by scientists, to provide a rationale for human ethics.

Humans are selfish and generous, aloof and empathic, hateful and loving, dishonest and honest, disloyal and loyal, cruel and kind, arrogant and humble; but most feel a little guilt over an excessive display of the first member of these seven pairs. The resulting dysphoria, which is uncomfortable, is unique to humans, and they are eager to have it ameliorated. Confession or psychotherapy is effective for some, especially if the priest or therapist is respected. I suspect that some people feel better when they learn that their less social urges are natural consequences of their phylogenetic history. The current high status of the biological sciences has made it possible for students of evolution also to serve as therapists to the community.

In the final section of a recent book that presents an evolutionary account of human ethical behavior, the author surprisingly throws away all the examples of animal behavior described in the previous twelve chapters and pleads for an ethic that could only occur in humans. "We must encourage social and natural exchange between equals for that is the raw material of trust and trust is the foundation of virtue."[52] Precisely! Although I do not doubt the essential correctness of modern evolutionary theory, some Americans have become too accepting of the view that humans bear the indelible stamp of their lowly origins. An uncritical attitude toward that assumption could make it a self-fulfilling prophecy. Every time a judge excuses a violent act of aggression by a sane adolescent of average intelligence because the child grew up under harsh conditions, the court, speaking for all of us, declares that no person subject to extreme cruelty or deprivation should be required to use the universal knowledge that maliciousness is wrong.

The biological imperative for all animals is to avoid hunger and harm and to reproduce, and adult chimps spend much of each day doing just that. But humans in ancient societies established cities, wrote laws forbidding certain behaviors, built ships, wore finery, used slaves, attended plays, and, in Greece, admired the Parthenon. What is biologically special about our species is a constant attention to what is good and beautiful and a dislike of all that is bad and ugly. These biologically prepared biases render the human experience incommensurable with that of any other species.

The appeal of the ideas of evolutionary biology, and the elegant discoveries in genetics and molecular biology, have persuaded many that fitness in the service of reproductive success is the only legitimate definition of adaptation. If survival of one's genes, and the genes of one's relatives, is treated as the seminal feature of adaptation, then of course maximizing the number of offspring in the next generation is the correct criterion to apply. But "psychological adaptation" has a different set of features and therefore a different definition. It is easy to argue that a subjective feeling of virtue is psychologically adaptive because it minimizes distress and contributes, in a benevolent way, to health, longevity, and a feeling of well-being—three qualities that are critical to psychological adaptation. But most adults who conform to a moral standard that respects the dignity of another will be less sexually exploitative of others and therefore will be less fecund than those who seek a sexual liaison with anyone they can seduce. In this case, the criteria for biological and psychological adaptation are inconsistent. But inconsistencies are common in nature. Red blood cells with a sickled shape are not best for absorbing oxygen but they do protect against malaria, which is adaptive in some parts of the world. A moral motive and its associated emotions are psychologically adaptive features for a species that lives in groups and can harm conspecifics, even though these features may not maximize the meaning of reproductive fitness held by evolutionary biologists.

The number of acts of rudeness, vandalism, theft, abuse, rape, and murder that occurred yesterday, throughout the world, is infinitesimal when compared with the total number of opportunities each adult had to display any one of these behaviors. The ratio of asocial acts to total opportunities approaches zero every day. We are, as Blake understood, both lion and lamb. That insight should not breed indifference to our capacity for hatred, cruelty, and narcissism, but it is both incorrect and dangerous to deny the unique moral emotions that chance mutations made possible between 100,000 and 200,000 years ago. Our moral sense is "not a thin layer that covers a beastly and selfish makeup,"[53] but a necessary feature for a species with a frontal lobe so large it permits a person to harbor resentment, envy, jealousy, and hostility for a long time after acute anger has passed.

Perhaps that is why it was adaptive for the first sign of a moral sense to emerge so early in development, a half dozen years before the grammar of the local language has been mastered, and ten to twelve years before reproductive maturity. It is likely that an early appreciation of right and wrong was also necessary to control the resentment of an older sibling toward a younger one. Every four-year-old is jealous of the attention directed at a new infant who has joined the family, and every four-year-old has both the opportunity and strength to hurt the young child. Yet the frequency of such seriously violent acts is so tiny, each occurrence is a screaming headline in the local newspaper. The brutal 1993 murder of two-year-old James Bolger by a pair of ten-year-old Liverpool boys provoked full-length books because of the rarity of the event; the 1998 murders of schoolchildren and a teacher in Jonesboro, Arkansas, will provoke its set of books for the same reason. The human moral sense, like a spider's web, is a unique product of evolution that has been maintained because it ensures our survival.

Epilogue

A king once announced that the person who executed the most extraordinary act would be given permission to marry the princess. A herald carried this message to all parts of the kingdom and, following local competitions, three finalists were selected to display their creative products. When the first applicant brought forward a handcrafted harpsichord, the king declared it to be an extraordinary object of great beauty. When the second candidate displayed a painting of the forest behind the palace, the king declared it an even more extraordinary work of art than the harpsichord. When the final applicant carried in a porcelain clock, the king was so overwhelmed by its exquisite detail, he announced that it was the most extraordinary thing he had ever encountered. He was about to give his daughter to the clock maker when a young man in the audience leapt up, brought a hammer down on the clock, and smashed it into pieces. The king gasped and, after a pause, declared, "*That* is the most extraordinary thing I have ever experienced!" and awarded the princess to the aggressor.

Even though the scientific view of human nature is like a mirror that shatters every two or three generations, I am unwilling to be viewed as the man with the hammer and wish to make four constructive suggestions for those who work in the social and behavioral sciences.

The first is a plea for a moratorium on free-floating words like fear, learn, approach, altruism, avoid, and regulate, for which the observational situation is unspecified and the agent could be a snail, mouse, monkey, or college sophomore. I am aware of, and troubled by, the fact that the severity of this suggestion makes me appear more like Georges Cuvier than Geoffroy Etienne Saint-Hilaire in their famous 1830 debates in the French Academy. Geoffroy went far beyond the facts when he suggested that all animals share a basic body plan. However, modern biology has proven him correct, in ways he never could have imagined. Cuvier, the conservative empiricist, with the consensual facts on his side, ridiculed Geoffroy's wild suggestion that flies and monkeys share any aspect of body architecture.[1] It is possible that a rat's conditioned freezing to a tone that had been paired with shock shares important elements with a mother's guilt over returning to work two months after giving birth to her first child. However, at this moment I side with Cuvier.

The imperative to specify agent and situation should be heeded especially by those who argue that adult qualities are the partial products of early experiences. Unless these scientists state, in more detail than they have, the specific form of the association between past and present, it is fair to question the general claim that early events must have some future consequences. When psychologists studying human memory specified exactly what the individual was doing, and distinguished among declarative, episodic, implicit, and procedural memories, major insights followed. It is likely that equally stunning progress will be the reward for adopting a similar analytic strategy for many concepts in the social sciences. This maxim, developed in detail in Chapter 1, might be: *Full sentences, please.*

The second maxim urges: *A plenitude of procedures.* Social and behavioral scientists rely on three sources of information to make guesses about habits, feelings, and the contents of minds: (1) verbal statements, including self-reports and descriptions provided by informants; (2) observed behaviors, whether in the laboratory or in natural settings; and (3) measurements of central and peripheral physiology. Each source can lead to different conclusions. The descriptions of a person based only on verbal information—provided by self or by others—can be coherent but will be different from the descriptions based on the person observed and descriptions inferred from physiological information. When we limit ourselves to one source of information, we pay the price of limited understanding.

A serious problem in current studies of human personality is that the referents for the five so-called major personality types are not observations of behaviors and moods, as most laymen assume, but responses to questionnaires. The questions do not inquire about psychological processes that are not conscious, and, of course, are completely indifferent to the physiology that contributes to variation in human mood and action. No biologist would rely on the verbal reports of hikers, hunters, and forest rangers to decide on the number and nature of animal species. It should not be a source of pride that social scientists prefer a person's verbal descriptions to direct evaluations of action, mood, and physiology. That strategy does not reflect an epistemological difference between the social sciences on the one hand and biology or chemistry on the other. Rather, it reflects a failure to appreciate that deep understanding is not attainable with one source of information. Progress can only occur when varied sources of evidence are combined.

Although the meaning of current psychological concepts will be both changed and enriched by new facts about the brain, the psychological meanings will not be totally replaced by the biological concepts. In a book entitled *Conversations on Mind, Matter, and Mathematics,* Jean Pierre Changeaux, a biologist, and Alain Connes, a mathematician, engaged in a dialogue on the relation between mental products and their biological foundations.[2] The mathematician surprised and frustrated the biologist by insisting that any mathematical equation imagined by a mind is as real, natural, and autonomous an event as neurotransmitter molecules released into a synapse. The mathematician implied that, in principle, neuroscientists will never be able to reduce the content of a thought to a neural profile. The mental event will always retain some ontological independence from its neurophysiological base, just as the pain of a headache or the mood following exercise is not totally explained by the underlying physiology, no matter how complete the physiological description. The first three sentences of the Gettysburg Address will produce different patterns of activity in the sensory receptor cells on the basilar membrane of the inner ear, as well as in the ensemble of neurons in the auditory cortex. But the meanings of those sentences will not be discernible from the patterns of neural activity. Meaning transcends its elementary foundations.

Despite these inherent limitations of physiological measurements, I suspect that the addition of biological evidence to psychological information will create new, fruitful concepts by replacing notions that originate in phenomenology with theoretically more useful constructs that are more faithful to nature. A similar advance occurred in physics when the discovery of radioactivity, almost a century ago, motivated scientists to look for the constituents of what they thought were indivisible atoms. If psychologists possessed relevant physiological information on those adults we now call extroverts (based on their answers to a questionnaire), they would detect several different types. No present concept in personality will survive the next half century; every one is heterogeneous in its history and physiology, and therefore each is a candidate for fruitful analysis.

A third maxim suggests: *Consider categories.* Rather than viewing all individual differences as quantitative variations that fall on a continuum (for example, from low to high sociability, low to high aggression, or low to high impulsivity), we ought to consider the potential usefulness of qualitative categories that represent individuals at the extremes of a dimension or those who possess a particular combination of traits. Some extremely sociable adults are qualitatively, not quantitatively, different from those who are only mildly extraverted. Adults who are sociable as well as reflective in time of crisis are qualitatively different from extraverts who are impulsive. Very few useful biological categories are defined by one feature or dimension. Categories of people are analogous to closely related species, with each species defined by a correlated cluster of features. Each current personality type should be replaced with a family of categories that acknowledges the person's temperament, developmental history, and adult characteristics. Comprehension of these classes of persons requires multiple views.

The final maxim—*Acknowledge minds*—urges those who study humans to ask how the person interprets experience. Most social scientists study the influence of events that can be quantified easily—violence on television, parental punishment, or divorce—because they do not possess methods that permit insight into the child's or adult's private constructions. We must invent novel methods in order to discover the large number of tacit, yet informative, associations people possess, especially those that are derivatives of identifications with gender, family, class, and ethnic groups. There is no set of events observers could film that would reveal the existence of the close semantic association in children between the category "female" and the category "natural." The dramatic advances in biology, chemistry, and physics in this century could not have occurred without the invention of new methods, whether DNA technology or radio astronomy. Social scientists must create new sources of evidence if these disciplines are to progress.

The suggestion to acknowledge minds has two correlated implications. The first, discussed in Chapters 1 and 2, is that most of the time minds are aroused by discrepancy or relative difference rather than by a specific event defined absolutely. Feelings of hunger occur when blood sugar levels change, not at any particular concentration of blood sugar. The appearance of a rose on a screen produces a specific brainwave—called the P300—only when it is preceded by many pictures of objects other than roses and therefore is a discrepancy. A state of surprise automatically provokes an attempt at interpretation which is the critical governor of behavior. It is not timidity that makes some psychologists reluctant to tell parents how to behave with their children but rather the realization that it is not any specific parental action but the child's interpretation that shapes the child's development. Whether spanking a child for seizing a sibling's dessert has benevolent or malevolent consequences will depend on whether the child interprets the punishment as fair or unjust.

Humans interpret change in complex, symbolic ways— animals do not—and one of the first interpretations imposed on experience is whether the change is good or bad, for ourselves and for those we care about. No animal makes that calculation. The Serbs who murdered innocent neighbors are not to be compared with tigers killing gazelles. The humans killed because of threats to their belief in their virtue; the tigers killed because they were hungry. Efforts intended to reform asocial youth should be directed at changing their definition of what characteristics are good rather than focusing only on punishing them. Contemporary youth detect the profound cynicism that permeates our society but wish for more honesty, compassion, responsibility, and loyalty. Fans of the writer Isaac Bashevis Singer will remember that when the consistently dishonest and unfaithful wife of Gimpel the Fool learns that her husband is about to deviate from his old-fashioned moral code, she returns from the dead to tell her forgiving and always trusting spouse that it was he, not she, who chose the happier path.

Notes
Acknowledgments
Index

Notes

Prologue

1. J. M. Nash, "Fertile minds," *Time*, February 3, 1997, pp. 51, 55.
2. T. Parker, *The Violence of Our Lives* (New York: Holt, 1995).

1. A Passion for Abstraction

1. L. A. Dugatkin, *Cooperation among Animals* (New York: Oxford, 1997); B. A. Mellers, A. Schwartz, K. Ho, and I. Ritov, "Decision affect theory," *Psychological Science* 8 (1997): 423–429.

2. H. Feshbach, T. Matsui, and A. Olesen, eds., *Niels Bohr: Physics in the World* (New York: Harwood, 1988); A. N. Whitehead, *The Aims of Education and Other Essays* (New York: Macmillan, 1929), p. 158; L. Wittgenstein, *Culture and Value* (Chicago: University of Chicago Press, 1984), p. 41E.

3. D. A. Regier, W. E. Narrow, and B. S. Rae, "The epidemiology of anxiety disorders," *Journal of Psychiatric Research* 24 (1990): 3–14.

4. W. J. Magee, W. W. Eaton, H. U. Wittchen, K. A. McGonagle, and R. L. Kessler, "Agoraphobia, simple phobia, and social phobia in the national comorbidity survey," *Archives of General Psychiatry* 53 (1996): 159–168; M. B. Stein, J. R. Walker, and D. R. Forde, "Public speaking fears in a community sample," *Archives of General Psychiatry* 53 (1996): 169–174; J. R. T. Davidson, D. C. Hughes, L. K. George, and D. G. Blazer, "The boundary of social phobia," *Archives of General Psychiatry* 51 (1994): 975–983.

5. M. Myrtek, *Constitutional Psychophysiology* (New York: Academic, 1984). A potential problem with asking people to remember when they were anxious in the

past is that the memories are often inaccurate. A. Angold, A. Erkanli, E. J. Costello, and M. Rutter, "Precision, reliability and accuracy in the dating of symptom onsets in child and adolescent psychopathology," *Journal of Child Psychology and Psychiatry* 37 (1996): 657–664.

6. G. Roccatagliata, *A History of Ancient Psychiatry* (New York: Greenwood, 1986).

7. C. Chen, J. K. Kim, R. F. Thompson, and S. Tonegawa, "Hippocampal lesions impair contextual fear conditioning in two strains of mice," *Behavioral Neuroscience* 110 (1996): 1177–1180; J. A. Gray and N. McNaughton, "The neuropsychology of anxiety," *Nebraska Symposium on Motivation* 43 (1996): 61–134.

8. K. S. LaBar and J. E. LeDoux, "Partial disruption of fear conditioning in rats with unilateral amygdala damage," *Behavioral Neuroscience* 110 (1996): 991–997.

9. E. Laan, W. Everaerd, and A. Evers, "Assessment of female sexual arousal," *Psychophysiology* 32 (1995): 476–485.

10. P. J. Whalen, S. L. Rauch, N. L. Etcoff, S. C. McInerney, M. B. Lee, and M. A. Jenike, *Journal of Neuroscience* (in press).

11. D. L. Walker and M. Davis, "Involvement of the dorsal periaqueductal gray in the loss of fear-potentiated startle accompanying high foot shock training," *Behavioral Neuroscience* 111 (1997): 692–702.

12. P. J. Lang, M. M. Bradley, and B. N. Cuthbert, "Emotion, attention and the startle reflex," *Psychological Review* 97 (1990): 377–395.

13. S. K. Sutton, R. J. Davidson, B. Donzella, W. Irwin, and D. A. Dottl, "Manipulating affective state using extended picture presentations," *Psychophysiology* 34 (1997): 217–226.

14. O. V. Lipp, D. A. T. Siddle, and P. J. Dall, "The effect of emotional and attentional processes on blink startle modulation and on electrodermal responses," *Psychophysiology* 34 (1997): 240–347.

15. J. Kagan and N. Snidman, "Infant temperament and anxious symptoms in school-age children" (unpub. manuscript).

16. W. A. Falls, S. Carlson, and J. G. Turner, "Fear-potentiated startle in two strains of inbred mice," *Behavioral Neuroscience* 11 (1997): 855–861. See also N. Shanks and H. Anisman, "Stressor provoked behavioral changes in six strains of mice," *Behavioral Neuroscience* 102 (1988): 854–905.

17. G. J. Gagliardi, G. G. Gallup, and J. C. Boren, "The effect of different pupil-to-eye size ratios on immobility in chickens," *Bulletin of the Psychonomic Society* 8 (1976): 58–60.

18. M. E. Goddard and R. G. Beilharz, "A multivariate analysis of the genetics of fearfulness in potential guidedogs," *Behavioral Genetics* 15 (1985): 69–89.

19. S. H. Potter, "The cultural construction of emotion in rural Chinese social life," *Ethos* 16 (1988): 181–208. W. MacEwen, "Short communications," *Glasgow Medical Journal*, 1877, p. 80.

20. I. M. Marks, *Fears, Phobias, Rituals* (Oxford: Oxford University Press, 1987), p. 40.

21. R. J. Krawzlis, M. A. Basso, and R. H. Wurtz, "Shared motor error for multiple eye movement," *Science* 276 (1997): 1693–1695.

22. J. B. Watson and R. Rayner, "Conditioned emotional reactions," *Journal of Experimental Psychology* 3 (1920): 1–14.

23. D. L. Walker and M. Davis, "Double-dissociation between the involvement of the bed nucleus of the stria terminalis and the central nucleus of the amygdala in startle increases produced by conditioned versus unconditioned fear," *Journal of Neuroscience* (in press).

24. C. Belzung and G. LePape, "Comparison of different behavioral test situations used in psychopharmacology for measurement of anxiety," *Physiology and Behavior* 56 (1994): 623–628.

25. O. Berton, A. Ramos, F. Chaouloff, and P. Mormede, "Behavioral reactivity to social and nonsocial situations," *Behavior Genetics* 27 (1997): 155–166.

26. D. Treit, C. Pesold, and S. Rotzinger, "Dissociating the anti-fear effects of septal and amygdaloid lesions using two pharmacologically validated models of rat anxiety," *Behavioral Neuroscience* 107 (1993): 770–785; D. Treit, C. Pesold, and S. Rotzinger, "Noninteractive effects of diazepam and amygdaloid lesions in two animal models of anxiety," *Behavioral Neuroscience* 107 (1993): 1099–1105; F. K. Jellestad, A. Markowska, H. K. Bakke, and B. Walther, "Behavioral effects after ibotenic acid 6/OHDA and electrolytic lesions in the central amygdala nucleus of the rat," *Physiology and Behavior* 37 (1986): 855–862.

27. C. I. Thompson, J. S. Schwartzbaum, and H. F. Harlow, "Development of social fear after amygdalectomy in infant rhesus monkeys," *Physiology and Behavior* 4 (1969): 249–254.

28. J. P. Sartre, *Sketch for a Theory of Emotions* (London: Methuen, 1962).

29. H. Putnam, *Words and Life* (Cambridge: Harvard University Press, 1994), p. 478.

30. E. S. Valenstein, "Problems of measurement and interpretation with reinforcing brain stimulation," *Psychological Review* 71 (1964): 415–437; E. S. Valenstein, V. C. Cox, and J. W. Kakolewski, "The hypothalamus and motivated behavior," in J. Tapp, ed., *Reinforcement* (New York: Academic Press, 1969); K. C. Berridge and E. S. Valenstein, "What psychological process mediates feeding evoked by stimulation of the lateral hypothalamus?" *Behavioral Neuroscience* 105 (1991): 3–14.

31. A. Perkins and J. A. Fitzgerald, "Sexual orientation in domestic rams," in L. Ellis and L. Ebertz, eds., *Sexual Orientation* (London: Praeger, 1997), pp. 107–127.

32. W. H. Li, *Molecular Evolution* (Sunderlund, MA: Sinauer, 1997).

33. J. Cheever, *The Journal of John Cheever* (New York: Ballantine, 1993), p. 215; J. Strouse, *Alice James* (Boston: Houghton Mifflin, 1980), pp. 118, 131.

34. L. Weiskrantz, *Consciousness Lost and Found* (New York: Oxford, 1997).

35. A. Revonsuo, "Words interact with colors in a globally aphasic patient," *Cortex* 31 (1995): 377–386.

36. D. Dennett, *Consciousness Explained* (Boston: Little, Brown, 1991). In a critical review of David Chalmer's book on consciousness, John Searle notes that some scientists who are frustrated by the recalcitrant quality of subjective awareness have been willing to adopt a functional definition of this state. They argue that consciousness should be defined by sets of empirical (or causal) relations in which it participates. If, for example, the invoking of consciousness explains a child's answer

to the question, Do you love your mother? as well as an adult's report of low self-esteem and a chimpanzee's hiding a morsel of food, then consciousness can be treated as present in all three cases. But functional differences are often theoretically dangerous. Imbibing too much alcohol, a concussion of the skull, mainlining heroin, and Alzheimer's disease are all accompanied by a severe impairment in declarative memory. However, few would claim that these four conditions define the same brain or psychological state. Functional definitions are typically used when scientists do not understand the structure of a particular entity, be it a gene, brain molecule, or brain circuit. See J. Searle, "Consciousness and the philosophers," *New York Review of Books*, March 6, 1997, pp. 43–50.

37. G. M. Edelman, *The Remembered Present* (New York: Basic Books, 1989).

38. V. Mountcastle, "The evolution of ideas concerning the function of the neo-cortex," *Cerebral Cortex* 5 (1995): 289–295; E. Mayr, *Toward a New Philosophy of Biology* (Cambridge: Harvard University Press, 1988).

39. W. Wittling, "Brain asymmetry in the control of autonomic physiologic activity," in R. J. Davidson and K. P. Hugdahl, eds., *Brain Asymmetry* (Cambridge: MIT Press, 1995), pp. 305–357.

40. W. Schultz, P. Dayan, and P. R. Montague, "A neural substrate of prediction and reward," *Science* 275 (1997): 1593–1599; I. Wickelgren, "Getting the brain's attention," *Science* 278 (1997): 35–37.

41. J. M. Jennings, A. R. McIntosh, S. Kapur, E. Tulving, and S. Hule, "Image subtractions do not always add up: the interaction between semantic processing and response modes," in A. W. Toga, R. S. J. Frackowiak, and J. C. Mazziotta, eds., *Second International Conference on Functional Mapping of the Human Brain* (Boston: Academic Press, 1996), p. S226; G. Stemmler, *Differential Psychophysiology* (New York: Springer Verlag, 1992); T. W. Smith, J. B. Nealey, J. C. Kircher, and J. P. Limon, "Social determinants of cardiovascular reactivity," *Psychophysiology* 34 (1996): 65–73; P. D. Drummond, "The effect of adrenergic blockade on blushing and facial flushing," *Psychophysiology* 34 (1997): 163–168; see also R. M. Stelmack and N. Mandelzys, "Extraversion and pupillary response to affective and taboo words," *Psychophysiology* 12 (1975): 536–540.

42. A. Harrington, *Reenchanted Science* (Princeton: Princeton University Press, 1996).

43. D. Magnusson, *Individual Development from an Interactional Perspective* (Hillsdale, NJ: Erlbaum, 1988); R. B. Cairns, G. H. Elder, and E. J. Costello, *Developmental Science* (New York: Cambridge University Press, 1996).

44. M. M. Myers, S. A. Brunelli, H. M. Shair, J. M. Squire, and M. A. Hofer, "Relationship between maternal behavior of SHR and WKY dams and adult blood pressures of cross-fostered F1 pups," *Developmental Psychobiology* 22 (1989): 55–67; M. M. Myers, S. A. Brunelli, J. M. Squire, R. D. Shindeldecker, and M. A. Hofer, "Maternal behavior of SHR rats and its relationship to offspring blood pressure," *Developmental Psychobiology* 22 (1989): 29–53; Jean-Louis Gariepy, "The question of continuity and change in development," in R. B. Cairns, G. H. Elder, and E. J. Costello, eds., *Developmental Science* (Hillsdale, NJ: Erlbaum, 1996), pp. 78–96.

45. D. P. Hanes and J. D. Schall, "Control of voluntary movement initiation," *Science* 274 (1996): 427–429; T. Ruusuvirta, T. Koronen, M. Penttonen, J. Arikoski, and K. Kivirikko, "Hippocampal event-related potentials to pitch deviances in an auditory oddball situation in the cat," *International Journal of Psychophysiology* 20 (1995): 33–39.

46. A. Pais, *Niels Bohr's Times* (New York: Oxford University Press, 1991), p. 301.

47. V. Mountcastle, "The evolution of ideas concerning the function of the neo-cortex," *Cerebral Cortex* 5 (1995): 285–295; for a passionate defense of the emergent quality of psychological events, see G. A. Miller, "How we think about cognition, emotion and biology in psychopathology," *Psychophysiology* 33 (1996): 615–628.

48. N. Block, "On a confusion about a function of consciousness," in N. Block, O. Flanagan, and G. Guzeldere, eds., *The Nature of Consciousness* (Cambridge: MIT Press, 1997), pp. 375–415.

49. H. Ito, Y. Segyama, T. Mano, H. Okada, T. Matsukowa, and S. Iwase, "Skin sympathetic nerve activity and event-related potentials during auditory oddball paradigms," *Journal of the Autonomic Nervous System* 60 (1996): 129–135.

50. P. D. Wall, "My foot hurts me: an analysis of a sentence," in R. Blairs and E. G. Gray, eds., *Essays on the Nervous System* (Oxford: Clarendon Press, 1974), pp. 39–406; P. Rainville, G. H. Duncan, D. D. Price, B. Carrier, and M. C. Bushnell, "Pain affect encoded in anterior cingulate but not somatic sensory cortex," *Science* 277 (1997): 968–971; D. Armstrong, "What is consciousness?" in N. Block et al., *Nature of Consciousness*, pp. 721–728.

51. E. Tulving, *Elements of Episodic Memory* (Oxford: Clarendon Press, 1983).

52. M. M. Bradley, B. N. Cuthbert, and P. J. Lang, "Picture media and emotion: effects of a sustained affective content," *Psychophysiology* 33 (1996): 662–670.

53. Weiskrantz, *Consciousness Lost and Found*, p. 229.

54. M. K. Mullen, "Earliest recollections of childhood," *Cognition* 52 (1994): 55–79.

55. F. Galton, *Hereditary Genius* (London: Macmillan, 1869).

56. J. B. Carroll, "The measurement of intelligence," in R. J. Sternberg, ed., *Handbook of Human Intelligence* (Cambridge: Cambridge University Press, 1982), pp. 29–120.

57. C. Spearman, *The Abilities of Man* (New York: Macmillan, 1927); C. Spearman, *The Nature of Intelligence and the Principles of Cognition* (London: Macmillan, 1923); L. L. Thurstone and T. G. Thurstone, *Factorial Studies of Intelligence* (Chicago: University of Chicago Press, 1941); L. L. Thurstone, *The Vectors of the Mind* (Chicago: University of Chicago Press, 1935).

58. R. C. Tryon, "Studies in individual differences in maze ability," *Journal of Comparative Psychology* 12 (1931): 95–115; F. A. Mote, "Correlations between conditioning and maze learning in the white rat," *Journal of Comparative Psychology* 30 (1940): 197–219.

59. H. Gardner, *Frames of Mind* (New York: Basic Books, 1983).

60. Robert Sternberg agrees: "It is doubtful that there exists any best approach to studying intelligence, because intelligence can mean such diverse things in different

settings." R. J. Sternberg and W. Salter, "Conceptions of intelligence," in Sternberg, ed., *Handbook of Human Intelligence*, pp. 3–28.

61. G. E. McClearn, B. Johansson, S. Berg, N. L. Pedersen, F. Ahern, S. A. Petrill, and R. Plomin, "Substantial genetic influence on cognitive abilities in twins 80 or more years old," *Science* 276 (1997): 1560–1563.

62. J. S. Reznick, R. Corley, and J. Robinson, "A longitudinal twin study of intelligence in the second year," in *Monographs of the Society for Research in Child Development* 62, ser. 249 (1997): 1–162.

63. J. B. Carroll, "The measurement of intelligence," in Sternberg, ed., *Handbook of Human Intelligence*, pp. 29–120.

64. P. Bateson and B. D'Udine, "Exploration in two inbred strains of mice and their hybrids," *Animal Behavior* 34 (1986): 1026–1032.

65. J. C. Christian, S. Morzorati, J. A. Norton, C. J. Williams, S. O'Connor, and T. K. Li, "A genetic analysis of the resting electroencephalographic power spectrum in human twins," *Psychophysiology* 33 (1996): 584–591.

66. R. Greenberg, "Differences in neophobia between naive song and swamp sparrow," *Ethology* 91 (1992): 17–24.

67. W. T. Keaton and J. L. Gould, *Biological Science* (New York: Norton, 1993).

68. A. Diamond, M. Prevar, G. Callender, and D. P. Druin, "Prefrontal cortex in children tested early and continuously for PKU," *Monographs of the Society for Research in Child Development* 62, ser. 252 (1997): 1–207.

69. S. W. Jacobson, J. L. Jacobson, R. J. Sokol, S. S. Martier, and L. M. Chiodu, *Journal of Pediatrics* 129 (1996): 581–590.

70. A. Sankaranaryanon, unpub. ms.

71. J. Colombo, *Infant Cognition* (London: Sage, 1993).

72. H. M. Lenhoff, P. P. Wang, F. Greenberg, and U. Bellugi, "Williams syndrome and the brain," *Scientific American* 277 (1997): 68–73.

73. Reznick, Corley, and Robinson, "A longitudinal twin study of intelligence in the second year."

74. G. Gigerenzer and U. Hoffrage, "How to improve Bayesian reasoning without instruction," *Psychological Review* 102 (1995): 684–704.

75. M. K. Johnson, S. F. Nolde, M. Mather, J. Kounios, D. L. Schacter, and T. Curran, "Test format can affect the similarity of brain activity associated with true and false recognition memories," *Psychological Science* 8 (1997): 250–257.

76. N. E. Adler, T. Boyce, M. A. Chesney, S. Cohen, S. Folkman, R. L. Kahn, and S. L. Sime, "Socioeconomic status and health," *American Psychologist* 49 (1994): 15–24.

77. R. B. Cattell, *Description and Measurement of Personality* (New York: World Book, 1946).

78. F. Vargha-Khadem, D. G. Gadian, K. E. Watkins, A. Connolly, W. Van Raessahen, and M. Mishkin, "Differential effects of early hippocampal pathology on episodic or semantic memory," *Science* 277 (1997): 376–380.

79. M. Schiff, M. Duyme, A. Dumaret, J. Stewart, S. Tomkiewicz, and J. Feingold, "Intellectual status of working-class children adopted early into upper-middle-class families," *Science* 200 (1978): 1503–1504.

80. R. Plomin, D. W. Fulker, R. Corley, and J. L. De Fries, "Nature, nurture, and cognitive development from one to sixteen years," *Psychological Science* 8 (1997): 442–447.

81. R. B. McCall, "Childhood IQ as predictors of adult educational and occupational status," *Science* 197 (1976): 482–483.

82. E. Mach, *The Analysis of Sensations* (1886; New York: Dover, 1959), p. 37.

83. U. Neisser, "Rising scores on intelligence tests," *American Scientist* 85 (1997): 440–447. See also J. R. Flynn, "Massive IQ gains in 14 nations," *Psychological Bulletin* 101 (1987): 171–191.

84. U. Neisser, G. Boodoo, T. J. Bouchard, A. W. Boykin, N. Brody, S. J. Ceci, F. Halpern, J. C. Loehlin, R. Perloff, R. J. Sternberg, and S. Urbina, "Intelligence: knowns and unknowns," *American Psychologist* 51 (1996): 77–101.

85. R. J. Herrnstein and C. Murray, *The Bell Curve* (New York: Free Press, 1994).

86. K. H. Rubin, "The Waterloo Longitudinal Project," in K. H. Rubin and J. B. Asendorpf, eds., *Social Withdrawal, Inhibition, and Shyness in Childhood* (Hillsdale, NJ: Erlbaum, 1993), pp. 291–314; K. H. Rubin, P. D. Hastings, S. L. Stewart, H. A. Henderson, and X. Chen, "The consistency and concomitants of inhibition," *Child Development* 68 (1997): 467–483.

87. K. Coleman, and D. S. Wilson, "Shyness and boldness in pumpkin seed sunfish," *Animal Behavior* (in press).

88. J. Kagan, *Galen's Prophecy* (New York: Basic Books, 1994).

89. J. Kagan, N. Snidman, and D. Arcus, "Childhood derivatives of high and low reactivity in infancy," *Child Development* (in press).

90. J. Kagan, unpub. manuscript.

91. Ibid.

92. P. Kosso, *Appearance and Reality* (New York: Oxford University Press, 1998).

93. H. Putnam, *The Many Faces of Realism* (LaSalle, IL: Open Court, 1987).

94. S. P. Stich, *Deconstructing the Mind* (New York: Oxford University Press, 1996).

95. M. Barinaga, "Social status sculpts activity of crayfish neurons," *Science* 271 (1996): 290–291.

96. F. Jackson, "What Mary didn't know," in N. Block et al., *Nature of Consciousness*, pp. 567–570.

97. J. A. Gray, "Three fundamental emotion systems," in P. Ekman and R. J. Davidson, eds., *The Nature of Emotion* (New York: Oxford University Press, 1994), pp. 243–247.

98. B. Russell, *Philosophical Essays* (New York: Simon and Schuster, 1966).

99. G. Frege, *Posthumous Writings* (Chicago: University of Chicago Press, 1979).

2. The Allure of Infant Determinism

1. J. J. Rousseau, *Emile*, trans. B. Faxler (New York: Dutton 1911), pp. 13–14.

2. S. Bernfeld, *The Psychology of the Infant* (New York: Brentanos, 1929), pp. 138, 213.

3. J. C. Fenton, *The Practical Side of Babyhood* (Boston, 1925), pp. 293–294.

4. G. Gorer, "Theoretical approaches," in M. Mead and M. Wolfenstein, eds., *Children in Contemporary Cultures* (Chicago: University of Chicago Press, 1955), pp. 31–36.

5. J. G. Bremner, *Infancy*, 2nd ed. (London: Blackwell, 1994), p. 232.

6. M. E. Lamb and M. H. Bornstein, *Development in Infancy*, 2nd ed. (New York: Random House, 1987), pp. 395, 396.

7. J. Bowlby, *Attachment and Loss*, vol. 1 (New York: Basic Books, 1969); E. H. Erikson, *Childhood and Society* (New York: Norton, 1963). In January 1998 the governor of Georgia asked the state legislature for funds to supply every infant with exposure to music. *Science* 279 (1998): 663.

8. N. Eldredge and S. J. Gould, "Punctuated equilibria: an alternative to phyletic gradualism," in T. J. M. Schopf, ed., *Models in Paleobiology* (San Francisco: Freeman, 1972); C. H. Waddington, *The Evolution of an Evolutionist* (Ithaca: Cornell University Press, 1975).

9. W. H. Li, *Molecular Evolution* (Sunderland : Sinauer, 1997).

10. P. G. Bateson, "The characteristics and context of imprinting," *Biological Review* 41 (1966): 177–220.

11. D. H. Hubel and T. N. Wiesel, "Receptive fields and functional architecture in two nonstriate visual areas (18 and 19) of the cat," *Journal of Neurophysiology* 28 (1965): 229–289.

12. M. H. Klaus and J. H. Kennell, *Maternal Infant Bonding* (St. Louis: Mosby, 1976).

13. C. Rathbun, L. DiVirgilio, and S. Waldfogel, "A restitutive process in children following radical separation from family and culture," *American Journal of Orthopsychiatry* 28 (1958): 408–415; M. Winick, K. K. Meyer, and R. C. Harris, "Malnutrition and environmental enrichment by early adoption," *Science* 190 (1975): 1173–1175.

14. B. M. Flint, *The Child and the Institution* (Toronto: University of Toronto Press, 1966), pp. 138–139. Although it is not good practice to draw strong conclusions from a single case history, these life stories have value. During the period when London was being bombed by Hitler's planes, Anna Freud accepted and cared for young children in a home outside of the city that was relatively safe from attack. One girl, who came to the home at 33 months of age, reacted with extreme anxiety to the stress of separation from her mother. She sat for hours sucking her hand or turned toward a wall. One of the psychologists working in the home followed this child's development and established a relationship with her. When the girl became an adult, she stayed with the psychologist while looking for a job in London. The psychologist felt that this young woman was well adjusted, free of serious conflict or pathology. The prolonged separation from the parent, and the accompanying anxiety, "had neither stopped ongoing development nor left a disturbing mark on her adult life." I. Hellman, "Hamstead nursery follow-up studies," *Psychoanalytic Study of the Child* 17 (1962): 159–174.

15. D. E. Eyer, *Mother-Infant Bonding* (New Haven: Yale University Press, 1992).

16. *Time*, February 3, 1997, p. 221. The same warning appeared in the April 17, 1997, issue of the *New York Times*.

17. M. West, *Infant Care*, ser. 2, Bureau Publication 8 (Washington, D.C.: U.S. Government Office, 1914), p. 59.

18. E. E. Werner and R. S. Smith, *Vulnerable But Invincible* (New York: McGraw Hill, 1982).

19. H. B. D. Kettlewell, "A résumé of investigations on the evolution of melanism in the Lepidoptera," *Proceedings of the Royal Society* B145 (1956): 297–303.

20. C. B. Alberti, *Della Famiglia*, trans. G. A. Guarrino (Lewisberg, PA: Bucknell University Press, 1971).

21. J. Robinson, "New essay," in R. Ashton, ed., *The Works of John Robinson, Pastor of the Pilgrim Fathers*, vol. 1 (Boston: Doctrinal Tract and Book Society, 1851), pp. 242–250.

22. F. Wayland, *The Elements of Moral Science* (1835; Cambridge: Harvard University Press, 1963).

23. J. Bowlby, "Separation, anxiety, and anger," in Bowlby, *Attachment and Loss*, vol. 1., p. 321.

24. M. D. S. Ainsworth, M. C. Blehar, E. Waters, and S. Wall, *Patterns of Attachment* (Hillsdale, NJ: Erlbaum, 1978).

25. R. Seifer, M. Schiller, A. J. Sameroff, S. Resnick, and K. Riordan, "Attachment, maternal sensitivity, and infant temperament during the first year of life," *Developmental Psychology* 32 (1996): 12–25; P. M. Kroonenberg, M. Van Dam, M. H. von IJzendoorn, and A. Mooijaart, "Dynamics of behavior in the Strange Situation," *British Journal of Psychology* 88 (1997): 311–332.

26. NICHD Early Child Care Research Network, "The effects of infant-child care on infant-mother attachment security," *Child Development* 68 (1997): 860–879.

27. M. S. De Wolff and M. H. von Ijzendoorn, "Sensitivity and attachment," *Child Development* 68 (1997): 571–591.

28. S. Ozment, *Three Behaim Boys* (New Haven: Yale University Press, 1990).

29. R. LeVine, unpub. manuscript.

30. M. Main, N. Kaplan, and J. Cassidy, "Security and infancy, childhood and adulthood: a move to the level of representation," *Monographs of the Society for Research in Child Development* 50, ser. 209 (1985).

31. M. Lewis, C. Feiring, and S. Rosenthal, "Attachment over time" (unpub. manuscript).

32. L. A. Sroufe, "The role of infant caregiver attachment in development," in J. Belsky and T. Mezworski, eds., *Clinical Implications of Attachment* (Hillsdale, NJ: Erlbaum, 1978): 18–38; E. A. Carlson and L. A. Sroufe, "Contribution of attachment theory to developmental psychopathology," in D. Cicchetti and D. J. Cohen, eds., *Developmental Psychopathology*, vol. 1 (New York: John Wiley, 1995), pp. 594, 598.

33. V. H. Denenberg, "Critical periods, stimulus input, and emotional reactivity," *Psychological Review* 71 (1964): 335–351.

34. T. J. Fillion and E. M. Blass, "Infantile experiences with suckling odors determines adult sexual behavior in rats," *Science* 231 (1986): 729–731.

35. F. Rebelsky, "Infancy in two cultures," *Psychologie* 22 (1967): 379–385.

36. D. B. Gardner and L. G. Burchinal, "Noncontinuous mothering in infancy and development in later childhood," *Child Development* 32 (1962): 225–234; for institutional infants see W. Dennis, *Children of the Creche* (New York: Appleton Century Crofts, 1973); for World War II orphans see C. Rathburn, L. DiVirgilio, and A. Waldfogel, "A restitutive process in children following radical separation from family and culture," *American Journal of Orthopsychiatry* 28 (1958): 408–415. Wayne Dennis reported an unusual experiment, performed fifty years ago, that would be regarded as unethical today. Dennis and his wife reared twin girls in their home for the first seven months of their lives under conditions most would evaluate as depriving. The infants remained in one room and were neither played with nor spoken to unless these acts were part of routine care. Nonetheless, both infants attained the usual milestones of the first year at the expected times. Dennis concluded: "Normal behavioral development can occur in some infants when most of the first year is spent under conditions of minimal social stimulation and of very restricted practice." W. Dennis, "Infant development under conditions of restricted practice and of minimum social stimulation," *Journal of Genetic Psychology* 53: 149–157.

37. M. Rutter, personal communication.

38. J. Kagan, *The Nature of the Child* (New York: Basic Books, 1984).

39. J. Kagan and H. A. Moss, *Birth to Maturity* (New York: John Wiley, 1962).

40. Werner and Smith, *Vulnerable But Invincible*, p. 159.

41. A. M. Clarke and A. D. B. Clarke, *Early Experience: Myth and Evidence* (London: Open Books, 1976).

42. C. Ernst, "Are early childhood experiences overrated?" *European Archives of Psychiatry and Neurological Science* 237 (1988): 80–90.

43. M. C. Jones, N. Bayley, J. W. MacFarlane, and M. P. Honzik, eds., *The Course of Human Development* (Lexington, MA: Xerox, 1971). See also D. S. Pine, D. Gurley, J. Brook, and Y. Ma, "The risk for early adulthood anxiety and depressive disorders in adolescents with anxiety and depressive disorders," *Archives of General Psychiatry* 55 (1998): 56–64.

44. M. Rutter, "Continuities and discontinuities from infancy," in J. D. Osofsky, ed., *Handbook of Infant Development*, 2nd ed. (New York: John Wiley, 1987), pp. 1256–1296.

45. B. Fish, J. Marcus, S. C. Hans, J. G. Auerbach, and S. Perdue, "Infants at risk for schizophrenia," *Archives of General Psychiatry* 49 (1992): 221–235.

46. W. T. Greenough and J. E. Black, "Induction of brain structure by experience," in M. R. Gunnar and C. A. Nelson, eds., *Developmental Behavioral Neuroscience: Minnesota Symposium on Child Psychology*, vol. 24 (Hillsdale, NJ: Erlbaum, 1992), pp. 155–200.

47. A. Diamond, M. Prevar, G. Callender, and D. P. Druin, "Prefrontal cortex in children tested early and continuously for PKU," *Monographs of the Society for Research in Child Development* 62, ser. 252 (1997): 1–207.

48. Kagan, *Birth to Maturity*.

49. M. K. Mullen, "Earliest recollections of childhood," *Cognition* 52 (1994): 55–79.

50. J. Ungerer, personal communication.

51. C. Rovee-Collier, "Learning and memory in infancy," in Osofsky, ed., *Handbook of Infant Development*.

52. J. R. Saffron, R. N. Aslin, and E. L. Newport, "Statistical learning by eight month old infants," *Science* 274 (1996): 1926–1928.

53. S. J. Chew, D. S. Vicario, and F. Nottebohm, "Quantal duration of auditory memories," *Science* 274 (1996): 1909–1914.

54. F. McCourt, *Angela's Ashes* (New York: Scribner, 1996).

55. T. Gregor, *Mehinaku* (Chicago: University of Chicago Press, 1977).

56. J. S. Mill, *Autobiography of John Stuart Mill* (New York: Columbia University Press, 1927), pp. 36–37.

57. H. Wagatsuma, "Some aspects of the contemporary Japanese family," *Daedalus* 106 (1977): 181–210.

58. M. Holroyd, *Bernard Shaw*, vol. 1 (New York: Vintage, 1990).

59. J. L. Briggs, *Never in Anger* (Cambridge: Harvard University Press, 1970).

60. G. H. Herdt, *Guardians of the Flutes* (New York: McGraw Hill, 1981).

61. E. H. Adelson, "Perceptual organization and the judgment of brightness," *Science* 262 (1993): 2042–2044.

62. D. Liu, J. Diorio, B. Tannenbaum, C. Caldji, D. Francis, A. Freedman, S. Sharma, D. Pearson, D. M. Plotsky, and M. M. Meaney, "Maternal care, hippocampal glucocorticoid receptors, and hypothalamic-pituitary-adrenal responses to stress," *Science* 277 (1997): 1659–1662.

63. T. A. Appel, *The Cuvier-Geoffroy Debate* (New York: Oxford, 1987).

64. C. Darwin, *On the Origin of Species*, 6th ed. (1859; New York: Avenel Books, 1979), p. 453.

65. I. Pavlov, *Lectures on Conditioned Reflexes*, trans. W. H. Gantt (London: Laurence and Wishart, 1928), p. 95.

66. S. H. Podolsky and A. I. Teuber, *The Generation of Diversity* (Cambridge: Harvard University Press, 1997).

67. N. E. Adler, T. Boyce, M. A. Chesney, S. Cohen, S. Folkman, R. L. Kahn, and S. L. Syme, "Socioeconomic status and health," *American Psychologist* 49 (1994): 15–24.

68. M. Weber, *Ancient Judaism* (Blanco, IL: Free Press, 1952).

69. C. N. Degler, *At Odds: Women and the Family in America from the Revolution to the Present* (New York: Oxford University Press, 1980).

70. C. Ernst and J. Angst, *Birth Order: Its Influence on Personality* (Berlin: Springer Verlag, 1983).

71. W. D. Altus, "Birth order and its sequelae," *Science* (1966) 151: 44–49; B. Sutton-Smith and B. G. Rosenberg, *The Sibling* (New York: Holt, Rinehart and Winston, 1970); E. E. Sampson and F. T. Hancock, "An examination of the relationship between ordinal position, personality, and conformity," *Journal of Personality and Social Psychology* 5 (1967): 398–407.

72. F. Sulloway, *Born To Rebel: Birth Order, Family Dynamics, and Creative Lives* (New York: Pantheon, 1996).

73. L. M. Baskett, "Ordinal position differences in children's family interactions," *Developmental Psychology* 20 (1984): 1026–1031.

74. Sulloway, *Born To Rebel*.

75. C. Darwin, *The Autobiography of Charles Darwin* (1887; New York: Norton, 1958), p. 141.

76. M. K. Mullen, "Children's classifications of nature and artifact pictures into female and male categories," *Sex Roles* 23 (1990): 577–587.

77. M. Douglas, *Purity and Danger* (London: Routledge and Kegan Paul, 1966); C. Fabre-Vassas, *The Singular Beast* (New York: Columbia University Press, 1997).

78. L. A. Hirschfeld, "Do children have a theory of race?" *Cognition* 54 (1995): 209–252.

79. R. Rodriguez, *The Hunger of Memory* (Boston: D. R. Godine, 1982).

80. F. E. Manuel, *A Requiem for Karl Marx* (Cambridge: Harvard University Press, 1995).

81. J. Updike, *Self-Consciousness: Memoirs* (New York: Knopf, 1989).

82. F. Kermode, *Not Entitled* (New York: Farrar, Straus & Giroux, 1995).

83. R. Nozick, *Philosophical Explanations* (Cambridge: Harvard University Press, 1981), p. vii.

84. J. Kagan, J. S. Reznick, J. Davies, J. Smith, H. Sigal, and K. Miyake, "Selective memory and belief: a methodological suggestion," *International Journal of Behavioral Development* 9 (1986): 205–218.

85. E. Mayr, *Toward a New Philosophy of Biology* (Cambridge: Harvard University Press, 1988).

86. J. E. Wideman, *Brothers and Keepers* (New York: Holt, Rinehart and Winston, 1984).

87. G. C. Homans, *Coming to My Senses* (New Brunswick, NJ: Transaction Books, 1984).

88. G. H. Elder, Jr., *Children of the Great Depression* (Chicago: University of Chicago Press, 1974).

89. R. Bendix, *Max Weber* (New York: Doubleday, 1960).

90. W. J. Greenough, "We can't focus just on ages zero to three," *Monitor* 28 (1997): 19.

91. R. J. Geller, D. P. Jackson, Y. Y. Kagan, and F. Molargia, "Earthquakes cannot be predicted," *Science* 275 (1997): 1616–1617.

3. The Pleasure Principle

1. Although Freud waffled over whether the increase in excitation was only sensory in origin, he was bold, but wrong, when he declared that pleasure was a diminution and displeasure an increase in the quantity of excitation. S. Freud, *Beyond the Pleasure Principle* (Vienna: International Psychoanalytic Publications, 1920; New York: Liveright, 1950).

2. Bertrand Russell argued in "The Elements of Ethics" that "good" cannot be defined in terms of any specific action. An act is morally good, Russell wrote, when the agent approves of it subjectively. B. Russell, *Philosophical Essays* (New York: Simon and Schuster, 1966). One of the new Chinese entrepreneurs who manages a bar and massage parlor in Beijing captured the difference between sense and mind. After telling an interviewer that he hated his business because the activities went against his moral beliefs, he added, "My attitude is: If my eyes don't see it, my mind won't be troubled." J. Spence and A. Chin, "Deng's heirs," *New Yorker*, March 10, 1997, p. 76.

3. C. Darwin, "Notebooks," in H. E. Gruber, *Darwin on Man* (London: Wildwood House, 1974), p. 400.

4. J. Olds and P. Milner, "Positive reinforcement produced by electrical stimulation of septal areas and other regions of rat brain," *Journal of Comparative and Physiological Psychology* 47 (1954): 419–427. C. R. Gallistel, "Self-stimulation," in J. A. Deutsch, ed., *Physiological Basis of Memory* (New York: Academic Press, 1983), pp. 265–349; I. Wickelgren, "Getting the brain's attention," *Science* 278 (1997): 35–37.

5. A. MacIntyre, *After Virtue* (Notre Dame: University of Notre Dame Press, 1981), pp. 61–62.

6. A. O. Hirschman, *Passions and Interests* (Princeton: Princeton University Press, 1977).

7. A. Smith, *The Theory of the Moral Sentiments* (New Rochelle: Arlington House, 1959), p. 84.

8. C. Darwin, *The Descent of Man, and Selection in Relation to Sex* (London: Murray, 1871); G. Broberg, "Linnaeus's classification of man," in T. Frangsmyr, ed., *Linnaeus: The Man and His Work* (Berkeley: University of California Press, 1983), p. 167.

9. S. Lee and A. Kleinman, "Mental illness and social change in China," *Harvard Review of Psychiatry* 5 (1997): 43–46.

10. B. S. Thornton, *Eros* (Boulder: Westview Press, 1997).

11. R. A. Shweder, N. A. Much, M. Mahapatra, and L. Park, "The 'big three' of morality (autonomy, community, and divinity) and the 'big three' examples of suffering," in J. A. Brandt and P. Rozin, eds., *Mortality and Health* (New York: Routledge and Kegan Paul, 1997).

12. L. Pollock, *A Lasting Relationship* (Hanover, NH: University Press of New England, 1987).

13. T. Hobbes, *Leviathan*, ed. M. Oakeshott (1651; Oxford: Oxford University Press, 1957); J. Rawls, *A Theory of Justice* (Cambridge: Harvard University Press, 1971); P. Riley, *Leibniz' Universal Jurisprudence* (Cambridge: Harvard University Press, 1996).

14. H. White, *The Content of the Form* (Baltimore: Johns Hopkins University Press, 1987).

15. R. Nozick, *Philosophical Explanations* (Cambridge: Harvard University Press, 1981).

16. T. H. Huxley, *Life and Letters of Thomas Henry Huxley* (New York: Appleton, 1901).

17. J. Dewey, *Reconstruction in Philosophy* (1920; Boston: Beacon Press, 1957), p. 103.

18. E. O. Wilson, *Sociobiology* (Cambridge: Harvard University Press, 1975).

19. P. H. Abelson, "Diet and cancer in humans and rodents," *Science* 255 (1992): 141.

20. P. M. H. Mazumdar, *Species and Specificity* (New York: Cambridge University Press, 1995).

21. M. Ridley, *The Origins of Virtue* (New York: Viking, 1996).

22. R. Levi-Montalcini, "The nerve growth factor 35 years later," *Science* 237 (1987): 1154–1162.

23. W. A. Mason and J. P. Capitanio, "Formation and expression of filial attachment in rhesus monkeys raised with living and inanimate mother substitutes," *Developmental Psychobiology* 21 (1988): 401–430.

24. "Darwin revisited," *Economist*, August 30, 1997, p. 11.

25. R. D. Alexander, *The Biology of Moral Systems* (New York: DeGruiter 1987); F. de Waal, *Good Natured* (Cambridge: Harvard University Press, 1996); J. Q. Wilson, *The Moral Sense* (New York: Free Press, 1993); E. Mayr, *This Is Biology: The Science of the Living World* (Cambridge: Harvard University Press, 1996).

26. W. Koehler, *The Mentality of Apes*, trans. E. Winter (1917; New York: Harcourt Brace & World, 1925); R. M. Yerkes, *Almost Human* (London: Jonathan Cape, 1925).

27. D. J. Povinelli and T. J. Eddy, "What young chimpanzees know about seeing," *Monographs of the Society for Research in Child Development* 61 (1996): 3.

28. M. Tomasello, J. Call, and A. Gluckman, "Comprehension of novel communicative signs by apes and humans in children," *Child Development* 68 (1997): 1067–1080.

29. Povinelli and Eddy, "What young chimpanzees know about seeing."

30. B. Herman, *The Practice of Moral Judgment* (Cambridge: Harvard University Press, 1993).

31. D. Hume, *An Enquiry Concerning the Principles of Morals* (1751; La Salle, IL: Open Court, 1966); J. Monod, *Chance and Necessity* (New York: Knopf, 1971).

32. J. Kagan, N. Snidman, and D. Arcus, "Childhood derivatives of reactivity in infancy," *Child Development* (in press).

33. C. L. Gerstadt, Y. J. Hong, and A. Diamond, "The relationship between cognition and action," *Cognition* 53 (1994): 129–157.

34. J. Kagan, *The Nature of the Child* (New York: Basic Books, 1984).

35. L. Menand, "The gods are anxious," *New Yorker*, December 16, 1996, pp. 5–6.

36. A. Damasio, *Descartes' Error* (New York: Putnam, 1994); W. Wittling, "Brain asymmetry in the control of autonomic-physiologic activity," in R. J. Davidson and K. Hugdahl, eds., *Brain Asymmetry* (Cambridge: MIT Press, 1995), pp. 305–358; A. Ehlers and B. Breuer, "Increased cardiac awareness in panic disorder," *Journal of*

Abnormal Psychology 101 (1992): 371–382; C. H. Rouse, G. E. Jones, and K. R. Jones, "The effect of body composition and gender on cardiac awareness," *Psychophysiology* 25 (1988): 400–407.

37. S. Taylor, W. J. Koch, S. Woody, and P. McLean, "Anxiety, sensitivity and depression," *Journal of Abnormal Psychology* 105 (1996): 474–475.

38. W. James, "What is emotion?" *Mind* 9 (1984): 188–205; C. Lange, *Ueber Gemuthsbewegungen* (Leipzig: Theodor Thomas, 1887).

39. Pollock, *A Lasting Relationship*.

40. J. Joyce, *A Portrait of the Artist as a Young Man* (New York: Modern Library, 1916), p. 287.

41. R. Rhees, ed., *Recollections of Wittgenstein* (New York: Oxford, 1981), p. 174; L. Wittgenstein, *Culture and Value*, trans. P. Winch (Chicago: University of Chicago Press, 1984), pp. 20, 21, 36, 72; R. Monk, *Ludwig Wittgenstein* (New York: Free Press, 1990), p. 442.

42. C. Miłosz, *The Year of the Hunter* (New York: Farrar, Straus, Giroux, 1994).

43. R. F. Christian, *Tolstoy's Diaries* (New York: Scribner, 1985), pp. 4–12, 329.

44. M. Benson, ed., *Notebooks of Athol Fugard (1960/1977)* (London: Faber and Faber, 1983).

45. D. Grossman, *On Killing* (New York: Little, Brown, 1995).

46. Ibid., pp. 201, 88.

47. R. Yehuda, S. M. Southwick, and E. L. Giller, "Exposure to atrocities and severity of chronic posttraumatic stress disorder in Vietnam combat veterans," *American Journal of Psychiatry* 149 (1992): 333–336; A. Bleich, M. Koslowsky, A. Dolev, and B. Lerer, "Posttraumatic stress disorder and depression," *British Journal of Psychiatry* 170 (1997): 479–482.

48. D. P. Valentiner, E. B. Foa, D. S. Riggs, and B. S. Gershuny, "Coping strategies and posttraumatic stress disorder in female victims of sexual and nonsexual assault," *Journal of Abnormal Psychology* 105 (1996): 455–458.

49. N. McCall, *Makes Me Wanna Holler* (New York: Vintage, 1995), p. 49.

50. C. S. North, E. M. Smith, E. L. Spitznagel, "One year follow-up of survivors of a mass shooting," *American Journal of Psychiatry* 154 (1997): 1696–1702; Z. Soloman, *Coping with War-Induced Stress* (New York: Plenum, 1995).

51. Soloman, *Coping with War-Induced Stress*.

52. M. Ridley, *The Origins of Virtue*, p. 265.

53. de Waal, *Good Natured*, p. 218.

Epilogue

1. T. A. Appel, *The Cuvier-Geoffroy Debate* (New York: Oxford, 1987).

2. M. B. DeBevoise, ed., *Conversations on Mind, Matter, and Mathematics* (Princeton: Princeton University Press, 1995).

Acknowledgments

I am grateful to Loyal Rue, William Damon, J. Steven Reznick, Richard Hackman, and Marc Hauser for critiques of one or more chapters and to Susan Wallace Boehmer for, once again, helping me to clarify meaning and untangle dense prose. Paula Mabee and Blair Boudreau deserve special appreciation for manuscript preparation. The research on temperament described in Chapter 1 was collaborative with Nancy Snidman and supported by grants from the John D. and Catherine T. MacArthur Foundation Network on Psychopathology and Development, directed by Dr. David Kupfer, William T. Grant Foundation, and the National Institute of Mental Health. Many ideas in this book profited from fruitful discussions with participants in the Mind/Brain/Behavior Initiative at Harvard University.

Index